ILLUSTR.......NG

C

ILLUSTRATING

C

(ANSI/ISO VERSION)

Donald Alcock

Reigate Manual Writers

 CAMBRIDGE UNIVERSITY PRESS

CAMBRIDGE
NEW YORK   PORT CHESTER
MELBOURNE SYDNEY

Published by the Press Syndicate of the University of Cambridge,
The Pitt Building, Trumpington Street, Cambridge CB2 1RP
40 West 20th Street, New York, NY 10011, USA
10 Stamford Road, Oakleigh, Melbourne 3166, Australia

© Cambridge University Press 1992

First published 1992

Printed in Great Britain at the University Press, Cambridge

British Library cataloguing in publication data available

Library of Congress cataloguing in publication data available

ISBN 0 521 42483 6

Acknowledgements

My warmest thanks to the following people without
whom the job of writing this book would have been
lonely and terrifying: Paul Burden, for patiently
steering my rambling thoughts from nonsense to sense
during many telephone conversations; Mike Ingham,
for the same thing, and making it worth while to
continue instead of throwing it all in the bin; Paul
Shearing, for his enthusiasm and indispensable help
with production; Andrew, my elder son, for help with
just about everything.

CONTENTS

PREFACE

The original C programming language was devised by Dennis Ritchie. The first book on C, by Kernighan and Ritchie, came out in 1978 and remained the most authoritative and best book on the subject until their second edition, describing ANSI standard C, appeared in 1988. In all that time, and since, the availability and use of C has increased exponentially. It is now one of the most widely used programming languages, not only for writing computer systems but also for developing applications.

There are many books on C but not so many on ANSI standard C which is the version described here.

This book attempts three things:

- to serve as a text book for introductory courses on C aimed both at those who already know a computer language and at those entirely new to computing

- to summarize and present the syntax and grammar of C by diagrams and tables, making this a useful reference book on C

- to illustrate a few essential programming techniques such as symbol state tables, linked lists, binary trees, doubly linked rings, manipulation of strings, parsing of algebraic expressions.

For a formal appreciation of C ⇌ its power, its advantages and disadvantages ⇌ see the references given in the Bibliography. As an *informal* appreciation: all those I know who program in C find the language likeable and enjoy its power. Programming C is like driving a fast and powerful car. Having learned to handle the car safely you would not willingly return to the family saloon.

The hand-written format of this book has evolved over several years, and over six previous books on computers and programming languages. The pages contain the kind of diagram an able lecturer draws on the blackboard and annotates with encircled notes. Written text has been kept short and succinct. I have tried to avoid adverbs, cliches, jargon and unnecessarily formal language.

I hope the result looks friendly.

REIGATE

Surrey, U.K.

Donald Alcock

February 1992

1

INTRODUCTION

The introduction starts with the concept of a stored program. The concept is second nature to anyone who has programmed anything on any computer in any language, but to a complete novice it can be difficult to grasp. So a simple program is written in English and then translated into C.

The chapter explains principles of running a C program on the computer. The explanation is sketchy because each implementation of C has different rules for doing so. Check the manuals for your own installation.

Finally the program is dissected, statement by statement.

CONCEPTION

If you ask to borrow £5,000 at 15.5% compound interest over 5 years, the friendly bank manager works out your monthly repayment, M, from the compound interest formula:

$$M = \frac{P \times R \times (1+R)^N}{12\,((1+R)^N - 1))}$$

Where:

P represents the principal ⟪ £5000 in this case ⟫

R represents the rate of interest ⟪ 0.155 is the *absolute* rate in the case of 15.5% ⟫

N represents the number of years ⟪ 5 in this case ⟫

To work this out the friendly bank manager might use the following 'program' of instructions:

1 Get math tables or calculator ready

2 Draw boxes to receive values for P, Rpct, N. Also a box for the absolute rate, R, and a box for the repayment, M

P ⬚ Rpct ⬚ N ⬚

R ⬚ M ⬚

⟪ smaller box for whole number ⟫

3 Ask the client to state the three values: Principal (P), Rate percent (Rpct), Number of years (N)

4 Write these values in their respective boxes

5 Write in box R the result of Rpct/100. For Rpct use the value to be found in box Rpct ⟪ don't rub out the content of box Rpct ⟫

6 Write in box M the result of the compound interest formula. Use for the terms P, R, N the values to be found in boxes P, R, N respectively ⟪ don't change anything in boxes P, R, N ⟫

7 Confirm to the client the values in boxes P, Rpct, N and the monthly installment read from box M

8 Work out ⟪ 12 × value in box M × value in box N ⟫ to tell tell the client how much will have to be repaid.

This program is good for any size of loan, any rate of interest, any whole number of years. Simply follow instructions 1 to 8 in sequence.

2   ILLUSTRATING C

A computer can be made to execute such a program, but first you must translate it into a language the computer can understand. Here is a translation into the language called C.

```c
#include <stdio.h>
#include <math.h>

int main (void)

{

    float P, Rpct, R, M;

    int N;

    printf ( "\nEnter: Principal, Rate%, No. of yrs.\n" );

    scanf ("%f %f %i", &P, &Rpct, &N );

    R = Rpct / 100;

    M = P * R * pow(1+R, N ) / ( 12 * ( pow(1+R, N) - 1));

    printf ("\n£%1.2f, @%11.2f %% costs  £%1.2f over %iyears", P, Rpct, M, N);

    printf ("\nPayments will total  £%1.2f", 12*M*N );

    return 0;

}
```

main program starts — 1, 2, 3, 4, 5, 6, 7, 8 *main program ends*

The above is a *program*. This particular program comprises:

- a set of *directives* to a *preprocessor*; each directive begins #
- a *function* called main( ) with one *parameter* named void.

A function comprises:

- a *header* conveying the function's name (main) followed by
- a *block*

A block { enclosed in braces } comprises:

- a set of *declarations* ('drawing' the little boxes)
- a set of *statements* (telling the processor what to do)

Each declaration and each statement is terminated with a semicolon.

The correspondence between the English program opposite, and the C program above, is indicated by numbers 1 to 8.

The C program is thoroughly dissected in following pages.

REALIZATION

The program on the previous page should work on any computer that understands C.

Unfortunately not all computer installations go about running C programs the same way; you have to have some understanding of the *operating system*, typical ones being Unix and DOS. You may be lucky and have an *integrated development environment* (IDE) such as that which comes with Turbo C or Microsoft C. In this case you do not have to learn much about Unix or DOS. You control Turbo C with mouse and menus; it really is easy to learn how.

Regardless of environment, the following essential steps must be taken before you can run the C program on the previous page.

- **Type.** Type the program at the keyboard using the editing facilities available. If these are inadequate, discover if it is feasible to use your favourite word processor.

    When typing, don't type **main** as **MAIN**; corresponding upper and lower case letters are distinct in the C language (except in a few special cases).

    Be sensible with spacing; don't split adjacent *tokens* and don't join adjacent tokens if both are words or letters;

    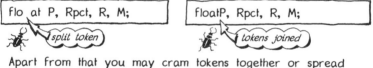

    Apart from that you may cram tokens together or spread them out ⤳ over several lines if you like:

    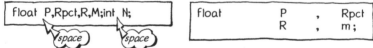

    To separate tokens, use any combination of whitespace keys:

    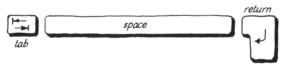

- **Store.** Store what you type in a file, giving the file a name such as WOTCOST.C (The .C is added automatically in some environments; it signifies a file containing a C program in character form, the .C being an *extension* of the name proper.)

- **C**ompile. Compile the program — which involves translating your C program into a code the computer can understand and obey directly.

  This step may be initiated by selecting Complie from a screen menu, or typing a command such as cc wotcost.c (Unix) and pressing the Return key. It all depends on your environment.

  The compiler reports any errors encountered. A good IDE displays the statements in which the errors were discovered, and locates the cursor at the point where the correction should be made.

- **E**dit. Edit the .C file and recompile as often as necessary to correct the errors discovered by the compiler. The program may still have *logical* errors but at least it should compile.

  You have now created a new file containing *object code*. The file of object code has a name related to the name of the original file. In a DOS environment it might have the name WOTCOST.OBJ (compiled from WOTCOST.C) . In a Unix environment, if you compiled **wotcost.c** your object code would be stored in **a.out** .

- **L**ink. In many environments a simple C program may be compiled and linked all in one go (type a.out, press Return, and away we go!) . In other environments you must link the program to functions in the standard libraries (pow, printf, scanf are functions written in C too) . The resulting file might have the name WOTCOST.EXE (linked from WOTCOST.OBJ) .

- **R**un. Run the executable program by selecting Run from a menu or enterng the appropriate command from the keyboard.

- **E**xecution. The screen now displays:

  Enter three items separated space, tab or new line. End by pressing Return.

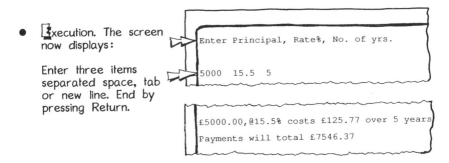

```
Enter Principal, Rate%, No. of yrs.
```

```
5000   15.5   5
```

```
£5000.00,@15.5% costs £125.77 over 5 years
Payments will total £7546.37
```

  The program computes and sends results to the standard output file (named std.out) . This 'file' is typically the screen.

Here is the compound interest program again ≈ with a title added for identification.

```
/* WOTCOST; Computes the cost of a loan */          ◁ comment
#include <stdio.h>
#include <math.h>                    ◁ directives - no semicolon
int main (void)      ◁ header
{
       float P, Rpct, R, M;
       int N;
       printf ("\nEnter: Principal, Rate%, No. of yrs.\n");
       scanf ("%f %f %i", &P, &Rpct, &N );
       R = Rpct / 100;
       M = P * R * pow(1+R, N) / ( 12 * ( pow(1+R, N) - 1 ) );
       printf ("\n£%1.2f, @%11.2f%% costs £%1.2f over %i years", P,Rpct,M,N);
       printf ("\nPayments will total £%1.2f", 12*M*N );
       return 0;
}
```

block

`/* WOTCOST ;   loan */` **A**ny text between /* and */ is treated as commentary. Such commentary is allowed wherever whitespace is allowed, and is similarly ignored by the processor.

`#include <stdio.h>`
`#include <math.h>` **T**he # ((which must be the first non-blank character on the line)) introduces an instruction to the *preprocessor* which deals with organizational matters such as including standard files. The standard libraries of C contain many useful functions; to make such a function available to your program, tell the preprocessor the name of its *header file*. In this case the header files are stdio.h ((standard input and output)) and math.h ((mathematical)). The header files tell the linker where to find the functions invoked in your program.

`int main (void)` **A** C program comprises a set of functions. Precisely one must be named **main** so the processor knows where to begin. The **int** and **void** are explained later; just accept them for now. The declarations and statements of the functions follow immediately; they are enclosed in braces, constituting a *block*. There is no semicolon between header and block.

`float P, Rpct, R, M;`
`int N;` **T**he 'little boxes' depicted earlier are called *variables*. Variables that hold decimal numbers like 15.5 are of a different *type* from variables that hold only whole numbers. These two statements declare that the variables named P, Rpct, R, M are of type **float** ((short for floating point number)) and the variable named N is of type **int** ((short for integer)). Other types are introduced later.

Declarations, such as those above, must all precede the first *statement*.

Each declaration and each statement is terminated by a semicolon. A *directive* is neither a declaration nor a statement; it has no semicolon after it.

You have freedom of layout. Statements may be typed several to a line, one per line, one to several lines. To the C compiler a space, new line, Tab, comment, or any number or combination of such things between statements $\rightleftharpoons$ or between the tokens that make up a statement $\rightleftharpoons$ are simply *whitespace*. One whitespace is as good as another, but not when between quotation marks as we see here.

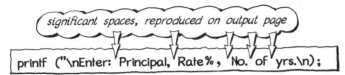

This is an invocation

of printf(), a much-used library function for printing. In some environments the processor includes standard input and output automatically $\rightleftharpoons$ without your having to write #include <stdio.h>

When printing, the processor watches for back-slash. On meeting a back-slash the processor looks at the next character for guidance: n says start a new line. \n is called an *escape sequence*. There is also \t for Tab, \f for form feed, \a for ring the bell (or beep) and others.

$It's$ no good pressing the Return key instead of typing \n. Pressing Return would start a new line on the screen, messing up the syntax and layout of your program. You don't *want* a new line *in the program*, you want your program to generate one when it obeys printf().

scanf ("%f %f %i", & P, & Rpct, & N);

This is an invocation of the scanf() function for

input. For brevity, most examples in this book use scanf(). Safer methods of input are discussed later.

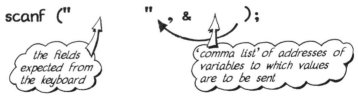

There is more about scanf() overleaf.

To obey the scanf( ) instruction the processor waits until you have typed something at the keyboard and pressed the return key (('something' means three values in this example)). The processor then tries to copy values, separated by whitespace, from the keyboard buffer. If you type fewer than three values the processor stays with the instruction until you have pressed Return after entering the third. If you type more, the processor reads and ignores the excess.

The processor now tries to interpret the first item as a floating point number ((%f)). If the attempt succeeds, the processor sends the value to the address of variable P ((& P)) ⇌ in other words stores the value in P. The second value from the keyboard is similarly stored in Rpct. Then the processor tries to interpret the third item from the keyboard as a whole number ((%i)) and stores this in variable N.

What happens if you type something wrong? Like:

where the 15000 is acceptable as 15000.00, but the second item involves an illegal sign, the third is not a whole number.

The answer is that things go horribly wrong. In a practical program you would *not* use scanf( ).

Why the '&' in &P, &Rpct, &N ? Just accept it for now. The art of C, as you will discover, lies in the effective use of:

&   'the address of...'   or 'pointer to...'

*   'the value pointed to by...'   or 'pointee of...'

```
R=Rpct/100;
M=P*R*pow(1+R,N)/(12*pow(1+R,N)-1));
```

These statements specify the necessary arithmetic: Rpct/100 means divide the value found in Rpct by 100. The /, *, +, - mean respectively: divide by, multiply by, add to, subtract from. They are called *operators*, of which there are many others in C.

pow(1+R,N) is a *function* which *returns* the value of (1+R) raised to the power N. If you prefer to use logs you could write exp(log(1+R)*N) instead. The math library ((#include <math.h>)) would be needed in either case; exp( ), log( ), pow( ) are all math.h functions.

The terms 1+R and N are *arguments* ((*actual* arguments)) for the function pow( ), one for each of that function's *parameters* ((*dummy* parameters)). In some books on computing the terms *argument* and *parameter* are used interchangeably.

ILLUSTRATING C

```
printf ("\n%8.2f,@%.2f%% costs £%.2f over %i years", P,Rpct,M,N);
```

This is like the earlier printf( ) invocation; a string between quotes in which \n signifies *Start a new line on the output screen.*

printf ("   "   ,   );

characters to be printed, interspersed with format specifications for values to be printed

comma list of names of variables whose values are to be printed in the format specified

But this time the string contains four *format* specifications: %8.2f, %.2f, %.2f, %i for which the values stored in variables P, Rpct, M, N are to be substituted in order. You can see this better by rearranging over two lines using whitespace:

```
printf ("\n£ %8.2f  @ %.2f %% costs £ %.2f over %i years" );
            ,P      ,Rpct        ,M        ,N
```

Take %8.2f as an example. The % denotes a format specification. f denotes a field suitable for a value of type **float** ≈ in other words a number with a fractional part after a decimal point. The 8 specifies eight character positions for the complete number. The .2 specifies a decimal point followed by two decimal places:

```
| | | | | • | | |     %8.2f
 1 2 3 4 5 6 7 8
          2
```

A single percentage sign introduces a format specification as illustrated. So how do you tell the processor to *print* an ordinary percentage sign? The answer is to write %% as demonstrated in the printf( ) statement above.

The second ((and subsequent)) format specification is %.2f. How can the field be zero characters wide if it has a decimal point and two places after? This is a dodge; whenever a number is too wide, the processor widens the field rightwards until the number just fits.

```
printf ("\nPayments will total £%.2f", N * 12 * M );
```
This is another printf( ) invocation with an 'elastic' field. This time the value to be printed is given by an *expression*, n∗12∗M, rather than the name of a variable. The processor evaluates the expression, converts the resulting value ((if necessary)) to a value of type **float**, and prints that value in the specified field.

printf ("   "   ,   )

comma list may contain expressions as well as names of variables

```
return Ø;
```
Just accept it for now: the opening **int main (void)** and closing **return Ø** are described later.

EXERCISES

1   Implement the loans program. This is an exercise in using the tools of your particular C environment. It can take a surprisingly long time to master a new editor and get to grips with the commands of an unfamiliar interface. If all else fails, try reading the manual.

2

CONCEPTS

One of the few troubles with C is that you can't formally define concept A without assuming something about concept B, and you can't define B without assuming something about A. Books on C have a bit in common with the novel Catch 22.

The aim of this chapter is to introduce, informally, enough simple concepts and vocabulary to make subsequent chapters comprehensible.

This chapter introduces decisions, loops, characters, arrays, functions, scope of variables, and recursion. Complete programs are included to illustrate the aspects introduced.

DECISIONS

If, in your program, Profit is greater than Loss (Profit and Loss being names of variables holding values) you may want the program to do one thing, otherwise another. The expression Profit > Loss is *true* if the value in Profit is greater than that in Loss; *true* is represented by 1. Conversely, if the value in Profit is *not* greater than that in Loss the expression is *false* and takes the value 0.

Thus 9.5 > 0.0 takes the value 1 (*true*); 9.5 < 0.0 takes the value 0 (*false*). A few other logical operators are shown here: ▷ Operators are defined in Chapter 3 and briefly summarized on page 196.

<	less than
>=	greater than or equal to
==	equal to
!=	not equal to
&&	logical *and*

There are no Boolean variables in C ⟿ you have to make do with integers; a value of zero represents *false*; *any non-zero value represents true.*

Statements concerned with the flow of control (if, while, do for) are based on values of logical expressions: non-zero for *true*, zero for *false*.

IF ELSE

The if statement may be used to select a course of action according to the logical value (true or false) of a parenthesized expression:

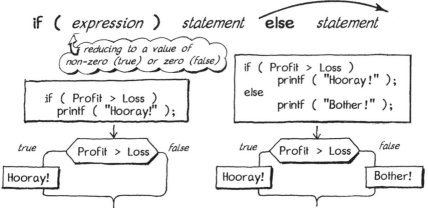

The *statement* is typically a compound statement or *block*. Anywhere a *statement* is allowed a *block* is also allowed. A block comprises an indefinitely long sequence, in braces, of declarations (optional) followed by statements. Some of the statements may be if statements ⟿ a *nested* pattern.

Be careful when nesting 'if' statements. Try to employ the pattern resulting from 'else if' rather than 'if if' which leaves 'elses' dangling in the brain. A sequence of 'if if' makes it difficult to match the associated 'elses' that pile up at the end.

In the illustration below, the operator ! means *not*. Thus if variable Lame holds the value ø (false) then the expression !Lame takes the value 1 (true). Conversely, if Lame holds a non-zero value (true) then the expression !Lame takes the value ø (false).

```
if ( Lame )
    Walk ( ø );
else
    if ( SoSo )
        Trot ( ø );
        else
            if ( Quiet );
                Canter ( ø );
                else
                    Gallop ( ø );
```

OK

```
if ( !Lame )
    if ( !SoSo )
        if ( !Quiet )
            Gallop ( ø );
        else
            Canter ( ø );
    else
        Trot ( ø );
else
    Walk ( ø );
```

confusing

Each 'else' refers to the closest preceding 'if' that does not already have an 'else', paying due respect to parentheses. Careful indentation shows which 'else' belongs to which 'if', but remember that *the processor* pays no attention to indentation. Careless indentation can present a misleading picture.

Here is a program that uses a *block* in the 'if' statement as discussed opposite. The program does the same job as the introductory example but first checks that all items of data are positive.

Complicated logic based on 'if else' can be clumsy; we meet more elegant methods of control later.

```
/* WOTCOST with data check */
#include <stdio.h>
#include <math.h>
void main (void)
{
    float P, Rpct, R, M;
    int N;
    printf ("\nEnter: Principal, Rate%, No. of yrs.\n");
    scanf ("%f %f %i", &P, &Rpct, &N );
    if ( ( P>ø ) && ( Rpct > ø ) && ( N > ø ) )
    {
        R = Rpct / 100;
        M = P*R*pow(1+R, N) / (12*(pow(1+R, N) - 1 ) );
        printf ("\n£%.2f, @%.2f%% costs £%.2f over %i years",P,Rpct,M,N);
        printf ("\nPayments will total %1.2f", 12*M*N );
    }
    else
        printf ( "Non-positive Data" );
}
```

the initial 'void' means the program returns no signal of success or failure to its environment *there is no 'return ø'*

&& says 'and'

block

All real programs have *loops*. When a program has finished computing one person's salary it works through the same set of instructions to compute the *next* person's salary, and so on through the payroll. That is a loop.

There are, however, different *kinds* of loop. This one is a 'counted' loop; you specify in advance how many times to go round.

```
/* Humbug */
#include <stdio.h>
void main ( void )
{
    int j;
    for ( j=0; j<3; ++j )
        printf ("\nWe wish you a merry Christmas");
    printf ("\nAnd a happy New Year!");
}
```

In this loop, j has a test for continuation (j<3) and stands at zero. Zero satisfies the test, so round we go, wishing you a merry Christmas. Then j is incremented by 1 (++j is short for j=j+1) to become 1. The test (j<3) is again satisfied, so round we go for another merry Christmas. This process continues until j reaches 3, at which stage the test is no longer satisfied; we don't offer any more merry Christmases; we drop out of the loop with New Year greetings.

for (*expression* ; *expression* ; *expression*) *statement*

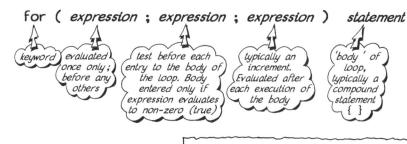

keyword | *evaluated once only; before any others* | *test before each entry to the body of the loop. Body entered only if expression evaluates to non-zero (true)* | *typically an increment. Evaluated after each execution of the body* | *'body' of loop, typically a compound statement { }*

You can specify an infinite loop by omitting the second expression (implying 1 = *true*) and get out of the loop with **break**.

getc(stdin) *defined on opposite page*

```
/* Count characters until new line */
#include <stdio.h>
void main ( void )
{
    int count = 0;   char ch;
    for ( ; ; )
    {
        Ch = getc ( stdin );
        if ( Ch = '\n' ) break;
        else ++count;
    }
    printf ("\nEntry has %i chars", count );
}
```

Later we meet 'tested' loop structures; the **while** loop and **do** loop:

while (*expression*) *statement*   **do** *statement* **while** (*expression*)

14   ILLUSTRATING C

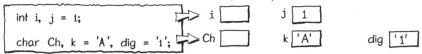

CHARACTERS

INTRODUCING CHARACTER CONSTANTS
"STRINGS" COME LATER

Previous examples illustrated type **int** (*integer*) and **float** (*floating-point number*, one that has a decimal point). Another type is **char**, short for *character*. A character is a letter, digit or symbol.

```
int i, j = 1;
```
⟹ i [ ]   j [1]

```
char Ch, k = 'A', dig = '1';
```
⟹ Ch [ ]   k ['A']   dig ['1']

What can we assume about the relationship of characters? Some aspects depend on the character set employed. In ANSI C:

• 'a' < 'b' < 'c' etc.

> *both alphabets (lower & upper case) are stored in ascending order*

• 'A' < 'B' < 'C' etc.

• 'ø' < '1' < '2' etc.

> *digits are stored in ascending order*

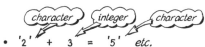

> *character   integer   character*

• '2' + 3 = '5' etc.

> *digits are stored contiguously*

If you work exclusively in the ASCII character set, the following relationships (*not* defined in ANSI C) also hold:

• 'i' + 1   gives   'j'
• 'I' + 1   gives   'J'

> *ASCII alphabets (not EBCDIC) are stored contiguously*

• 'i' + ('A' − 'a') gives 'I' etc.
• 'I' + ('a' − 'A') gives 'i' etc.

> *these relationships hold for EBCDIC letters also*

The previous examples featured scanf( ) and printf( ) for formatted items. For input of a single character from the keyboard use getc(stdin), and for output of a single character to the screen use putc(Ch, stdout). Both functions are defined in stdio.h. The parameters stdin and stdout indicate standard input and output streams defined by the system as depicted below.

Ch = getc (stdin)

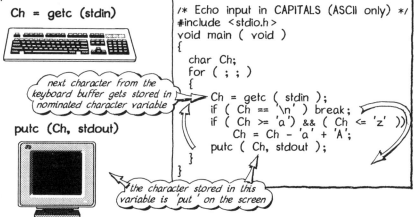

> *next character from the keyboard buffer gets stored in nominated character variable*

putc (Ch, stdout)

```
/* Echo input in CAPITALS (ASCII only) */
#include <stdio.h>
void main ( void )
{
    char Ch;
    for ( ; ; )
    {
        Ch = getc ( stdin );
        if ( Ch == '\n' ) break;
        if ( Ch >= 'a') && ( Ch <= 'z' ))
            Ch = Ch - 'a' + 'A';
        putc ( Ch, stdout );
    }
}
```

> *the character stored in this variable is 'put' on the screen*

 **ARRAYS**

The little boxes illustrated earlier are individual boxes for values of type int, float and char. You may also declare *arrays* of such boxes (∥ arrays of *elements* ∥). In any one array all elements are of the same type.

```
int M[6];
```

```
float Wow[3] = { 36, 18.5, 34 };
```

```
char Letter[14];
```

int

subscripts run from [ø]

float

initial-izer { , }

char

M[ø]
M[1]
M[2]
M[3]
M[4]
M[5]

Wow[ø] 36.ø
Wow[1] 18.5
Wow[2] 34.ø

[5] is called a subscript

Letter[ø]
Letter[1]
Letter[2]
Letter[3]
Letter[4]
Letter[5]
Letter[6]
Letter[7]
Letter[8]
Letter[9]
Letter[1ø]
Letter[11]
Letter[12]
Letter[13]

An array may be initialized as shown for Wow[ ] above. If you initialize *all* the elements you may leave the brackets empty and let the processor do the counting:

3 is implied by the initializer

```
float Wow [ ] = { 36, 18.5, 34 };
```

If the size is declared you may supply fewer initializing values; the processor pads out with zeros.

```
float M[5] = { 1, 2 };
```
implies { 1, 2, ø, ø, ø, ø }

Arrays may have any number of *dimensions*. Here is a two-dimensional array:

```
int Coeffs [5][3]
```

int Coeffs	[ø]	[1]	[2]
[ø]	1	1	ø
[1]	1	2	1
[2]	1	3	3
[3]	1	4	6
[4]	1	5	1ø

The array is stored by rows.

Multi dimensional arrays may be initialized using nested braces:

```
int Coeffs[5][3]={{1, 1 }, {1, 2, 1}, {1, 3, 3}, {1, 4, 6}, {1, 5, 1ø} }
```
missing items imply zero

If you arrange values by rows, and include all of them, you may ignore the inner braces:

```
int Coeffs [ ][3] = { 1, 1, ø, 1, 2, 1, 1, 3, 3, 1, 4, 6, 1, 5, 1ø };
```
5 not necessary *3 is necessary* *ø is necessary*

MATRIX MULTIPLICATION

Non-mathematicians don't go away! This is business. There are three sales people selling four products. Quantities sold are tabulated in Table A:

A

		PRODUCT			
		[∅]	[1]	[2]	[3]
SALES PERSON	[∅]	5	2	∅	1∅
	[1]	3	5	2	5
	[2]	2∅	∅	∅	∅

B

		MONEY	
		[∅]	[1]
PRODUCT	[∅]	1.5∅	∅.2∅
	[1]	2.8∅	∅.4∅
	[2]	5.00	1.00
	[3]	2.00	∅.5∅

Table B shows the price of each product and the commission earned by selling each item.

The money brought in is calculated thus:

SALES PERSON
[∅] $5 * 1.5∅ + 2 * 2.8∅ + ∅ * ∅.5∅ + 1∅ * 2.00 = 33.1∅$
[1] $3 * 1.5∅ + 5 * 2.8∅ + 2 * ∅.5∅ + 5 * 2.00 = 38.5∅$
[2] $2∅ * 1.5∅ + ∅ * 2.8∅ + ∅ * ∅.5∅ + ∅ * 2.00 = 3∅.00$

And the commissions earned thus:

SALES PERSON
[∅] $5*∅.2∅ + 2 * ∅.4∅ + ∅ * 1.00 + 1∅ *∅.5∅ = 6.8∅$
[1] $3*∅.2∅ + 5 * ∅.4∅ + 2 * 1.00 + 5 *∅.5∅ = 7.1∅$
[2] $2∅*∅.2∅ + ∅ * ∅.4∅ + ∅ * 1.00 + ∅ * ∅.5∅ = 4.00$

This computation is called matrix multiplication and looks best as set out below.

$$
\begin{array}{c}
 & [∅] \ [1] \ [2] \ [3] \\
A[∅] \\ A[1] \\ A[2]
\end{array}
\begin{bmatrix}
5 & 2 & ∅ & 1∅ \\
3 & 5 & 2 & 5 \\
2∅ & ∅ & ∅ & ∅
\end{bmatrix}
\times
\begin{array}{c}
 & [∅] \ [1] \\
B[∅] \\ B[1] \\ B[2] \\ B[3]
\end{array}
\begin{bmatrix}
1.5∅ & ∅.2∅ \\
2.8∅ & ∅.4∅ \\
5.00 & 1.00 \\
2.00 & ∅.5∅
\end{bmatrix}
=
\begin{array}{c}
 & [∅] \ [1] \\
C[∅] \\ C[1] \\ C[2]
\end{array}
\begin{bmatrix}
33.1∅ & 6.8∅ \\
38.5∅ & 7.1∅ \\
3∅.∅∅ & 4.00
\end{bmatrix}
$$

the number of columns of A must be the same as the number of rows of B and the result has as many rows as A & as many columns as B

Here is a program to input data for matrices A and B, multiply them together, then display their product, matrix C.

```
/* MATMUL Matrix multiplication */
#include <stdio.h>
float A[3][4], B[4][2], C[3][2];
int   n, i, j, k;
void main (void)
{
   for ( n=∅; n<3; ++n )
      scanf ( "%f %f %f %f", &A[n][∅], &A[n][1], &A[n][2], &A[n][3] );
   for ( n=∅; n<4; ++n )
      scanf ( "%f %f", &B[n][∅], &B[n][1] );
   for ( i=∅; i<2; ++i )
      for ( j=∅; j<3; ++j )
      {
         C[i][j] = ∅;
         for ( k=∅; k<4; ++k )
            C[j][i] += A[j][k] * B[k][i];
      }
   for ( n=∅; n<3; ++n )
      printf ( "%.2f %.2f, C[n][∅], C[n][1] );
}
```

enter A by rows
```
5       2       0       10
3       5       2       5
20      0       0       0
```

enter B by rows
```
1.50    0.20
2.80    0.40
5.00    1.00
2.00    0.50
```

```
33.10          6.80
38.50          7.10
30.00          4.00
```
program displays C by rows

2: CONCEPTS   17

HOOKE'S LAW

At school we hung little weights on the end of a spiral spring and measured its extension. If the spring extended 12mm on adding a one-gram weight we found it extended a further 12mm on adding the next gram. In other words we showed that extension is proportional to the force applied.

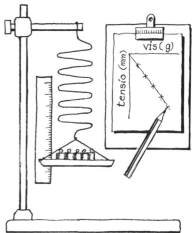

Robert Hooke (1635 – 1703) discovered this law and expressed it in Latin as 'ut tensio sic vis' (as the extension, thus the force). Then he tried to patent his discovery. To establish ownership before disclosing the secret, he published an *anagram* of 'ut tensio sic vis', made by arranging the letters of that sentence in alphabetical order.

Here is a program to compile Hooke's anagram. Run the program to see the anagram he published.

```c
/* Anagram of Hooke's Law */
#include <stdio.h>

void main (void)
{                        the number of letters
    char Letter[14] = {'u','t', 't','e','n','s','i','o', 's','i','c', 'v','i','s'};
    int j, k, Tempry;            j = j + 1
    for ( j=0; j<13; ++j)             k = k - 1
        for ( k=13; j<k; --k)
            if ( Letter[k-1]>Letter[k])
                {
                    Tempry = Letter[k-1];
                    Letter[k-1] = Letter[k];       swop
                    Letter[k] = Tempry;            adjacent
                }                                  letters
    printf ("\nHooke's anagram is ");
    for (j=0; j<14; ++j)
        putchar ( Letter[j] );
}
```

This program illustrates the technique called 'bubble sort' which is suitable for sorting small lists. For longer lists there are better methods such as Quicksort which is explained on Page 62.

Here is how the bubble sort works. To keep the illustration simple we shorten the quotation for uttensiosicvis to utten.

The outer loop is controlled by j which starts at ø as depicted in the first row of the table below. k is set pointing to the bottom letter. That letter is compared with the letter immediately above it (Letter [k-1] > Letter [k]) . If these two letters are out of order they are exchanged, otherwise left alone. Notice that the first two letters to be compared (n below, e above) are in the correct order.

Still with j set to zero, k is decremented by 1 so that it indicates the next letter up. This letter is compared with the letter immediately above it as before. If the two are out of order they are exchanged. In this case (e below, t above) they are out of order and therefore exchanged.

Again k is decremented so as to indicate the next letter up. Again this letter is compared with the letter above it and an exchange made if the two are out of order. And so on until k has risen to a position just below j. That completes the first cycle of j. The lightest letter has now risen to the top.

Back to the outer loop; j is incremented so that it indicates the second letter in the list. k is set to the bottom of the list. Then the whole procedure, described above, is started again. But this time there is less to do because k does not have to rise so high. In the second cycle of j the second lightest letter rises to the second position in the list.

And so on until the list has been sorted.

read table row by row

FUNCTIONS

MORE CONCEPTS *
IN PARTICULAR THAT OF 'CALL BY VALUE'

The introductory example used a function from the **math** library called pow( ) (short for *power*).

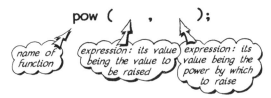

pow (,);

- name of function
- expression: its value being the value to be raised
- expression: its value being the power by which to raise

Example: $2.0^{3.0}$ would be expressed pow(2.0, 3.0); the value returned would be 8.0.

The parameters of the library function pow( ) are, in general, both of 'floating' type. In the introductory example, however, the second parameter was constrained to whole numbers by being declared of type int. This constraint is essential to what follows.

Here is the first example again, but instead of using pow( ) from the math library we supply and invoke our own function, Powr( ).

```
/* WOTCOST with home-made Powr() */
#include <stdio.h>
float Powr ( float x, int n )
{
  float v;
  for ( v=1.0 ; n>0 ; --n )
    v = v * x;
  return ( v );
}
void main ( void )
{
  float P, Rpct, R, M;
  int N;
  printf ("\nEnter: P, Rate%, Nyrs\n" );
  scanf ("%f %f %i", &P, &Rpct, &N );
  R = Rpct/100 ;
  M = P * R * Powr(1+R, N)/(12 *(Powr(1+R, N)-1));
  printf ("Costs £%1.2f per month", M );
}
```

- don't include math.h
- header of home-made function, Powr()
- declarations before statements
- block of code for home-made function, Powr ( )
- main ( ) much as before
- invoke Powr ( ) twice

- program
- user
- program

```
Enter P, Rate%, Nyrs
5000 15.5 5
Costs £125.77 per month
```

The home-made function is dissected below:

float Powr ( );   The header gives the name of the function being defined and the type of value the function will return. If the function returns no value at all, write **void**.

`float Powr ( float x, int n )` **T**he header also shows how many parameters there are, and the type of each. The names of parameters in the header are names of *dummy* parameters ⇆ private to the block that follows the header. It does not matter if these names coincide with names in **main** (⟨ or in any other function that might invoke Powr ⟩). In this example, **n** could just as well be **N** ⇆ without confusion with the **N** declared in **main**.

`float v ;` **V**ariable v is private to the function; a local variable. Outside the function any reference to v would be treated as an error. But when the program obeys a statement that invokes the function, a new variable v is created. When the program has finished with the function (⟨ having returned a value to the invoking statement ⟩) the variable v, together with its content, evaporates.

`for ( v=1.∅ ; n>∅ ; n=n-1 )` **V**ariable v is initialized to 1.∅ before the loop is executed for the first time. If Powr() were invoked with a value of 3 for n, the body of the loop would be executed 3 times. n=n-1 may be abbreviated to n-=1 or --n as we shall see.

`v = v * x;` **T**his is the body of the loop. v begins at 1.∅. The accumulating value in v is multiplied by the value found in x (⟨ computed from 1+R in this example ⟩) on every circuit of the loop. This statement may be abbreviated to v *= x as we shall see.

`return (v);` **T**his is an instruction (⟨ return is a keyword ⟩) to stop executing statements of the function and offer the value in variable **v** as the value to be returned by this function. The 'return ∅' at the end of a main() program returns ∅ to its *environment* if execution has been successful.

CALL BY VALUE

FUNDAMENTAL TO C-LANGUAGE

When you write a statement that *invokes* the function (⟨ in this case the relevant part of that statement is Powr(1+R, N) ⟩) you substitute appropriate *expressions* for the dummy parameters x and n. Here we substitute 1+R for x and substitute N for n.

When the processor comes to obey the statement in which you invoke the function, it works out the value of 1+R (⟨ this might be 1.1, for example ⟩) and the *value* of N (⟨ this might be 3, for example ⟩). The program then starts obeying the statement { in the function block } with x initialized to 1.1 and n initialized to 3. This concept is known as *call by value*.

Although you invoke the function with Powr(1+R, N) the function is incapable of changing the content of variables N or R. In general, *no* function in C can change the content of a variable offered as an argument.

A function *can* change the contents of *global* variables, as demonstrated on the next page. A function can also change values to which pointers point, but this topic is left until later.

RATE OF INTEREST

INTRODUCING GLOBAL & LOCAL VARIABLES

The program in the first example computed the monthly repayment for a loan, given the size of the loan, the rate of interest and the term. But here is a more difficult problem; a loan of P is to be repaid at M per month over N years; what rate of interest is being charged?

$$M = \frac{PR(1+R)^N}{12((1+R)^N-1)}$$

$$where\ R = P/100$$

The equation shown above may be solved for R by trial and error. Guess R, substitute in the formula to compute Mt, then:

- if Mt is the same 《 very nearly 》 as M the guess was correct; accept R

- if Mt is too small it means R was guessed too low, so multiply the rate by M/Mt to make it bigger and try again

- if Mt is too big it means R was guessed too high, so multiply the rate by M/Mt to make it smaller and try again.

This algorithm causes the ratio M/Mt to get closer and closer to 1. Make the program continue as long as the difference between M/Mt and 1 is more than 0.005 《 say 》. The difference may be positive or negative, so we must ask if its *absolute value* 《 value ignoring sign 》 is greater than 0.005.

Here are some global declarations and three functions:

```
/* WOTRATE: computes rate of loan interest */
#include <stdio.h>
float P, M, R = 0.01;
int N;
float Powr (float x, int n)
{
   float v;
   for (v=1.0; n>0; n=n-1)
      v = v * x;
   return (v);
}
```

variables P, N, M, R declared globally (at file level). R is initialized at 1 % before first entry to loop

n--

v= x*

```
float Formula (void)
{
   float v;
   v = Powr (1+R, N);
   return(P*R*v)/(12*(v-1));
}
```

computes formula at top of page, referring to global P, R, N, hence no need for parameters. Formula( ) invokes Powr( )

this v is local to Formula( ). no connection with v in Powr( )

local P

```
float Absolute (float P)
{
   if ( P >= 0.0) return P;
   else return -P;
}
```

local P 'hides' global P

more concisely
float Absolute(float P)
{ return (P<0.0)? -P: P;}

Finally function main( ):

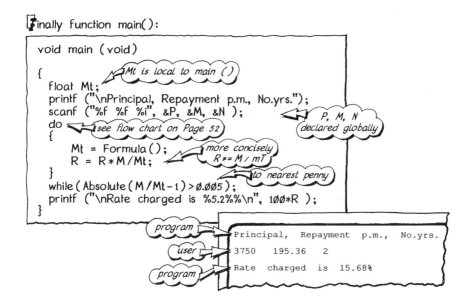

```
void main ( void )

{
    float Mt;                          [Mt is local to main ( )]
    printf ("\nPrincipal, Repayment p.m., No.yrs.");
    scanf ("%f %f %i", &P, &M, &N );                    [P, M, N declared globally]
    do          [see flow chart on Page 52]
    {
        Mt = Formula ();         [more concisely R *= M / mT]
        R = R*M/Mt;
    }                                    [to nearest penny]
    while ( Absolute ( M /Mt-1 ) >Ø.ØØ5 );
    printf ("\nRate charged is %5.2%%\n", 1ØØ*R );
}
```

program →	Principal, Repayment p.m., No.yrs.
user →	3750 195.36 2
program →	Rate charged is 15.68%

SCOPE OF VARIABLES

A FEW FUNDAMENTALS

Variables P, M, R, N are declared *at file level* or *globally* which means outside every function. Implications of global declarations are:

- the processor reserves space for the variables declared. Declarations that reserve space are called *definitions*

- global variables retain the space reserved for them throughout the run. Their contents do not evaporate during the run

- variables may be referred to by statements in functions provided that:

    (i) any reference *follows* a declaration in the same file ⟨ or follows an **extern** declaration if in a different file ☞ see later ⟩

    (ii) the name referred to is not *hidden* by a local variable ⟨like variable P in function Absolute( ) opposite⟩.

Variable v in Powr( ), and variable v in Formula( ), have only a transient existence. Although v is *declared* in Powr( ) on the first line after the header, it is not *defined* until Powr( ) is invoked. It then exists only until control reaches **return** (v). At this instant control leaves Powr( ), and variable v evaporates, together with its contents. Puff! Next time Powr( ) is invoked, variable v could find itself somewhere else in memory. Such variables are called *automatic* to distinguish them from the *static* variables which retain identity throughout the run.

RECURSION

The highest common factor ((hcf)) of 1470 and 693 is 21. In other words 21 is the biggest number that will divide into 1470 and 693 without leaving a remainder in either case. To verify this, factorize both numbers to prime factors:

$$1470 = 2 \times 3 \times 5 \times 7 \times 7$$
$$693 = 3 \times 3 \times 7 \times 11$$

and pair off any common factors ≈ in this case 3 and 7. The highest common factor ((also called the greatest common divisor)) is the product of these: in this case 3 x 7 = 21.

Euclid's method of finding the hcf is more elegant. Find the remainder when 1470 is divided by 693. ((The % operator gives this remainder)):

1470 % 693 ⟹ 84

Because this remainder is not zero, repeat the process, substituting the second number for the first and the remainder for the second:

693 % 84 ⟹ 21

This remainder is still not zero so repeat the process:

84 % 21 ⟹ 0

This remainder is zero, so the hcf is 21. Nice!

Here is a C function based on Euclid's method:

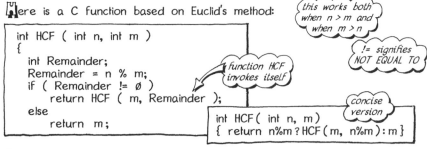

```
int HCF ( int n, int m )
{
    int Remainder;
    Remainder = n % m;
    if ( Remainder != 0 )
        return HCF ( m, Remainder );
    else
        return  m;
}
```

*this works both
when n > m and
when m > n*

*!= signifies
NOT EQUAL TO*

*function HCF
invokes itself*

*concise
version*

```
int HCF ( int n, m )
{ return n%m ? HCF ( m, n%m ) : m }
```

It is easy to see what would happen with HCF(84, 21) because Remainder would become zero, making the function return 21. But with HCF(1470, 693) Remainder becomes 84, so the function invokes itself as HCF(693, 84). In so doing, Remainder becomes 21, therefore the function invokes itself as HCF(84, 21). It is as though C provided a fresh copy of the code of function HCF() on each invocation.

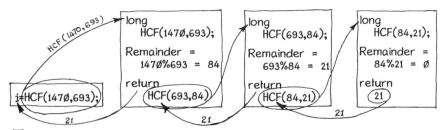

The ability of a function to invoke a fresh copy of itself is called *recursion.*

ILLUSTRATING C

If you find the function opposite confusing, here is a simpler example; the hackneyed *factorial*:

The factorial of 5 is 5 x 4 x 3 x 2 x 1 = 12Ø. Mathematicians indicate a factorial by a post-fixed exclamation mark:

  5! = 12Ø

It is obvious that the factorial of 5 is 5 times the factorial of 4:

  5! = 5 x 4!

So what is the factorial of n? Clearly:

  n! = n x (n-1)!

But that's too hasty. What if n is 1? If n is 1 then factorial n is 1.

Tell this to the computer by encoding:

  'if n is 1 then factorial n is 1,
  otherwise factorial n is n times factorial (n-1) '

```
#include <stdio.h>

long int Factorial (long int n)
{
  if (n==1)
      return 1;
  else
      return n*Factorial(n-1);
}
```

And try out the function by appending a simple main() function:

```
void main (void)
{
  long int m, k;
  printf ("Integer please\n");
  scanf ("%f", &m );
  k = Factorial(m);
  printf ("%lf", k);
}
```

```
Integer please
4
24
```

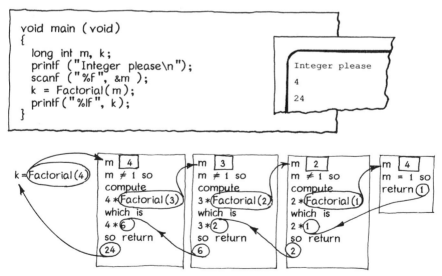

EXERCISES

1 Program MATMUL multiplies matrices of fixed size (3 rows, 4 columns; 4 rows, 2 columns). Make the program deal with any specified sizes up to an arbitrary 100 by 100.

Read three sizes: the number of rows of A, the number of columns of A (implying also the number of rows of B), the number of columns of B. Read A and B by rows, then print C by rows. For this exercise you have to change each simple reading loop to a nested pair of loops. Similarly the printing loop.

2 Alter the Hookes's Law program to read and sort a list of numbers (type double) into numerical order, then display the sorted list. Make the program request the length of list, then ask for the numbers one by one.

3 For the math library functions sin(x) and cos(x), the value of x must be expressed in radians. Write functions Sine(a) and Cosine(a) for which the argument, a, must be expressed in degrees of arc. All types are double.

4 Write function Reverse(A, N) to display an array of integers in reverse order. An obvious way to do this is print A[--N] in a loop until N stores zero. Instead of using a loop, write the function so that it employs recursion.

3

COMPONENTS

This chapter defines most of the basic components of C. Their syntax is defined using a pictorial notation. Characters, names and constants (the simple building blocks) are defined first. Important principles of the language are next explained; these include the concept of scalar 'types', the precedence and associativity of 'operators', the concepts of 'coercion' and 'promotion' in expressions of mixed type.

The operators are summarized on a single page for ease of reference.

The syntax of expressions and statements is defined in this chapter. Declarations are discussed, but their syntax is not defined because it involves the concept of pointers and dynamic storage. These topics are left to later chapters.

 *TO DESCRIBE THE WRITTEN FORM (SYNTAX)*
OF THE BUILDING BLOCKS OF C

For a precise definition of the syntax of ANSI C, see the definitions in ANSI X 3.159. These are expressed in BNF (Backus Naur Form).

To appreciate the syntactical form of an entity the practical programmer needs something different; BNF is not a self evident notation. Some books employ railway track diagrams, potentially easier to comprehend than BNF, but the tracks grow too complicated for defining structures in C. So I have devised a pictorial notation from which a programmer should be able to appreciate syntactical forms at a glance. The notation is fairly rigorous but needs a little help from notes here and there.

italics

Italic letters are used to name the entities being defined: *digit, token, integer* and so on

The broad arrow says that the nominated entity 'is defined to be ...' (in this example 'An *integer* is defined to be ...')

Romans,
& + (* /
Ø12 etc.

These stand for themselves. Copy them from the diagram just as they are. Do not change case; R and r are *not* the same letter

Vertical bars contain two or more rows and offer the choice of *one* row. Vertical bars may be nested

Forward arrow says the item or items beneath may be skipped over; in other words they are optional. In some cases a word is written over the arrow: this defines the implication of skipping the item under the arrow

Backward arrow says you may return to go through this part of the diagram again (typically choosing another item from vertical bars)

This also says you may return, but must insert a comma before the next item; it defines a 'comma list'

Notes may be explanatory or definitive. A typical definitive note points to *expression* and says *'must be integral'*

▶

This symbol is put in front of illustrations; it says 'for example' or 'e.g.'

CHARACTERS

```
character  ⟩  letter
              digit
              symbol
              escape
```
⟵ **T**he diagram says 'A character is defined as a *letter* or *digit* or *symbol* or *escape*'

```
letter ⟩
```

```
symbol ⟩
```

```
digit ⟩   Ø
           1
           2
           3
           4
           5
           6
           7
           8
           9
```

Upper and lower case letters are distinct in C. Z is not the same letter as z.

Digits Ø to 9 are decimal digits. Octal and hex digits are defined on Page 197.

A few characters, such as $, £, @, are available in most implementations of C. They may be used as character constants and in strings but are not defined by ANSI C.

Not every installation can manage the full range of *symbols*. The Standard gets round this problem by defining a range of *trigraphs*. If you type ??<, for example, the implementation should substitute the code for a left brace. And similarly for the other trigraphs. Substitution is carried out before any other operation on the text.

In Chapter 1 you saw the *escape* sequence \n which is effectively a single character, although compounded of two. It represents the new line character. It is no good pressing Return to get a new line character because that would mess up the layout of the program. You don't *want* a new line *in your program*; you want the computer to make a new line when printing results. \n does the trick.

An *'escape sequence'* is needed whenever the character to be conveyed would upset something, or has no corresponding key on the keyboard ⮐ like 'ring the bell'.

symbol column:
```
'
,
.
:
;
?
"
!
|
/
\
~
%
&
^
*
-
=
+
<
>
(
)
[
]
{
}
#
```

??/ \
??- ~
??' ^
??([
??)]
??> }
??< {
??= #

letter column:
```
A a
B b
C c
D d
E e
F f
G g
H h
I i
J j
K k
L l
M m
N n
O o
P p
Q q
R r
S s
T t
U u
V v
W w
X x
Y y
Z z
```

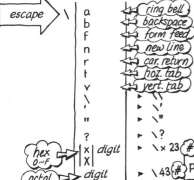

```
escape ⟩  \   a ── ring bell
              b ── backspace
              f ── form feed
              n ── new line
              r ── car. return
              t ── hoz. tab
              v ── vert. tab
              \ ── ► \\
              " ── ► \"
              ? ── ► \?
       hex ── x│ digit ── ► \x 23 #
       0~F    X│
       octal ── digit ── ► \43 #
       0~7   Ø ── ► \Ø NULL
```

An example of 'upsetting something' is a double quote in printf (" "); which would close the quotation prematurely. You can include a double quote in a quotation as the single *escape* sequence \" as follows:

```
printf("\"Ooh!\" I exclaimed.");
```

NAMES

The example programs in the first chapter illustrate several names invented by the programmer to identify variables. Such names are also called *identifiers*. Names are used to identify other things in C apart from objects such as variables.

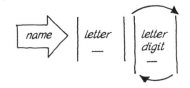

The diagram shows that a *name* starts with a letter or underscore, that the first character may be followed by other letters, digits, underscores. Examples are: LengthOfWall, Lenth_Of_Wall, __DATE__.

The name you invent should not clash with a keyword. There are thirty-two keywords in ASCII C as listed here. Remember that upper and lower case letters are distinct, so Auto and Break are *not* keywords and may be used as names of variables.

The names chosen for use in the programs of this book are safe from clashing with keywords or with names of standard library functions. The names used are:

• single letters *e.g.* i, N

• capitalized words *e.g.* Length

• capitalized phrases *e.g.* NewLength, Old_Height

You may not give the same name to an array and to a variable in the same piece of program.

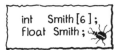

```
int    Smith[6];
float  Smith;
```

In general, functions and *objects* (*i.e.* variables, arrays, structures, unions, enumerations) have unique names in the same piece of program. If an object that is local to a function has the same name as a global object, the global object becomes hidden from view.

Not all names behave in this way; names of *tags* and *labels*, for example, do not clash; they occupy a different *name space*. Name space is explained in Chapter 5.

auto
break
case
char
const
continue
default
do
double
else
enum
extern
float
for
goto
if
int
long
register
return
short
signed
sizeof
static
struct
switch
typedef
union
unsigned
void
volatile
while

SCALAR TYPES

WE MEET AGGREGATES
AND COMPLEX TYPES LATER

A typical declaration at the beginning of a program is:

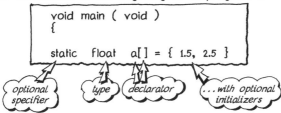

```
void main ( void )
{
static   float   a[ ] = { 1.5, 2.5 }
```

optional specifier — *type* — *declarator* — *...with optional initializers*

The implications of specifiers, declarators, initializers are far-reaching and complicated. All are explained in subsequent pages. For the moment, consider a declaration of a simple scalar (single valued) variable.

```
float b;
```

type — *declarator just a name*

The syntax for scalar *type* is defined as follows:

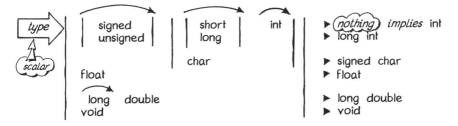

type (*scalar*)

signed		short	int
unsigned		long	
		char	
float			
long double			
void			

▶ (*nothing*) *implies* int
▶ long int

▶ signed char
▶ float

▶ long double
▶ void

The diagram is simplified for clarity; the syntax of C allows permutations. For example, the following are all allowed and equivalent: signed long int, long signed int, signed int long, *etc.*

You can define an *alias* (synonym) for a phrase using the **typedef** facility:

typedef   *type   name* ◀ *alias*

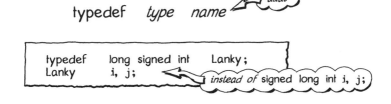

```
typedef    long signed int    Lanky;
Lanky      i, j;
```
◀ *instead of* signed long int i, j;

3: COMPONENTS   31

ON YOUR MACHINE

The number and arrangement of binary digits (bits) representing each scalar type depends on the implementation, subject to certain minimal requirements if the implementation is to comply with ANSI C. The following implementation is typical.

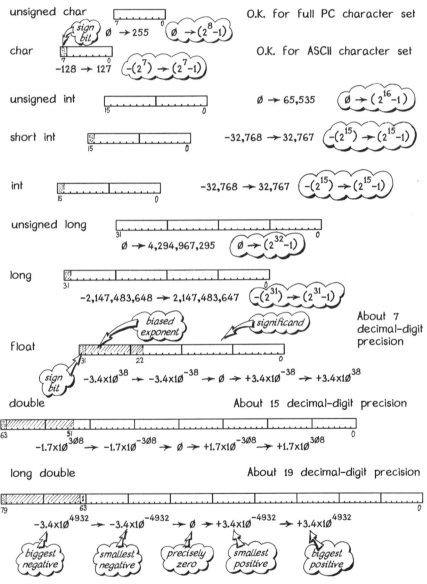

unsigned char — O.K. for full PC character set

sign bit $\emptyset \to 255$ $(\emptyset \to (2^8 - 1))$

char — O.K. for ASCII character set

$-128 \to 127$ $(-(2^7) \to (2^7 - 1))$

unsigned int — $\emptyset \to 65{,}535$ $(\emptyset \to (2^{16} - 1))$

short int — $-32{,}768 \to 32{,}767$ $(-(2^{15}) \to (2^{15} - 1))$

int — $-32{,}768 \to 32{,}767$ $(-(2^{15}) \to (2^{15} - 1))$

unsigned long — $\emptyset \to 4{,}294{,}967{,}295$ $(\emptyset \to (2^{32} - 1))$

long — $-2{,}147{,}483{,}648 \to 2{,}147{,}483{,}647$ $(-(2^{31}) \to (2^{31} - 1))$

biased exponent · significand · About 7 decimal-digit precision

float — sign bit · $-3.4 \times 10^{38} \to -3.4 \times 10^{-38} \to \emptyset \to +3.4 \times 10^{-38} \to +3.4 \times 10^{38}$

double — About 15 decimal-digit precision

$-1.7 \times 10^{308} \to -1.7 \times 10^{-308} \to \emptyset \to +1.7 \times 10^{-308} \to +1.7 \times 10^{308}$

long double — About 19 decimal-digit precision

$-3.4 \times 10^{4932} \to -3.4 \times 10^{-4932} \to \emptyset \to +3.4 \times 10^{-4932} \to +3.4 \times 10^{4932}$

biggest negative · smallest negative · precisely zero · smallest positive · biggest positive

CONSTANTS

The introductory program has the line R = Rpct / 100; The 100 is a *literal constant.* The program on Hooke's anagram illustrates character constants, 'u', 't', *etc.* These are also *literal* constants. *Named* constants are introduced over the page.

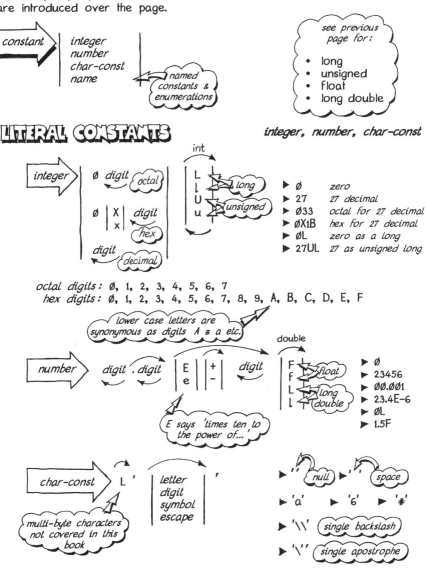

constant → integer
number
char-const
name

→ *named constants & enumerations*

see previous page for:
- long
- unsigned
- float
- long double

LITERAL CONSTANTS

integer, number, char-const

integer

ø *digit* (octal)

ø | X / x | *digit* (hex)

digit (decimal)

int
L / l → (long)
U / u → (unsigned)

▶ ø   *zero*
▶ 27   *27 decimal*
▶ ø33   *octal for 27 decimal*
▶ øX1B   *hex for 27 decimal*
▶ øL   *zero as a long*
▶ 27UL   *27 as unsigned long*

octal digits : ø, 1, 2, 3, 4, 5, 6, 7
hex digits : ø, 1, 2, 3, 4, 5, 6, 7, 8, 9, A, B, C, D, E, F

lower case letters are synonymous as digits A ≡ a etc.

number → *digit* . *digit* | E / e | | + / - | *digit*

double
F / f → (float)
L / l → (long double)

▶ ø
▶ 23456
▶ øø.øø1
▶ 23.4E-6
▶ øL
▶ 1.5F

E says 'times ten to the power of...'

char-const → L ' | letter digit symbol escape | '

multi-byte characters not covered in this book

▶ '' (null)   ▶ ' ' (space)

▶ 'a'   ▶ '6'   ▶ '#'

▶ '\\' (single backslash)

▶ '\'' (single apostrophe)

STRING LITERALS

"STRINGS" ARE DEFINED IN CHAPTER 6

NAMED CONSTANTS

If your program deals with the geometry of circles you may write the value of π as a literal constant:

```
Area = 3.141593 * d * d / 4;
```

Or give π a name and value as shown here:

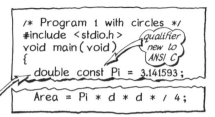

```
/* Program 1 with circles */
#include <stdio.h>          qualifier
void main ( void )           new to
{                            ANSI C
    double const Pi = 3.141593;

    Area = Pi * d * d * / 4;
```

The const is a *qualifier*. It qualifies the variable declared next on its right. The nominated variable should be initialized in the same declaration. Thereafter, the processor will not allow you to change the initialized value ⇌ by assignment or any other means. You may not use this kind of constant in 'constant expressions' evaluated at compile time.

The traditional way to name a C constant is to write a name (⟮ PI say ⟯) and tell the *preprocessor* to substitute a value for it.

Write #define with # as the first visible character on the line and no semicolon at the end as shown. From there on the preprocessor will substitute 3.141593 for every independent occurrence of PI (⟮ not in comments or where PI is part of a longer token ⟯). The preprocessor is covered in Chapter 5.

```
/* Program 2 with circles */
#include <stdio.h>
#define PI    3.141593
void main ( void )
{
                      substitution

    Area = PI * d * d * / 4;
    /* substitute value for PI */
                untouched

    PIPE = 6;
```

ENUMERATIONS

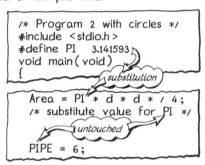

```
                              tag                    integral
enumeration >enum   name {   name  =  expression }  name ;
                                                     ← , ↲
```

Integral constants may be named in an *enumeration*. You may nominate **int** variables capable of storing **int** values in the range of the enumeration

- ► enum { No, Yes }; ⟸ *synonyms for ø and 1 respectively*
- ► enum Boolean { False, True }; ⟸ *defines a type, enum Boolean*
- ► enum Boolean Ok; ⟸ *declares variable of type 'enum Boolean'*
- ► enum Imperial {Inch=1, Foot=12*Inch} L; ⟮ *L, type 'enum Imperial', may take the value Inch (1) or Foot (12)* ⟯

```
Ok = ( a > b ) ? True : False;      variable Ok correctly used in
if ( Ok != Yes ) break;             range of its enumeration

Ok = ( a > b );          ⟸ probably allowable
Ok = 2 * Yes;            ⟸ not nice; out of range
Yes = No;                ⟸ error: Yes is a CONSTANT
```

EXPRESSIONS

Expressions are used in earlier examples without formal definition. The definition of *expression* is simple:

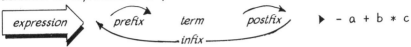

expression ⟩ prefix   term   postfix ▶ - a + b * c
                      — infix —

Operators are described individually later in this chapter; here they are defined syntactically under the names *prefix*, *postfix* and *infix*:

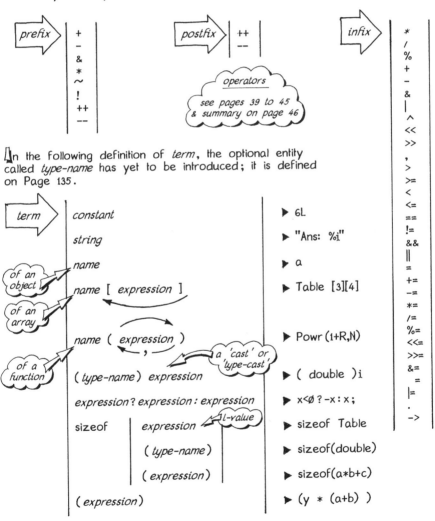

In the following definition of *term*, the optional entity called *type-name* has yet to be introduced; it is defined on Page 135.

prefix	postfix	infix
+	++	*
-	--	/
&		%
*		+
~		-
!		&
++		|
--		^

operators see pages 39 to 45 & summary on page 46

infix: * / % + - & | ^ << >> , > >= < <= == != && || = += -= *= /= %= <<= >>= &= = |= . ->

term:
- constant ▶ 6L
- string ▶ "Ans: %i"
- name ▶ a   *(of an object)*
- name [expression] ▶ Table [3][4]   *(of an array)*
- name (expression) ▶ Powr (1+R,N)   *(of a function)*
- (type-name) expression ▶ (double)i   *(a 'cast' or 'type-cast')*
- expression? expression : expression ▶ x<Ø ? -x : x ;
- sizeof expression ▶ sizeof Table   *(l-value)*
- sizeof (type-name) ▶ sizeof(double)
- sizeof (expression) ▶ sizeof(a*b+c)
- (expression) ▶ (y * (a+b))

STATEMENTS AND PROGRAM

Here is the syntax of *statement*. Some control statements have already been introduced (if, for, break, return), others are covered in Chapter 4.

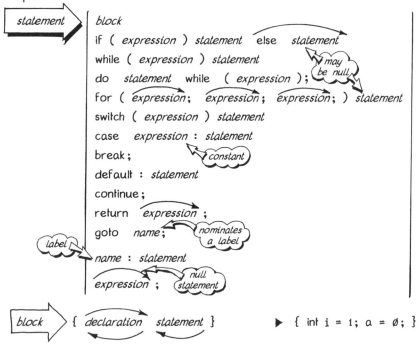

statement

block

if (*expression*) *statement*   else   *statement*

while (*expression*) *statement*   *may be null*

do   *statement*   while   (*expression*);

for (*expression*; *expression*; *expression*;) *statement*

switch (*expression*) *statement*

case   *expression* : *statement*

break;   *constant*

default : *statement*

continue;

return   *expression* ;

goto   *name*;   *nominates a label*

label

name : *statement*

expression ;   *null statement*

block   { *declaration*   *statement* }   ▶ { int i = 1; a = Ø; }

Because a *statement* may be a *block*, and because a *block* contains at least one *statement*, it follows that *blocks* may be 'nested'. All the *declarations* in each block must precede the first *statement* of that block.

Below is the syntax of *program*:

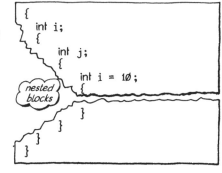

```
{
    int i;
    {
        int j;
        {
            int i = 1Ø;
            {
nested
blocks
            }
        }
    }
}
```

program   declaration

A *program* comprises a set of *declarations*, each of which may declare a global object, a function prototype or a function definition. You must give precisely one function the name *main*.

DECLARATIONS

OF 'OBJECTS' AND FUNCTIONS
(FOR FULL SYNTAX SEE CHAPTER 8)

'Objects' (or 'data objects') are variables, arrays, enumerations, structures and unions. We meet structures and unions in Chapter 8.

Objects are things which have a name and a *type* (or *shape*) and can store data. An object must be declared before it can be used.

Because structures and unions have not yet been introduced, the full syntax of a declaration must wait until later (Chapter 8). Some examples of typical declarations of simple types are shown here:

```
int     j, k;
char  Letter[ ] = { 'a', 'b', 'c' };
float   x = 3.45;
```

Each declaration applies as far as the end of the current file (the 'scope' of the declaration). But in a block of program within this scope, a contradictory declaration may 'hide' the original (the 'visibility'). Scope and visibility are further described below.

DECLARATION *VERSUS* DEFINITION

A SEMANTIC DIFFERENCE

When an object is initialized (*e.g.* float x = 3.45) the declaration becomes a *definition*; any further defining of x would make the processor report an error during compilation or linking.

An object *declared* but not initialized (*e.g.* int i) is, in general, automatically initialized to zero at the end of compilation as though you had originally declared int i = Ø. The object is then *defined*.

The differences between *declaration* and *definition* are semantic rather than syntactic. The differences are, in fact, more complicated than suggested above, and are further described in Chapter 5.

FUNCTION DEFINITION

SEQUENCE OF DECLARATIONS

Function Absolute( ), introduced earlier, is defined again here. Statements inside this function, and statements inside functions that follow this definition, may all invoke Absolute( ). Invocations from inside functions that precede this definition would be errors.

Referring back to the program on Page 22, notice that function Powr( ) precedes function Formula( ) in which Powr( ) is invoked, and that Formula( ) precedes main( ) in which Formula( ) is invoked.

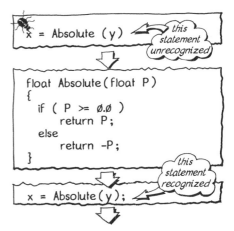

```
x = Absolute ( y )
```
this statement unrecognized

```
float Absolute( float P )
{
    if ( P >= Ø.Ø )
        return P;
    else
        return -P;
}
```

```
x = Absolute( y );
```
this statement recognized

PROTOTYPES

The restriction on sequence of declarations explained above may be removed by employing a *function declaration* as well as a *function definition*.

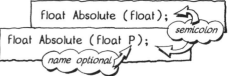

A function declaration is called a *prototype*; a concept new to ANSI C.

A prototype has the same form as the header of a function definition except:

• names of variables are simply comments; they may be different from those in the definition or omitted altogether

• every prototype ends with a semicolon.

Each prototype must be placed somewhere before the first invocation of the corresponding function; an obvious place is near the top of the file.

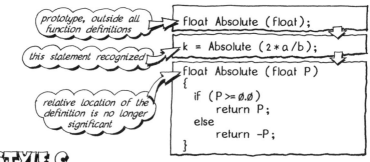

OLD~STYLE C

Prototypes did not exist in 'old-style' C. Furthermore, the shape of a function *definition* was different, the parameters being declared between the header and its block. Although this syntax is permitted by ANSI C, it is not illustrated further in this book.

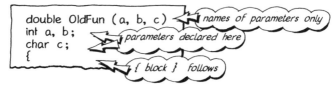

HEADER FILES

To keep a program tidy, collect all the prototypes in a file and give the file a name such as MYHDR.H (where .H signifies a *header file*). At the top of your main program write #include "MYHDR.H" which has the same effect as copying out all the prototypes ahead of the main program.

OPERATORS

On Page 35 operators are grouped according to their role in the syntax of expressions ⟨ *prefix, infix, postfix* ⟩. Here they are classified according to the kind of work they do.

The term *operand* signifies *expression*, the expression conforming to any special requirements noted ⟨ such as integral value ⟩.

ARITHMETIC OPERATORS   +   -   %   /   *

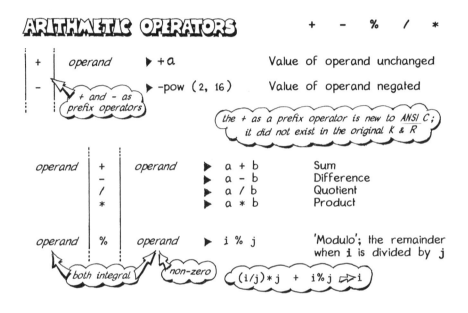

	+	operand	▶ +a	Value of operand unchanged

	-		▶ -pow (2, 16)	Value of operand negated

+ and - as prefix operators

the + as a prefix operator is new to ANSI C; it did not exist in the original K & R

operand	+	operand	▶ a + b	Sum
	-		▶ a - b	Difference
	/		▶ a / b	Quotient
	*		▶ a * b	Product

operand	%	operand	▶ i % j	'Modulo'; the remainder when i is divided by j

both integral   *non-zero*   (i/j)*j + i%j ⟹ i

LOGICAL OPERATORS   !   >   >=   <   <=   ==   && ||

Logical *not* is a prefix operator

	!		operand	▶ !Try

If Try contains a non-zero value ⟨true⟩ then !Try indicates a zero value ⟨false⟩. And vice versa

operand	
≠ Ø	= Ø
Ø	1

 ! operand

Each comparison made using the following six infix operators takes the result 1 (❨ type **int** ❩) if the comparison proves to be *true*; zero if it proves *false*.

operand		*operand*			
	>		▶	n > m	Greater than (❨6>5 gives 1❩)
	>=		▶	n >= m	Greater than or equal to
	<		▶	n < m	Less than (❨6<5 gives Ø❩)
	<=		▶	n <= m	Less than or equal to
	==		▶	n == m	Equal to
	!=		▶	n != m	Not equal to

Truth tables for the operators && (❨ and ❩) and || (❨ or ❩) are shown. The symmetry of the tables shows that these operations are *commutative*. For example, i && j gives the same result as j && i;

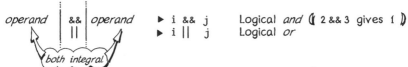

operand	&&	*operand*			
	||		▶	i && j	Logical *and* (❨ 2 && 3 gives 1 ❩)
			▶	i || j	Logical *or*

both integral

and &&		operand	
		≠ Ø	= Ø
operand	≠ Ø	1	Ø
	= Ø	Ø	Ø

or ||		operand	
		≠ Ø	= Ø
operand	≠ Ø	1	1
	= Ø	1	Ø

BITWISE OPERATORS
& / ^ ~ << >>

Bitwise operators are vital for screen graphics, for packing and unpacking data, and other devices of the programmer's craft.

All operands of bitwise operators must be integral. Because computers have different ways of representing negative integers, use bitwise operators *only on the unsigned* types.

unsigned int on your installation may be represented as a 16-bit word. If so, 26 will be stored like this:

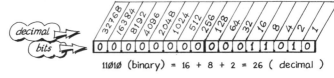

decimal ⟶
bits ⟶

32768	16384	8192	4096	2048	1024	512	256	128	64	32	16	8	4	2	1
0	0	0	0	0	0	0	0	0	0	0	1	1	0	1	0

11Ø1Ø (binary) = 16 + 8 + 2 = 26 (decimal)

Zero is stored as sixteen Ø's. The biggest number (❨ 1+2+4+8+16+...+32768 = 65536 ❩) is stored as sixteen 1's.

Ø `0 0 0 0 0 0 0 0 0 0 0 0 0 0 0 0`

65536 `1 1 1 1 1 1 1 1 1 1 1 1 1 1 1 1`

ILLUSTRATING C

operand | & | operand   ▶ X & XII   Bitwise *and*
       | | ▶ X | XII   Bitwise *or*
       | ^   ▶ X ^ XII   Bitwise *exclusive or*

these operators are commutative: X & XII gives the same result as XII & X, and similarly for the others, as evident from symmetry of truth tables.

~ | operand   ▶ ~ X   Bitwise *not*

prefix operator

operand | << | operand   ▶ X << N   Shift left N places: right fill with 0's
       | >> | ▶ X >> N   Shift right N places: left fill with 0's

```c
#include <stdio.h>
void main (void)
{
  unsigned int  Zero = 0, X = 10, XII = 12;
  printf ( "%u", ~ Zero);
```

%u is the conversion code for unsigned int. don't use %i

`65536`

Zero   `0 0 0 0 0 0 0 0  0 0 0 0 0 0 0 0`
~ Zero   `1 1 1 1 1 1 1 1  1 1 1 1 1 1 1 1`

~	operand	
	≠0	=0
	0	1

```c
  printf ("%u", X & XII );
```

`8`

X   `0 0 0 0 0 0 0 0  0 0 0 0 1 0 1 0`
XII   `0 0 0 0 0 0 0 0  0 0 0 0 1 1 0 0`

X & XII   `0 0 0 0 0 0 0 0  0 0 0 0 1 0 0 0`

&	operand	
	≠0	=0
operand ≠0	1	0
operand =0	0	0

```c
  printf ("%u", X | XII );
```

`14`

X   `0 0 0 0 0 0 0 0  0 0 0 0 1 0 1 0`
XII   `0 0 0 0 0 0 0 0  0 0 0 0 1 1 0 0`

X | XII   `0 0 0 0 0 0 0 0  0 0 0 0 1 1 1 0`

		operand	
	≠0	=0
operand ≠0	1	1
operand =0	1	0

```c
  printf ("%u", X ^ XII );
```

`6`

X   `0 0 0 0 0 0 0 0  0 0 0 0 1 0 1 0`
XII   `0 0 0 0 0 0 0 0  0 0 0 0 1 1 0 0`

X ^ XII   `0 0 0 0 0 0 0 0  0 0 0 0 0 1 1 0`

^	operand	
	≠0	=0
operand ≠0	0	1
operand =0	1	0

```c
  printf ("%u", X <<1, X >>1);
}
```

`20  5`

ASSIGNMENT OPERATORS

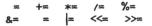

```
=   +=  *=  /=  %=
&=   =  |=  <<=  >>=
```

The operand on the left of an assignment is typically the name of a variable or array element.

n = 3; *makes sense*   3 = n; *is nonsense*

The term *l-value* (or *lvalue*) is short for 'left value' and is used in the jargon ↝ with blatant disregard for the sanctity of English ↝ to identify items that make sense only on the left of an assignment. In general, l-values are names of storage locations ↝ or expressions that point to storage locations ↝ in which the content may be altered. We meet pointers later.

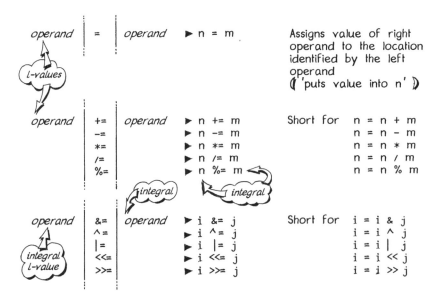

operand	=	*operand*	► n = m	Assigns value of right operand to the location identified by the left operand ('puts value into n')

l-values

operand	+=	*operand*	► n += m	Short for n = n + m
	-=		► n -= m	n = n - m
	*=		► n *= m	n = n * m
	/=		► n /= m	n = n / m
	%=		► n %= m	n = n % m

integral   *integral*

operand	&=	*operand*	► i &= j	Short for i = i & j
	^=		► i ^= j	i = i ^ j
	|=		► i |= j	i = i | j
	<<=		► i <<= j	i = i << j
	>>=		► i >>= j	i = i >> j

integral l-value

If you include one of the above assignments *as a term in a larger expression* the term contributes the value assigned. Thus in the expression:

$$4 + (n = a[i])$$

The term (n = a[i]) contributes the value assigned to n. If array element a[i] contained 3, this 3 would be assigned to n, and the value of (n = a[i]) would be 3.

The value of the whole expression would therefore be 4 + 3 = 7.

INCREMENTING OPERATORS   ++   --

Incrementing operators are special assignment operators. Each may be used as a prefix operator or postfix operator, the behaviour being different in each case.

► ++i   Short for i = i + 1
► --i   Short for i = i - 1

If you include i++ as a term of a larger expression, the *original value* of i is taken as the value of the term. Similarly for i--.

► i++   Short for i = i + 1
► i--   Short for i = i - 1

If you include ++i as a term of a larger expression, the *incremented* value of i is taken as the value of the term. Similarly with --i the *decremented value* is taken as the value of the term.

The following program demonstrates the difference in result between prefixing and postfixing the operator.

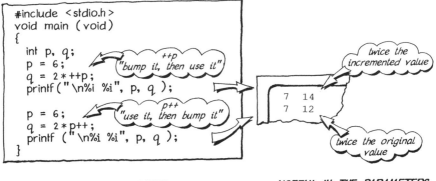

```
#include <stdio.h>
void main (void)
{
   int p, q;
   p = 6;               "bump it, then use it"  ++p
   q = 2 * ++p;
   printf ("\n%i %i", p, q );

   p = 6;               "use it, then bump it"  p++
   q = 2 * p++;
   printf ("\n%i %i", p, q );
}
```

twice the incremented value

7   14
7   12

twice the original value

SEQUENCE OPERATOR   , USEFUL IN THE PARAMETERS
                                             OF A for LOOP

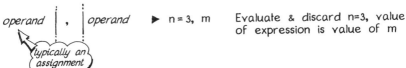

► n = 3, m   Evaluate & discard n=3, value
               of expression is value of m

The expression comprising the first operand is evaluated (any side effects being implemented) and the value of the expression discarded. Then the second operand is evaluated, its value being made the value of the complete expression.

REFERENCE OPERATORS   &   *   .   ->

The reference operators are concerned with pointers and structures. These topics are introduced later. Here, for sake of completeness, are definitions in mechanistic terms.

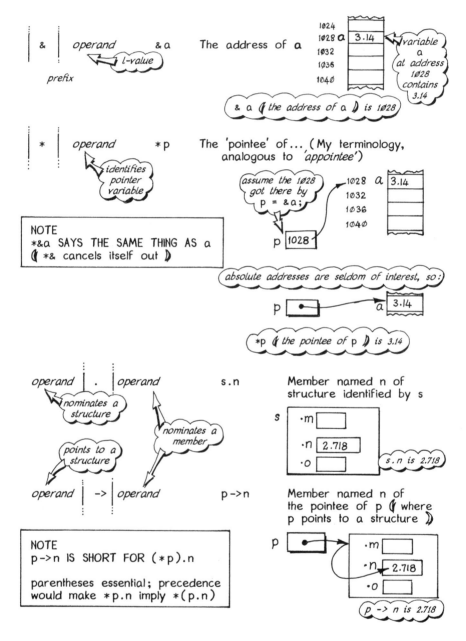

& | operand   &a   The address of a

l-value

prefix

& a ⟨ the address of a ⟩ is 1028

1024
1028 a 3.14
1032
1036
1040

variable a at address 1028 contains 3.14

* | operand   *p   The 'pointee' of... (My terminology, analogous to 'appointee')

identifies pointer variable

assume the 1028 got there by p = &a;

1028 a 3.14
1032
1036
1040

p 1028

NOTE
*&a SAYS THE SAME THING AS a
⟨ *& cancels itself out ⟩

absolute addresses are seldom of interest, so:

p •———→ a 3.14

*p ⟨ the pointee of p ⟩ is 3.14

operand | . | operand   s.n   Member named n of structure identified by s

nominates a structure

nominates a member

points to a structure

s •m
   •n 2.718
   •o

s.n is 2.718

operand | -> | operand   p->n   Member named n of the pointee of p ⟨ where p points to a structure ⟩

NOTE
p->n IS SHORT FOR (*p).n

parentheses essential; precedence would make *p.n imply *(p.n)

p •———→ •m
        •n 2.718
        •o

p -> n is 2.718

44   ILLUSTRATING C

OTHER OPERATORS ?: (*type*) ($\curvearrowleft$) [$\frown$] sizeof

First the ternary operator; exceedingly useful. All three operands are expressions, the first of which is integral.

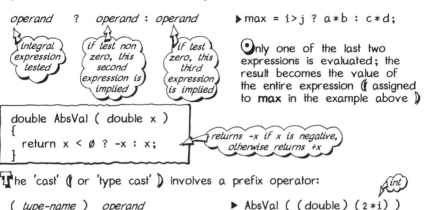

operand   ?   operand : operand

- *integral expression tested*
- *if test non zero, this second expression is implied*
- *if test zero, this third expression is implied*

▶ max = i > j ? a*b : c*d;

Only one of the last two expressions is evaluated; the result becomes the value of the entire expression (assigned to **max** in the example above)

```
double AbsVal ( double x )
{
    return x < Ø ? -x : x;
}
```
returns -x if x is negative, otherwise returns +x

The 'cast' (or 'type cast') involves a prefix operator:

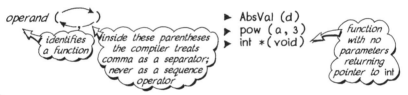

(*type-name*) *operand*   ▶ AbsVal ((double) (2*i))

nominates the type to which the value of the operand is to be converted before use.

Parentheses constitute a postfix operator, establishing that the operand is a function.

operand ($\curvearrowleft$)

- *identifies a function*
- *inside these parentheses the compiler treats comma as a separator; never as a sequence operator*

▶ AbsVal (d)
▶ pow (a , 3)
▶ int *(void) — *function with no parameters returning pointer to int*

Brackets constitute a postfix operator for subscripting the array identified by the operand.

operand [$\frown$]

identifies an array

▶ int a[] = {1Ø, 2Ø, 3Ø};
▶ a[i + 1]
▶ int (*) [] — *pointer to array of integers*

Prefix operator, sizeof, is for discovering the number of storage units (bytes) occupied by a particular object or by an object of particular type. This operator is used for dynamic storage (Chapter 1Ø) .

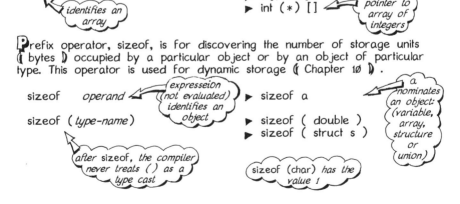

sizeof   *operand* — *expresseion (not evaluated) identifies an object*

sizeof (*type-name*)

after sizeof, the compiler never treats ( ) as a type cast

▶ sizeof a — *a nominates an object: (variable, array, structure or union)*

▶ sizeof (double)
▶ sizeof (struct s)

sizeof (char) has the value 1

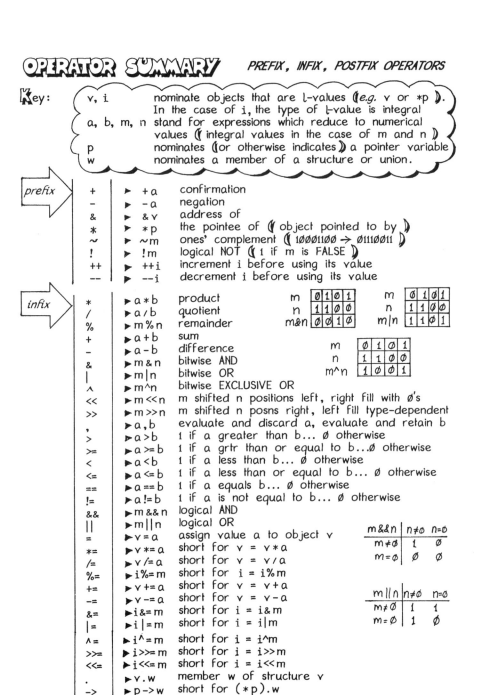

OPERATOR SUMMARY — PREFIX, INFIX, POSTFIX OPERATORS

Key:

v, i — nominate objects that are ℓ-values (e.g. v or *p). In the case of i, the type of ℓ-value is integral

a, b, m, n — stand for expressions which reduce to numerical values (integral values in the case of m and n)

p — nominates (or otherwise indicates) a pointer variable

w — nominates a member of a structure or union.

prefix

+	►	+ a	confirmation
–	►	– a	negation
&	►	& v	address of
*	►	*p	the pointee of (object pointed to by)
~	►	~ m	ones' complement (10001100 → 01110011)
!	►	! m	logical NOT (1 if m is FALSE)
++	►	++ i	increment i before using its value
--	►	-- i	decrement i before using its value

infix

*	►	a * b	product
/	►	a / b	quotient
%	►	m % n	remainder
+	►	a + b	sum
–	►	a – b	difference
&	►	m & n	bitwise AND
|	►	m | n	bitwise OR
^	►	m ^ n	bitwise EXCLUSIVE OR
<<	►	m << n	m shifted n positions left, right fill with 0's
>>	►	m >> n	m shifted n posns right, left fill type-dependent
,	►	a , b	evaluate and discard a, evaluate and retain b
>	►	a > b	1 if a greater than b... 0 otherwise
>=	►	a >= b	1 if a grtr than or equal to b...0 otherwise
<	►	a < b	1 if a less than b... 0 otherwise
<=	►	a <= b	1 if a less than or equal to b... 0 otherwise
==	►	a == b	1 if a equals b... 0 otherwise
!=	►	a != b	1 if a is not equal to b... 0 otherwise
&&	►	m && n	logical AND
||	►	m || n	logical OR
=	►	v = a	assign value a to object v
*=	►	v *= a	short for v = v * a
/=	►	v /= a	short for v = v / a
%=	►	i %= m	short for i = i % m
+=	►	v += a	short for v = v + a
-=	►	v -= a	short for v = v - a
&=	►	i &= m	short for i = i & m
|=	►	i |= m	short for i = i | m
^=	►	i ^= m	short for i = i ^ m
>>=	►	i >>= m	short for i = i >> m
<<=	►	i <<= m	short for i = i << m
.	►	v . w	member w of structure v
->	►	p -> w	short for (*p).w

Truth tables:

	m	0 1 0 1
	n	1 1 0 0
m&n		0 0 1 0

	m	0 1 0 1
	n	1 1 0 0
m|n		1 1 0 1

	m	0 1 0 1
	n	1 1 0 0
m^n		1 0 0 1

m && n	n≠0	n=0
m≠0	1	0
m=0	0	0

m || n	n≠0	n=0
m≠0	1	1
m=0	1	0

postfix

++	►	i ++	use value of i, then increment
--	►	i --	use value of i, then decrement

ILLUSTRATING C

PRECEDENCE AND ASSOCIATIVITY *OF OPERATORS*

What does a+b%c mean? (a+b)%c or a+(b%c)? The question can be asked another way: which of + and % takes *precedence*? The following table shows the precedence of all operators; those in the top row take precedence over those in the second, and so on. In any one row, all operators have equal precedence.

What does a/b/c mean? (a/b)/c or a/(b/c)? (Try 8/4/2 both ways and see the difference.) This question can be asked another way: When successive operators have *equal* precedence, in which direction are parentheses applied? Left to right or right to left? The required direction is the *associativity*. The table shows by an arrow the direction of associativity (left to right or right to left) at every precedence level.

In the placing of parentheses, *precedence* is relevant where successive operators are found in different rows of the table; *associativity* is relevant where successive operators are found in the same row of the table.

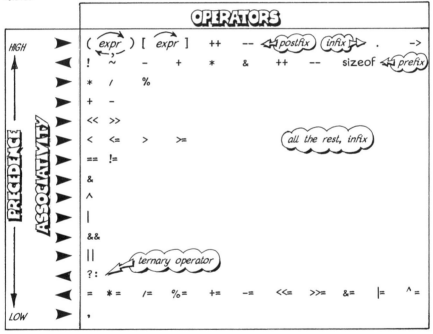

Example: precedence

```
5 + -3 * 4 > -8           value is 1
5 + (-3) * 4 > (-8)       ( true )
5 + ((-3) * 4 ) > (-8)
(5 + (( -3 ) * 4 )) > (-8)
```

Example: associativity   *R to L*

```
a *= b = c += d /= e
a *= b = c += ( d /= e )
a *= b = ( c += ( d /= e ))
a *= ( b = ( c += ( d /= e )))
```

MIXED TYPES

When terms of an expression are of different type, the processor 'coerces' values to a consistent type. Coercion may cause a short integer to become long (('promotion')) or a long to become short (('demotion')) according to the context of the expression. If you wish to override coercion you may include a *cast* to specify the precise promotion or demotion required.

PROMOTION & DEMOTION   'LOWER' TO 'HIGHER' & VICE VERSA

The processor cannot *directly* obey the statement d = 2, where d is of type double, because 2 is of 'lower' type than d; you cannot store an int in a location declared double. In obeying d = 2 the processor first takes a copy of 2 and promotes the copy to double ≈ as though you had written 2.0 instead of 2. The promoted value is then assigned to d.

The converse, i = 2.0, where i is of type int, also involves conversion before assignment is possible. But there can be trouble when a 'higher' value is demoted to a 'lower'. With i = 2.1, for example, the .1 would be lost and you would probably receive a warning. Some processors would collapse on meeting i = 70000.

CAST   OVERRIDES COERCION

When assignment involves different types, the program coerces values to the type of the receiving object. The same effect can be achieved by a cast. For example, 'd = (double) i' causes a copy of the content of i to be promoted to type double and assigned to d. The expression i = (int) d causes the converse by demotion.

PARAMETERS   A FORM OF ASSIGNMENT

Invoking a function with parameters is a form of assignment; parameters of different type are coerced in the manner just described.

For example, in AbsVal(-3) ((where the parameter has been declared of type double)) the -3 would be coerced to type double as though you had written AbsVal(-3.0). Or you could avoid coercion by writing AbsVal((double)-3). Coercion of parameters works because the processor can see from the prototype declaration what types of arguments the function expects.

LITERAL CONSTANTS   USE SUFFIXES, NOT CASTS

Literal constants not of type int or double would be suffixed to specify type. L (long or long double), F (float), U (unsigned) are defined on Page 33 . Thus 2L represents the value 2 in a form suitable for storage as a long int, whereas 2.0L represents the same value, but in a form suitable for storage as a long double. Do not use casts with literal constants.

ACTION OF OPERATORS

In general, any infix operator can cause type promotion if given operands of different type: 3.141593/4 is a simple example involving the division operator. In such a case the processor promotes the operand of 'lower' type (‖ in this case 4 which is **int** ‖) to the 'higher' type (‖ in this case that of 3.141593 which is **double** ‖).

The rules obeyed by the processor for maintaining the principle of promotion to 'higher' type are as follows:

For each operand; if it is:

• **unsigned short int** *promote its value to* **signed int**

• **unsigned char** *promote its value to* **int** *with zero left fill*

• **signed char** *promote its value to* **int** *with sign extended*

• **char** *promote its value to* **int** (*form depends on implementation*)

Then ask if the type of either operand is one of the following:

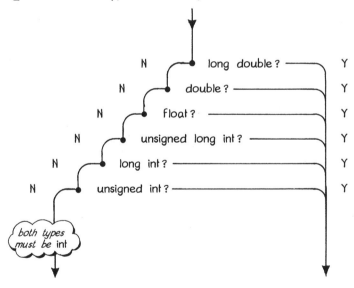

both types
must be int

Produce result of type **int**

Promote the value of the other operand to the same type, then produce a result of this same type.

4

CONTROL

This chapter describes the control statements of C and their use. These statements control the sequence of execution within a function. Without them, execution starts at the first statement after the heading of the function and proceeds sequentially to the last.

Control statements already introduced are: if, do, for, break, return.

Control statements are classified in this chapter as follows:

- Tested loops   while, do
- Counted loops   for
- Escape   break, continue, return
- Selection   if, switch
- Jump   goto

TESTED LOOPS

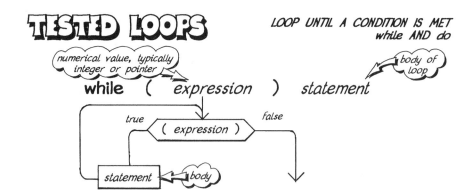

while (*expression*) *statement*

If, on entry to the while loop, *expression* reduces to zero ((or null)) then *statement* is not executed at all. The test for continuation is at the top.

An infinite loop may be constructed by writing a non-zero constant as the *expression* ((permanently *true*)). Escape from an infinite loop using 'break' or 'continue' as depicted opposite.

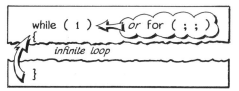

do *statement* while (*expression*) ;

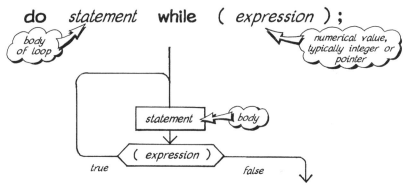

The *statement* is executed at least once, the test for continuation being at the bottom.

Tested loops are useful when you do not know in advance how many times ((if any)) a piece of program is to be executed. It may be executed again and again until some goal is achieved ≈ such as the difference between two quantities becoming very small. Whatever the goal, it must be expressed as a logical value, *true* or *false*.

The 'while' loop is needed more often than 'do', but an example in which 'do' is appropriate is given on Page 23.

 **COUNTED LOOP** PREDETERMINED NUMBER OF TIMES for

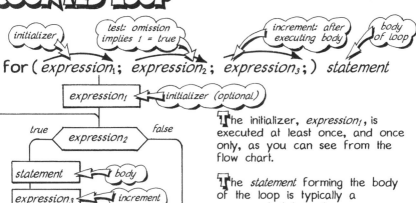

initializer

test: omission implies 1 = true

increment: after executing body

body of loop

for (*expression₁* ; *expression₂* ; *expression₃* ;) *statement*

expression₁ ← *initializer (optional)*

true *expression₂* *false*

statement ← *body*

expression₃ ← *increment*

The initializer, *expression₁*, is executed at least once, and once only, as you can see from the flow chart.

The *statement* forming the body of the loop is typically a compound statement.

Make an infinite loop by omitting the test, thereby implying constantly *true*.

Use the comma operator to extend any or all expressions. For example:

for (a=1, b=1; x>y; i++, j++)

ESCAPE GETTING OUT OF A LOOP BY break & continue
RETURNING FROM A FUNCTION BY return

'break' takes you out of the present loop altogether; 'continue' takes you to the end of the body of the loop, hence to the next execution of the body ≈ if the control mechanism so requires. (¶ You can escape from a complete nest of loops using the 'goto *label*' statement but use of 'goto', except for error recovery, is frowned upon.)

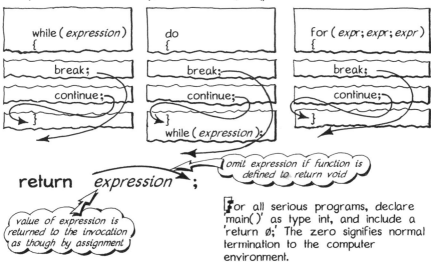

while (*expression*)
{

break;

continue;

}

do
{

break;

continue;

}

while (*expression*);

for (*expr*; *expr*; *expr*)
{

break;

continue;

}

omit expression if function is defined to return void

return *expression* ;

value of expression is returned to the invocation as though by assignment

For all serious programs, declare 'main( )' as type int, and include a 'return Ø;' The zero signifies normal termination to the computer environment.

AREA OF A POLYGON

Consider the diagam on the right: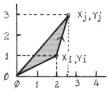
The shaded area is given by A_{ij}
where:

$$A_{ij} = \tfrac{1}{2}(X_iY_j - X_jY_i)$$
$$= \tfrac{1}{2}(2 \times 3 - 2.5 \times 1) = 1.75$$

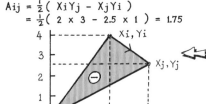

The same formula may be used for
computing the area on the left. But this
area turns out to be *negative*:
$$A_{ij} = \tfrac{1}{2}(X_iY_j - X_jY_i)$$
$$= \tfrac{1}{2}(3 \times 2.5 - 5 \times 4) = -6.25$$

The formula may be applied to sequential
sides of a polygon, and the triangular areas
summed to give the area shown here

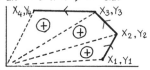

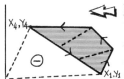

But if the polygon is *closed*, as shown on the left,
the sum of the areas will be the area enclosed.

The bounded surface must be kept to the *left* of
each arrow: the sides of the figure should not cross
each other as in a figure of eight.

Here is a program by which to input coordinates of boundary points
and compute the area enclosed:

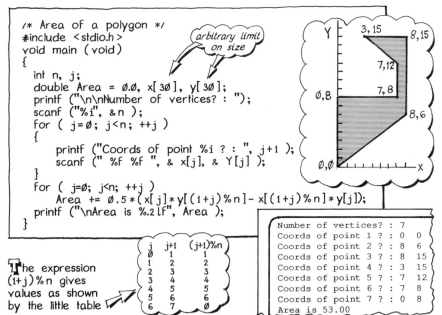

```
/* Area of a polygon */
#include <stdio.h>
void main ( void )
{
    int n, j;
    double Area = 0.0, x[30], y[30];
    printf ("\n\nNumber of vertices? : ");
    scanf ("%i", &n );
    for ( j=0; j<n; ++j )
    {
        printf ("Coords of point %i ? : ", j+1 );
        scanf (" %f %f ", & x[j], & Y[j] );
    }
    for ( j=0; j<n; ++j )
        Area += 0.5 *( x[j]*y[(1+j)%n]- x[(1+j)%n]*y[j]);
    printf ("\nArea is %.2lf", Area );
}
```

arbitrary limit on size

j	j+1	(j+1)%n
0	1	1
1	2	2
2	3	3
3	4	4
4	5	5
5	6	6
6	7	0

The expression
(1+j)%n gives
values as shown
by the little table

```
Number of vertices? : 7
Coords of point 1 ? :  0   0
Coords of point 2 ? :  8   6
Coords of point 3 ? :  8   15
Coords of point 4 ? :  3   15
Coords of point 5 ? :  7   12
Coords of point 6 ? :  7   8
Coords of point 7 ? :  0   8
Area is 53.00
```

SELECTION STATEMENT ~ IF

if (*expression*) *statement₁* **else** *statement₂*

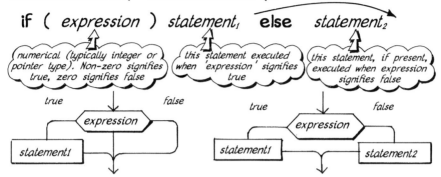

(numerical (typically integer or pointer type). Non-zero signifies true, zero signifies false)

(this statement executed when 'expression' signifies true)

(this statement, if present, executed when expression signifies false)

```
        true              false
          ↓
      ⬡ expression ⬡
   ┌──────┴──────┐
┌──────────┐
│ statement1 │
└──────────┘
          ↓
```

```
          true                    false
              ⬡ expression ⬡
      ┌───────────┴───────────┐
┌──────────┐            ┌──────────┐
│ statement1 │            │ statement2 │
└──────────┘            └──────────┘
          └──────────┬──────────┘
                     ↓
```

Ꞩee discussion on nesting and other features of if...else on pp 12 & 13.

```c
/* Areas of shapes */
#include <stdio.h>
#include <math.h>
void main (void)
{
    double Pi = 3.141593;
    double s, Area, a, b, c, d;
    char Letter;
    int Ok = 1;
    printf ("\nR, T, C ?\n");
    scanf ("%c", & Letter);
    if ( Letter == 'R' ) {
        printf ("\nb & d please");
        scanf ("%f %f ", &b, &d);
        Area = b * d;
    }
    else
        if ( Letter == 'T' ) {
            printf ("\na, b & c please");
            scanf ("%f %f %f", &a, &b, &c);
            s = ( a + b + c) / 2;
            Area = sqrt (s*(s-a)*(s-b)*(s-c));
        }
        else
            if ( Letter == 'C' ) {
                printf ("\nd please");
                scanf ("%f ", &d);
                Area = Pi * d * d / 4;
            }
            else
                Ok = ∅;
    if ( Ok )
        printf ("Area is %6.2f", Area);
    else
        printf ("Try again");
}
```

𝕋he example illustrates nested if's; *not* always the best way to express program logic.

```
                    ↓
         ┌─ input letter R,T or C ─┐
         f └──── letter R? ────┘ t
   f ┌─── letter T? ───┐ t        input b, d
 f ┌── letter C? ──┐ t    input a,b,c
                         ┌──────────────┐
                         │ s=(a+b+c)÷2  │
    input d              │   area=      │
                         │ √s(s-a)(s-b)(s-c) │
                         └──────────────┘
  ┌──────────┐   ┌──────────┐
  │ area=πd²÷4│   │ area = bd │
  └──────────┘   └──────────┘
   error         output area
                     ↓
```

```
                        |← b →|
                   R  ▨▨▨▨▨▨  ↕ d

                   T  ╱│  b
                    a ╱─│
                     |← c →|

                                 ○  ↕ d
                              C
```

```
R, T, C ?
R
b & d please
3.5   2
Area is    7.00
```

ROMAN NUMBERS

Programmers spend a lot of time writing input routines. Few are asked to input and decode Roman numbers like MCMXCII, but this presents no particular difficulty if you use a *symbol-state* table. This approach is tidier than logic based on if and else.

Assume Roman numerals to be composed of the following elements, never more than one from each consecutive list:

thousands	*hundreds*		*tens*		*units*	
		D=500		L=50		V=5
M=1000	C=100	DC=600	X=10	LX=60	I=1	VI=6
MM=2000	CC=200	DCC=700	XX=20	LXX=70	II=2	VII=7
MMM=3000	CCC=300	DCCC=800	XXX=30	LXXX=80	III=3	VIII=8
etc.	CD=400	CM=900	XL=40	XC=90	IV=4	IX=9

In fact the Romans felt less constrained. IIII was common. Some monuments have inscriptions of numbers starting with more than twenty Cs.

The logic of the program is contained in the following symbol-state table:

starting state	SYMBOL							
	M	D	C	L	X	V	I	error
00	1000:00	500:01	100:03	50:07	10:06	5:12	1:11	
01			100:02	50:07	10:06	5:12	1:11	
02			100:04	50:07	10:06	5:12	1:11	
03	800:05	300:05	100:04	50:07	10:06	5:12	1:11	
04			100:05	50:07	10:06	5:12	1:11	
05				50:07	10:06	5:12	1:11	
06			80:10	30:10	10:09	5:12	1:11	
07					10:08	5:12	1:11	
08					10:09	5:12	1:11	
09					10:10	5:12	1:11	
10						5:12	1:11	
11					8:15	3:15	1:14	
12							1:13	
13							1:14	
14							1:15	
15								

(STATE is the label for the rows 00–15.)

Take the Roman number CIX as an example. Begin with a value of zero. You are in *state 00* (where the arrow is). Look down from symbol C and find 100:03 which says 'Add 100 to the value and change state to 03.' So add 100 to zero and move the arrow to 03. Now look down from symbol I and find 1:11. So add 1 to the value (100 + 1 = 101) and move the arrow to state 11. Finally, look down from symbol X and find 8:15. So add 8 to the value (101 + 8 = 109) and move the arrow to state 15, a row of empty cells.

There are no more Roman digits, so CIX decodes as 109. Experiment with MCMXCII and you should get 1992. Experiment with MDDI and you should encounter an *empty* cell which means an *error of formation*.

56   ILLUSTRATING C

The program to implement this method of decoding is short and simple because the logic ⟶ the difficult part ⟵ is embodied in the table.

Two pieces of information are packed into each element of the table. To unravel, divide by 100 and use the quotient as the contribution to the final value and the remainder to give the next state. Thus 50001 gives a contribution of 50001 / 100 = 500 (integer division) and a new state of 50001 % 100 = 1 (remainder when 50001 is divided by 100). The array has to be declared as 'long' on installations that offer only 16 bits for an 'int'.

```
/* Roman Numerals */
#include <stdio.h>
char Symbol [ ] = { 'M', 'D', 'C', 'L', 'X', 'V', 'I' };
long Table [16] [8] =
{
    {  100000,   50001,  10003,  5007,  1006,   512,   111,   0   },
    {       0,       0,  10002,  5007,  1006,   512,   111,   0   },
    {       0,       0,  10004,  5007,  1006,   512,   111,   0   },
    {   80005,   30005,  10004,  5007,  1006,   512,   111,   0   },
    {       0,       0,  10005,  5007,  1006,   512,   111,   0   },
    {       0,       0,      0,  5007,  1006,   512,   111,   0   },
    {       0,       0,   8010,  3010,  1009,   512,   111,   0   },
    {       0,       0,      0,     0,  1008,   512,   111,   0   },
    {       0,       0,      0,     0,  1009,   512,   111,   0   },
    {       0,       0,      0,     0,  1010,   512,   111,   0   },
    {       0,       0,      0,     0,     0,   512,   111,   0   },
    {       0,       0,      0,     0,   815,   315,   114,   0   },
    {       0,       0,      0,     0,     0,     0,   113,   0   },
    {       0,       0,      0,     0,     0,     0,   114,   0   },
    {       0,       0,      0,     0,     0,     0,   115,   0   },
    {       0,       0,      0,     0,     0,     0,     0,   0   }
};

void main ( void )
{
    long   Entry = 1,   Number = 0;
    int    Column,      Row = 0;
    char   Ch;
    printf ("\nEnter a number\n");
    while ( (Ch = getchar()) != '\n' && Entry )
    {
        for ( Column = 0; Column < 7 && Ch != Symbol [Column]; ++Column)
            ;
        Entry = Table [Row] [Column];
        Number += Entry / 100;
        Row = Entry % 100;
    }
    if (Entry)
        printf ("=%i in Arabics", Number);
    else
        printf ("\nError");
    printf ("\nEnd of run");
}
```

stops looping if Entry picks up zero (false)

enter the table

accumulate Number

select next row of table

```
Enter a number
MCMXCII
= 1992 in Arabics
End of run
```

 **SWITCH**

switch **(** *expression* **)** *statement*

> *integral value (coerced if necessary to int or unsigned int) is compared with the value of each case expression in the block. Control jumps to the statement following the matching value. If there is no match, control jumps to the statement following default:*

> *typically a { block } containing case labels and a single default: label*

case *expression* **:** *statement*

> *no more than one default per switch*

> *may involve constants only: evaluated at compile time. Unique value essential after every case in the same block*

> *this statement is next to be executed if value of the case expression matches value of the switch expression*

default **:** *statement*

> *executed if no match. (Undefined behaviour if there is neither match nor default)*

break

> *break statement typically terminates each case*

```
printf ("How may legs did it have?");
scanf ("%i", & Legs );
switch ( Legs )
{
        case 8: printf ("A spider, perhaps?"); break;
        case 2: printf ("A double-glazing sales person"); break;
        case 3: case 5: case 1: printf ("That's odd!"); break;
        case 4: printf ("Probably a mouse"); break;
        case 6: printf ("Definitely a bug"); break;
        default: printf ("Could be dangerous");
}
```

> *no particular order*

> *multiple case expression:*

> *all breaks take you here*

The switch statement is useful wherever the logic demands selection of one case from a group of several. The Areas program could be improved using 'switch' in place of 'if' as shown below:

```
switch ( Letter ) {
```

> *allow r as well as R*

```
    case 'R': case 'r': {
            printf ("\nb & d please");
            scanf ("%f %f", & b, & d );
            area = b * d;
            break;
            }
    case 'T': case 't': {   etc.
```

> *terminates every case*

If you omit 'break' after the statements belonging to one particular case, control simply falls through to the next as illustrated by the following program which displays all twelve verses of a tedious Christmas carol.

```
/* 12 days of Christmas */
void main( void )
{
    int i, j;
    char Ord[] = { 's', 't', 'n', 'd', 'r', 'd', 't', 'h' };
    for ( i=1; i<= 12; i++ )
    {
        j = i<4 ? 2*(i-1) : 6;
        printf ("\n\nOn the ");
        printf ("%i%c%c ",i, Ord[j], Ord[j+1]);
        printf ("day of Christmas my true love sent to me,");
        if ( i==1) printf ("\nA ");
        switch (i)
        {
            case 12:    printf ("\nTwelve drummers drumming,");
            case 11:    printf ("\n'leven pipers piping,");
            case 10:    printf ("\nTen maids a-milking,");
            case 9:     printf ("\nNine lords a-leaping,");
            case 8:     printf ("\nEight ladies dancing,");
            case 7:     printf ("\nSeven swans a-swimming,");
            case 6:     printf ("\nSix geese a-laying,");
            case 5:     printf ("\nFive GO-OLD rings,");
            case 4:     printf ("\nFour calling birds,");
            case 3:     printf ("\nThree French hens,");
            case 2:     printf ("\nTwo-oo turtle doves,");
            printf ("\nAnd a ");
            case 1:     printf ("part ri-idge in a pear treeee.");
        }
    }
}
```

Note in the program the thought bubble: `Ord [6]` and `1st, 2nd, 3rd, 4th`

Nested switch statements are useful for implementing the logic contained in symbol-state tables. The outer switch is given a case for each state (row) of the table. The logic in each of these cases comprises an inner switch having a case for each symbol (column) of the table.

JUMP

RECOVERING FROM CHAOS

An error condition may be drastic enough to warrant a jump out of the mess.

goto   *name*   — a label marking a statement in the same function

matching label — *name* : *statement*

Names of labels do not clash with names of other entities.

CABLES

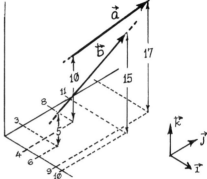

The power cables $\vec{a}$ and $\vec{b}$ look as if they are running uncomfortably close to one another. What is the closest distance between them?

This would be an awkward problem without vector algebra: here are enough of the principles to solve it.

A vector $\vec{v}$ is written as:
$$\vec{v} = v_0\vec{i} + v_1\vec{j} + v_2\vec{k}$$
where v_0, v_1, v_2 are its projections in the directions depicted. The length (modulus) of $\vec{v}$ is:

$$|\vec{v}| = \sqrt{v_0^2 + v_1^2 + v_2^2}$$

Divide $\vec{v}$ by its own length and you have a *unit* long vector in the same direction as $\vec{v}$:

$$\frac{v_0}{|\vec{v}|}\vec{i} + \frac{v_1}{|\vec{v}|}\vec{j} + \frac{v_2}{|\vec{v}|}\vec{k}$$

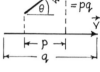

The scalar (or dot) product, $\vec{w}\cdot\vec{v}$, is given by $w_0v_0 + w_1v_1 + w_2v_2$. This expression represents the product of the length of one vector and the projected length of the other upon it. Another way to look at it is:

$$|w|\,|v|\,\cos\theta$$

The vector (or *cross*) product, $\vec{v}\times\vec{w}$ is given by this determinant. It is a vector having a direction normal *both* to $\vec{v}$ *and* to $\vec{w}$

$$\begin{vmatrix} \vec{i} & \vec{j} & \vec{k} \\ v_0 & v_1 & v_2 \\ w_0 & w_1 & w_2 \end{vmatrix}$$

That's all we need of vector algebra for this problem. In the sketch above, $\vec{a}$ and $\vec{b}$ can be expressed:

$$\vec{a} = (9-4)\vec{i} + (16-8)\vec{j} + (17-10)\vec{k} = 5\vec{i} + 8\vec{j} + 7\vec{k}$$
$$\vec{b} = (10-6)\vec{i} + (11-3)\vec{j} + (15-5)\vec{k} = 4\vec{i} + 8\vec{j} + 10\vec{k}$$

Their cross product, $a \times b$, is a vector normal to a and b:

$$\vec{a} \times \vec{b} = \begin{vmatrix} \vec{i} & \vec{j} & \vec{k} \\ 5 & 8 & 7 \\ 4 & 8 & 10 \end{vmatrix} = 24\vec{i} - 22\vec{j} + 8\vec{k}$$

a result of $0\vec{i} + 0\vec{j} + 0\vec{k}$ implies $\vec{a}$ lies parallel to $\vec{b}$

Its length is $\sqrt{(24)^2 + (-22)^2 + (8)^2} = 33.53$

So a *unit* vector, $\vec{c}$, connecting any point on $\vec{a}$ to any point on $\vec{b}$ is $(\vec{a} \times \vec{b}) \div 33.53$

$$0.72\vec{i} - 0.66\vec{j} + 0.24\vec{k}$$

Take a vector, $\vec{c}$, connecting any point on $\vec{a}$ to any point on $\vec{b}$. Here is one; it connects the tip of $\vec{a}$ to the tip of $\vec{b}$:

$$\vec{a} = (10-9)\vec{i} + (11-167)\vec{j} + (15-17)\vec{k} = 1\vec{i} - 5\vec{j} - 2\vec{k}$$

ILLUSTRATING C

Project this onto the unit vector to give the shortest distance between the cables:

$$d = (1) \times (0.72) + (-5) \times (-0.66) + (-2) \times (0.24) = 3.52 \text{ approximately}$$

If the cables run parallel, special action is needed as shown in the 'else' clause in the program.

```c
/* Power cables; are they too close? */
#include <stdio.h>
#include <math.h>          we need sqrt
void main( void )
{
    int       j,    k=1,   m=2;
    char      Cable[2] = {'A', 'B'};
    double    Coord[12], a[3], b[3], c[3], u[3];
    double    Clearance=0.0, Proj=0.0, asq=0.0, csq=0.0, usq=0.0;
    for (j=0; j<12; j++)
    {                                              alternating
                                                   [0], [1],...
        if (!(j%6))
            printf ( "\nCable %c\n",    Cable[k=1-k] );
        if (!(j%3))
            printf ( "End %i: x,y,z coords: ", m=3-m );
        scanf ("%lf", & Coord [j]);
    }                                              alternating
    for (j=0; j<3; ++j)                            1, 2, 1, 2,...
    {
        a[j] = Coord [3 + j] - Coord [j];
        b[j] = Coord [9 + j] - Coord [6 + j];
        c[j] = Coord [9 + j] - Coord [3 + j];
    }
    u[0] = a[1] * b[2] - b[1] * a[2];
    u[1] = a[2] * b[0] - a[0] * b[2];
    u[2] = a[0] * b[1] - b[0] * a[1];
        for (j=0; j<3; ++j)
        usq += u[j] * u[j];
    if (usq > 0.0)          non-parallel
    {                       cables
        for (j=0; j<3; ++j)
            csq += c[j] * u[j];
        csq /= sqrt (usq);
        Clearance = (csq < 0.0) ? -csq: csq;
    }
    else           parallel
    {              cables
        for (j=0; j<3; ++j)
        {                               Cable A
                                        End 1: x,y,z coords: 4    8    10
            asq  += a[j] * a[j];        End 2: x,y,z coords: 9    16   17
            csq  += c[j] * c[j];        Cable B
            Proj += a[j] * c[j];        End 1: x,y,z coords: 6    3    5
        }                               End 2: x,y,z coords: 10   11 15
        csq -= Proj * Proj / asq;       Clearance between A & B is  3.52
        Clearance = (csq > 0) ? sqrt( csq ) : 0.0;
    }
    printf ("\nClearance between A & B is %.2lf \n", Clearance);
}
```

The sorting method called Quicksort was devised by Prof. C. A. R. Hoare. The version described here is a bit different from the original but serves to explain the essential principles of the method.

Take some letters to sort:

G   B   L   I   C   N   M   H

i ⬆   ← ⬆ j

Set an arrow at either end of the list and prepare to move j towards i. If j indicates a 'bigger' letter than i does, move j another step towards i.

G   B   L   I   C   N   M   H

i ⬆   j ⬆←⬆←⬆←⬆

Now j indicates a *smaller* letter than i does. So swop the two letters indicated, and swop the arrows i and j as well:

C   B   L   I   G   N   M   H

j ⬆→   ⬆ i

Continue moving j towards i ((which now means stepping rightwards instead of leftwards)). If j indicates a *smaller* letter than i does, move j another step towards i:

C   B   L   I   G   N   M   H

⬆→⬆→⬆ j   ⬆ i

Now j indicates a *bigger* letter than i does. So swop letters, arrows, direction and condition exactly as before:

C   B   G   I   L   N   M   H

i ⬆   ← ⬆ j

And so on, swopping as necessary, until j reaches i:

C   B   G   I   L   N   M   H

i ⬆ j

At which stage it is true to say that every letter to the left of i is at least as small as the letter indicated: every letter to the right of i is at least as big. In other words the letter indicated has found its resting place. The letters to the left of i have not, however, been sorted, nor have those to the right of i. But having 'sorted' one letter, and split the group into two, it remains only to sort each sub-group, starting out in each case in the manner described in detail above.

C   B   G   I   L   N   M   H

secondly sort these   *first 'sort' one item*   *thirdly sort these*

A tidy way to sort is to *point* to the entities (such as personnel records) to be sorted, then rearrange the pointers. C language has special facilities for handling pointers but these must wait until Chapter 10; here we use integers to introduce the concept.

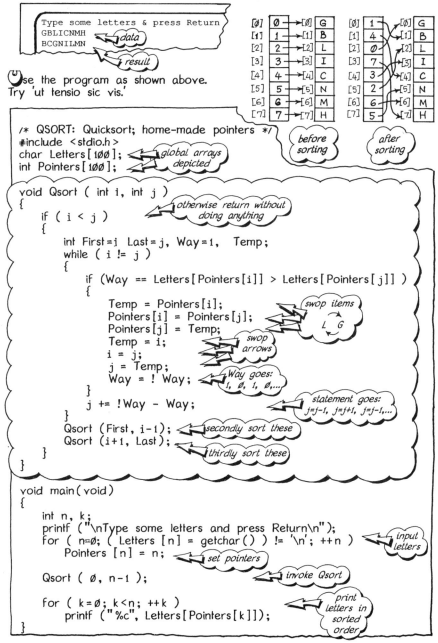

Type some letters & press Return
GBLICNMH ← *data*
BCGNILMN ← *result*

Use the program as shown above.
Try 'ut tensio sic vis.'

before sorting · *after sorting*

```
/* QSORT: Quicksort; home-made pointers */
#include <stdio.h>
char Letters [100];     ← global arrays
int Pointers [100];        depicted

void Qsort ( int i, int j )
{                              otherwise return without
    if ( i < j )                  doing anything
    {
        int First=i Last=j, Way=1,  Temp;
        while ( i != j )
        {
            if (Way == Letters[Pointers[i]] > Letters[Pointers[j]] )
            {
                Temp = Pointers[i];
                Pointers[i] = Pointers[j];     ← swop items
                Pointers[j] = Temp;               L ⇄ G
                Temp = i;
                i = j;                          ← swop arrows
                j = Temp;
                Way = ! Way;    ← Way goes: 1, 0, 1, 0,...
            }
            j += !Way - Way;   ← statement goes: j=j-1, j=j+1, j=j-1,...
        }
        Qsort (First, i-1);   ← secondly sort these
        Qsort (i+1, Last );   ← thirdly sort these
    }
}

void main(void)
{
    int n, k;
    printf ("\nType some letters and press Return\n");
    for ( n=0; ( Letters [n] = getchar() ) != '\n'; ++n )   ← input letters
        Pointers [n] = n;     ← set pointers

    Qsort ( 0, n-1 );   ← invoke Qsort

    for ( k=0; k<n; ++k )                ← print letters in sorted order
        printf ("%c", Letters[Pointers[k]]);
}
```

EXERCISES

1 Re-program 'Areas of shapes' using the logic of a switch statement in place of if...then...else. You should find the result simpler and tidier than the program on page 55.

2 Write a function, using a symbol-state table, to read an octal number from the keyboard, converting it to a decimal integer (of type long). Allow a preceding + or - sign. For example, the program should read -74 and get the result -5Ø.

Your state table should have four columns. These are: [Ø] to deal with the leading + or -, [1] to deal with any digit from Ø to 7, [2] to deal with a space character, [3] to deal with any other character (an error). The value in each cell should comprise a label (for use in an associated 'switch' statement) and the number of the next 'state', or row. The 'case' associated with valid digits should multiply the accumulating result by the number base, 8, then add the current digit.

Write a test-bed program to read octal numbers from the keyboard and display their decimal equivalents on the screen.

3 Extend your octal number program by making it read numbers to *any* base from 2 to 32. The digits for base 32 should be: Ø123456789ABCDEFGHIJKLMNOPQRSTUV (only as far as F for base 16 *etc.*). Hint: Store these as characters in an array; when accumulating a number, add the array *subscript* to the accumulation.

Let the program treat the first number it reads as a number base. Make it treat subsequent entries as numbers expressed to that base.

4 The Quicksort algorithm 'sorts' a single item, then calls itself to deal with those above and those below. You can apply similar logic to the bubble sort described on Page 19. Simply 'bubble' one number to the top of the list, then call the bubble function recursively to deal with the list below.

Write a recursive bubble sort function. To test it, use the program on Page 63, first replacing the Quicksort function.

5

ORGANIZATION

This chapter describes the organization of a C program in terms of *translation units* and *files*.

A C program is turned into an executable program by a *processor* comprising a *preprocessor*, a *compiler*, a *linker*.

The preprocessor is described in detail; its logical *passes*, the use of *directives*, the composition of a *macro*, and the use of macros for textual substitution and *conditional preprocessing*.

Storage class is explained; the use of storage class *specifiers* to establish the scope of an object or function, and whether objects and their contents evaporate or not when control moves on. The significance of storage class specifiers in different contexts ((outside and inside function definitions)) is carefully explained.

The chapter ends with an explanation of *name space*; the contexts in which different entities given the same name would clash.

A C program may be all in one file or shared among several. The contents of each file is called a *translation unit* and comprises a set of directives, declarations and function definitions.

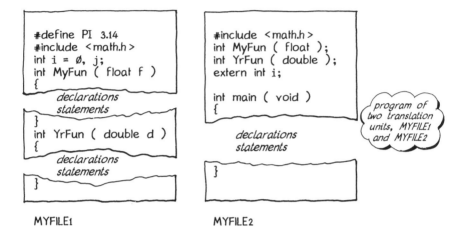

```
#define PI 3.14
#include <math.h>
int i = Ø, j;
int MyFun ( float f )
{
    declarations
    statements
}
int YrFun ( double d )
{
    declarations
    statements
}
```

MYFILE1

```
#include <math.h>
int MyFun ( float );
int YrFun ( double );
extern int i;

int main ( void )
{

    declarations
    statements

}
```

MYFILE2

program of two translation units, MYFILE1 and MYFILE2

Although some modern processors prepare a C program for execution in a single 'pass', the logical process of preparation is best described in terms of multiple passes made by three distinct parts of the processor;

- preprocessor
- compiler
- linker

The C *preprocessor* resembles a word processor; it simplifies and rationalizes spacing, removes comments, copies nominated files into the program, substitutes pieces of text. At the end of this stage, translation units contain nothing but C language.

The *compiler* translates C language into code the computer can obey directly. For each 'text file' of C language the compiler generates a corresponding 'object file' of executable code. Cross references between functions and between files are left open at this stage.

The *linker* deals with cross references. It copies the executable code of invoked library routines into the program, links all invocations to the functions invoked, cross refers local and global variables. The linkage of variables depends on their 'storage class', a subject described in detail below.

The final result is an 'executable file.'

ILLUSTRATING C

PREPROCESSOR

The preprocessor works with *tokens*. These are the indivisible atoms of a C program. All forms of token except *punctuator* have been introduced in other contexts; *punctuator* is defined below.

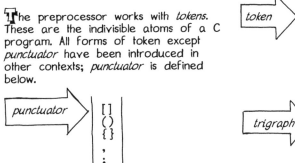

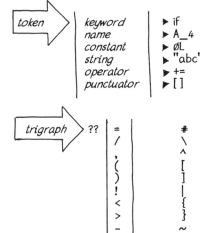

The C processor does the following things, effectively in the order listed below:

- It replaces each *trigraph* with code for the single character it represents. Thus ??< is everywhere replaced by a left brace. (❨ Trigraphs enable users of equipment based on a seven-bit character code to implement ANSI C.❩)

- Wherever \ is followed by a new line the preprocessor removes both the \ and the new-line character, thereby 'splicing' successive lines. The need for \ in this context is explained later.

  | Mind the\ rapist | | Mind therapist |

- It rearranges white space such that each token is minimally separated from its neighbours. It replaces each comment by a single space.

- It obeys each *directive* in turn. A directive begins with # as the first non-blank character on a new line. The directives (❨ all defined below ❩) are concerned with textual substitution by *macro*. Macros are described in subsequent pages.

- It replaces *escape sequences* in character constants and quoted strings with equivalent single codes. For example, \n (❨ as seen in '\n' or in printf ("\nFinish") ❩), gets replaced with the code for new-line generation. Escape sequences are summarized on Page 197.

- It concatenates adjacent strings, removing any space between them and removing redundant quotation marks:

  "Meth" "inks" " " "Pi" "rates"   ⟹   "Methinks Pirates"

SIMPLE MACROS

A name in association with a useful value, or useful piece of program, is called a *macro*.

In this program (which reads the radius of a circle from the keyboard and displays its area on screen) PI is a constant used in much the same way as an initialized variable. Before the compiler ever sees PI, however, the preprocessor meets #define PI 3.14 and substitutes 3.14 for each occurrence of PI ≋ except in the following circumstances:

```
#define PI 3.14
#define XXX return Ø;
int main ( void )
{
    float r;
    scanf ( "%f", &r );
    printf ( "%f", PI*r*r);
    XXX
}
```

replaced by return Ø

replaced by 3.14

- *not* if part of a longer token such as PIPE
- *not* inside quoted strings such as "Ratio PI"
- *not* in comments (all of which have been removed at this stage).

Much the same holds for '#define XXX   return Ø;' except that *three* tokens (return *and* Ø *and* ;) are substituted for each single occurrence of XXX. In general, the text for substitution may be of any length; it terminates at the end of the line. (So what if the cursor reaches the edge of the screen before you have finished typing the text for substitution? Press \ followed immediately by Return. The cursor jumps to the next line and you continue typing, but the preprocessor 'splices' what you type to the previous line as illustrated earlier.)

As explained above, #define PI 3.14 causes 3.14 to be substituted for each occurrence of PI throughout the file ≋ except for the three circumstances noted. Here is a fourth exception; substitution *ceases* when the preprocessor meets #undef PI. From that point onwards no further substitutions are made for PI.

MACROS WITH ARGUMENTS

no space here

```
#define ABS(x)    ((x)<Ø?-(x):(x))
```

Your macro may have *arguments*. These are names in parentheses following the macro's name and the opening parenthesis.

After the definition of ABS(X) the preprocessor might meet a term in an expression such as ABS(a) for which it would substitute: ((a)<Ø?-(a):(a)). This expression returns the absolute (*i.e. positive*) value of the number held in variable a.

Why all the parentheses? Wouldn't (x<Ø) ? -x : x suffice? No. Try with ABS(3-7) which would become (3-7) < Ø ? -3-7 : 3-7 and return -1Ø instead of 4. Put parentheses around the text and around every argument within it.

Watch out for side effects! ABS (i++) would expand into ((i++) < Ø ? -(i++) : (i++)) causing i to be incremented *twice* on each execution. (i++ is equivalent to i = i + 1).

ILLUSTRATING C

Macros may invoke each other:

```
#define ABS (X )  (( X ) < ø ? -( X ) : ( X ))
#define NEAR_EQL ((A),(B))  (ABS((A)-(B))>(TOL) ? ø : 1 );
#define TOL   ø.øø1
```

The NEAR_EQL macro returns 1 (*true*) if its arguments have nearly
equal values, otherwise ø (false). The criterion for 'nearly' is set by
the value associated with TOL. For the setting shown, NEAR_EQL (1.2345,
1.2349) would return 1 (*true*).

Macros that invoke one another may be arranged in any order; the
preprocessor re-scans to satisfy unmatched names (notice that ABS
precedes NEAR_EQL but TOL follows). However, if one macro involves
others, all participant macros must be defined ahead of any function
wanting to use it. For example, if NEAR_EQL is to be used in main( ) then
ABS, TOL and NEAR_EQL must all be defined ahead of the definition of
main( ).

STRING ARGUMENTS   operators: # 'string-izer'
                                      ## 'paster'

If # is placed in front of an argument inside the substitution text, the
preprocessor takes the argument literally, enclosing it in quotes. In this
example, if the preprocessor
subsequently met PLURAL(Cat)
it would expand it to
printf ("Cat" "s");

```
#define PLURAL(P) printf ( #P"s" );
```

Adjacent strings are always concatenated, and contiguous " " removed,
so the effect of PLURAL (Cat) would be printf ("Cats");

The \ and " in the actual argument are replaced by \\ and \"
respectively, and so should be treated literally. PLURAL (Cat\nip) is
replaced by printf ("Cat\nip") without an accident over the \n. But be
careful! My system goes berserk if it meets leading or trailing \ or
unbalanced " (\Cat, Cat\, C"at).

The preprocessor's 'operator',
##, concatenates arguments. If
the preprocessor subsequently

```
#define OYEZ(A, B)  printf ("A##B");
```

met OYEZ (Aster, ix) it
would substitute 'printf ("Asterix");' But here we are in dangerous
territory; see Kernighan & Ritchie and the manuals for your particular
system (or experiment boldly).

Here is a home-made header file. Name it MYHEAD.H

```
#define PI 3.14                          (MYHEAD.H)
int Print ( char c, int i );
int Post ( float, double );
#define ABS(X) ((X)<Ø ? -(X) : (X))
int Pick ( void );
```

You may start a program as below. Its first line then gets replaced by the contents of the

```
#include < stdio.h >
#include "MYHEAD.H"
int main ( void )
{
```

standard header file named stdio.h. Similarly, its second line gets replaced by the contents of the header file named MYHEAD.H

In general, the #include line tells the preprocessor to replace that line with the entire contents of the file nominated. If the name is in pointed brackets it means the file may be found in the usual directory for standard header files; if the name is in quotes it means the header file is in the same directory as the program being processed.

The organization of files and directories, and the limitations of allowable syntax in names of files, depends on your implementation. See local manuals for the precise implications of <name> and "name".

A header file is typically an ordinary text file that contains a selection of the following in any order:

* definitions of constants (| #define PI 3.14 |)
* definitions of macros (| #define ABS(x) ((x)<Ø?-(x):(x)) |)
* function prototypes (| int Pick(void); |)
* #include lines nominating similar files (| #include "YRHEAD.H" |)

Standard header files, such as stdio.h and math.h, are available at every C installation. When your program invokes a standard function (| for example printf("Hi"); |) you have to know which standard header file contains its prototype. In the case of printf() it is stdio.h. To make printf() available, place #include <stdio.h> somewhere ahead of the function in which printf("Hi") occurs. The usual place is ahead of all functions defined in the file.

FUNCTION PROTOTYPES

Home-made header files (| such as MYHEAD.H |) are useful for keeping a program tidy as it grows. Defining PI once only is better than defining it separately in each file. More importantly, an ANSI C processor will compile an invocation (| such as k = Pick(void) |) only if it knows what type of value (| int, float, double, *etc.* |) the function should return, and what type each argument should take. The processor knows these facts if it has already met your definition of Pick() and compiled it. But what if the processor met k = Pick() before having seen and compiled the definition? The answer is that you should already have shown the processor a *prototype* of Pick(): a prototype contains all information necessary for compiling the invocation k = Pick().

The tidiest way to show prototypes is to make a header file for them and include that header file (| #include "MYHEAD.H" |). Then you need not worry whether the processor meets an invocation before having compiled the function invoked.

CONDITIONAL PREPROCESSING

You can make the preprocessor deal with some sequences of lines in your input file and ignore others according to the conditions encountered during processing ⇌ such as including a file only if it is not already included.

The diagram shows the required arrangement of directives, expressions and lines to achieve conditional preprocessing.

The composition of *expression* is restricted to simple constants; don't include sizeof or a cast or an enumerated constant.

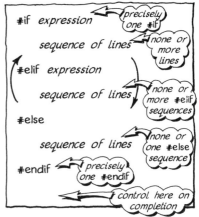

The preprocessor will deal with no more than *one* sequence of lines, and that's the first sequence encountered whose associated expression evaluates as non-zero (*true*). #elif means 'else if'. If all the #if and #elif expressions evaluate as zero (*false*) the preprocessor deals with the sequence following #else ⇌ but in the absence of an #else sequence the preprocessor does nothing. In every case the preprocessor ends by jumping to the line after the obligatory #endif.

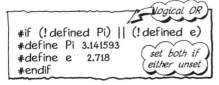

```
#if (!defined Pi) || (!defined e)
#define Pi 3.141593
#define e    2.718
#endif
```
set both if either unset

```
#if !defined MYTAG
#define MYTAG
```
receives null value
```
put contents of MYHEAD.H here;
they will be processed only once
#endif
```

```
#if !defined YRTAG
#include "YRHEAD.H"
#define YRTAG
#endif
```

An expression may involve the special 'operator' exclusive to the preprocessor. It has the form:

    defined (*name*)   or
    defined *name*

and takes the value 1L (*i.e.* unity expressed as a long int) if *true*; ØL if *false*. True signifies that the processor has already met the definition of *name* in the form:

    define *name*   *text*
                          (*null*)

The preprocessor coerces all its Boolean values to long int (1L, ØL).

Ansi C offers two directives, #ifdef and #ifndef, which you may use in place of #if in macros such as those illustrated above:

    #ifdef *name* is short for #if defined *name*
    #ifndef *name* is short for #if !defined *name*

There are no corresponding short cuts to use with #elif.

The following diagram summarizes the syntax of a preprocessor directive. Each directive must be on a line of its own (possibly extended by \ ) preceding the program it is to modify.

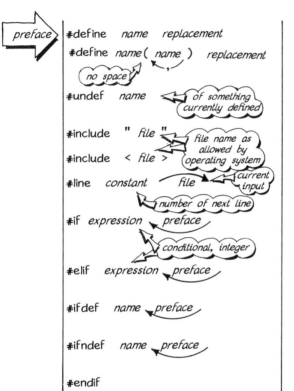

preface	
#define *name replacement*	▶ #define PI 3.14
#define *name(name) replacement* *no space*	▶ #define FAHR(cels) \ ((32)+(9)*(cels)/(5))
#undef *name* — *of something currently defined*	▶ #undef FAHR
#include " *file* " — *file name as allowed by operating system*	▶ #include "MYFIL.HED"
#include < *file* >	▶ #include < stdio.h >
#line *constant file* — *current input* — *number of next line*	▶ #line 22 MYFILE *(diagnostics)*
#if *expression preface* — *conditional, integer*	▶ #if !defined MyTag #define MyTag
#elif *expression preface*	▶ #elif !defined HerTag #define HerTag
#ifdef *name preface*	▶ #ifdef YourTag #undef YourTag
#ifndef *name preface*	▶ #ifndef MyTag #define MyTag
#endif	▶ #endif

where

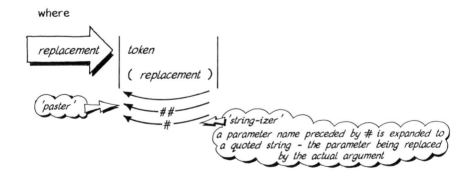

replacement	token
	(replacement)

'paster' ## *'string-izer'*
— *a parameter name preceded by # is expanded to a quoted string - the parameter being replaced by the actual argument*

STORAGE CLASS

The simple declarations illustrated earlier declare the type of a variable, and optionally supply an initial value. Such definitions may be preceded by a *qualifier* or *storage class specifier* or both:

```
int i = 6, j;
float f ;
```

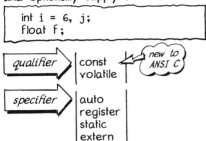

```
const float pi = 3.1416 ;
```

Any declaration qualified by const should be initialized ↝ because the processor refuses to permit a subsequent assignment to the object, either directly or indirectly; const means it is *constant.*

The volatile qualifier has to do with 'optimizing compilers'; its precise behaviour depends on the installation, so consult local manuals about its purpose and possible usefulness.

Storage class specifiers say whether an object should be remembered or allowed to evaporate when control leaves the current function, whether a global object is global to one file or all files, whether a function is accessible from all files or just one, and so on.

```
auto    int   i = 6,   j;

register   int   k = 3,  l;

static   float   a , b , c , d;

extern   int   p ,  q;
```

The significance of each storage class specifier depends on the context of the declaration. This subject is covered in detail in following pages. Here is a summary, much simplified :

 Means the object evaporates when control leaves the current block. Objects declared inside blocks are auto by default, so auto declarations are seldom used

 Means auto, plus a hint to the processor that it may store the variable in a fast register (|at the cost of being refused access to it via an address |).

 Outside all functions: 'static' means the object or function can be accessed within the current file only

 In a block; 'static' means the object and its contents are to be preserved when control leaves the current block

 Tells the processor to look for a full definition elsewhere outside the current block or current file ↝ and extend its scope to the current block or file.

OUTSIDE DECLARATIONS

'Outside' means outside all function definitions.

Objects declared outside function definitions are maintained throughout the program's run. They are said to be 'global.' Global objects provide a useful medium of communication between functions.

The 'scope' of an object is the region of program in which statements may refer to that object or change the contents of that object. This assumes the object is not hidden: 'visibility' is explained later.

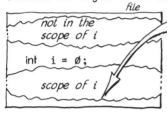

The scope of an object defined without a specifier runs from the point of declaration to the end of the same file.

The scope of such an object may be extended to other files, or another region of the same file, by extern declaration. Each extra scope runs from the point of extern declaration to the end of that file.

The scope of an object specified as static runs from the point of declaration to the end of the same file.

- In an outside declaration 'static' means private to the current file.

- An 'extern i' in the same file would refer to the same i.

- An 'extern i' in another file would not be associated with this static declaration.

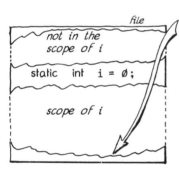

An outside declaration without an initializer is a *tentative definition*. There may be any number of tentative definitions throughout the program provided their types do not clash.

- If the linker finds a unique definition of the item it treats all tentative definitions as redundant declarations

- If the linker finds no unique definition it treats all tentative definitions as a single definition *initialized to zero* ((or zeros)).

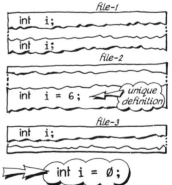

74

Although an object may be 'in scope' it may nevertheless be hidden by the scope of a local declaration inside a block. Global i becomes 'invisible' in the scope of local i.

In a deeper nested block you can hide the current scope of local i with an even more local i—and so on to any depth. ⟨ In this example we use 'extern' to make global i hide local i in the same block. ⟩⟩

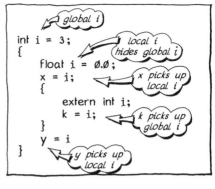

```
int i = 3;
{
    float i = Ø.Ø;
    x = i;
    {
        extern int i;
        k = i;
    }
    y = i
}
```

global i

local i hides global i

x picks up local i

k picks up global i

y picks up local i

A semicolon denotes a *prototype declaration*. The prototype declaration declares that statements between here and the end of the file may invoke Func(), whose *definition* is elsewhere.

In a prototype declaration the 'extern' is implied by default. In the example here, int Func(void); would be enough.

not in scope of Func( )

extern int Func (void);

extern *implied by default*

scope of Func( )

A *block* instead of a semicolon denotes a full *definition* of Func(), its scope running from the closing brace to the end of the file. It is unnecessary to write a prototype following a definition.

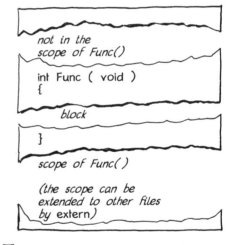

not in the scope of Func()

int Func (void)
{

block

}

scope of Func( )

(*the scope can be extended to other files by* extern)

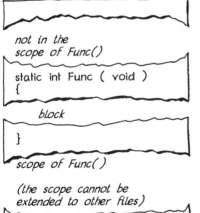

not in the scope of Func()

static int Func (void)
{

block

}

scope of Func( )

(*the scope cannot be extended to other files*)

The scope of a function may be kept private to the file in which it is defined by declaring the definition static. This feature is useful for 'encapsulating' information, together with corresponding access functions, where no other functions can see them. Encapsulation is a vital principle of OOP (object-oriented programming).

BLOCK DECLARATIONS

An auto object, whether declared auto explicitly or by default, evaporates together with its contents when control leaves the current block.

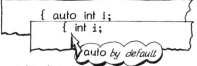

```
{ auto int i;
    { int i;
```
auto by default

```
{ register i;
```

A register variable behaves as an auto variable except that (i) you hint that storage in a fast register would be appropriate, and (ii) whether the processor takes the hint or not, ANSI C forbids taking a register variable's address.

```
{ int i = 2 * j + k;
```

Initialization of auto objects, or register variables, is 'dynamic', looking and behaving like assignment.

```
{ static int i;
```

Objects declared static are maintained throughout the program's run; they don't evaporate.

The initializer of a static object is evaluated at compile time; therefore it may involve only constants and sizeof.

```
{ static int i = 2 * sizeof ( int );
```

```
{ extern int i;
```

An extern declaration in a block makes the linker look first at outside definitions in the current file. If the linker finds the outside declaration 'int i=6;' it takes this to be the i referred to by extern. The same would apply if the linker found a static definition like 'static int i = 6;'

If the linker finds no outside definition of i in the current file, it assumes a unique definition exists elsewhere ⟿ in another file belonging to the program. (❲ 'int i=6' would be a valid definition of i, but 'static int i' in another file would be ignored because that particular i is exclusive to its own file. ❳)

Because extern says that the object or function is defined outside the current block (❲ whether in the same file or another ❳) it follows that an object declared 'extern int i' will not evaporate when control leaves the current block.

```
{ extern int Func ( void );
    { int Func ( void );
```
extern by default

This is a *prototype declaration*. It says that statements in the same block may invoke Func(), whose definition is outside (❲ in the same or another file ❳). The linker looks first in the current file. If it finds an outside definition (❲ beginning 'int Func (void) {' or 'static int Func (void) {' ❳) it takes this to be the Func() referred to by extern. If the linker finds no such definition of Func() in the current file it assumes the definition is to be found in another file (❲ disregarding any declared static ❳).

You cannot initialize an object declared extern *anywhere*. You cannot declare a function static if the prototype declaration is in a block.

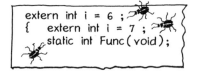

```
extern int i = 6 ;
{    extern int i = 7 ;
    static int Func ( void );
```

ILLUSTRATING C

PARAMETER DECLARATIONS

```
int Func ( int i ) {   ( block ) }
```

Object i is private to { *block* }.
When Func ( ) is subsequently invoked
from elsewhere (¶ say as x = Func (2 * 3) ;)) object i gets initialized to 6,
and the statements of *block* are obeyed. When control leaves the function,
object i and its contents evaporate.

Parameters are intrinsically *auto* objects:
don't specify auto, static or extern.

```
int Func (  auto
            static     int i )
            extern
```

```
int Func ( register int i )
```

The processor may take the hint
and store variable i in a fast
register rather than a memory location. Whether it does so or not, ANSI
C forbids taking the address of a register variable using &i or by indirect
means.

```
int Func ( int i, int j, int k )
```

On a call such as :
        s = Func (x*p, y*q, z*r) ;
you may *not* assume the order of evaluation of x*p, y*q, z*r. You *may*
assume all are evaluated before entry to Func ( ).

A parameter of a function may be
a function. For full understanding you
need to know about pointers (¶ next
chapter)) but here is an example:

```
int Func ( float   MyFun ( ) )
```

*short for (* MyFun)*

```
#include < stdio.h >
#include < math.h >
double Lookup ( double LibFun ( ), double Argument )
{
    return LibFun ( Argument ) ;
}

void main ( void )
{
    printf ("\n%f %f", Lookup (sqrt, 16 ), Lookup ( log, 2.718 ) ;
}
```

function as parameter of a function

*names of
< math.h >
functions*

`4.000000   0.999896`

```
int Func ( float MyArray [ ] )
```

*short for (* MyArray)*

A parameter of a function may be
an array. For full understanding you
need to know about pointers (¶ next
chapter)) but here is an example of
a function that swops array elements:

```
void Switch ( int A [ ], int i, int j )
{

    int Temp = A [ i ] ;
        A [ i ] = A [ j ] ;
        A [ j ] = Temp ;
}
```

match

*exchange elements
3 & 6 of array B [ ]
as follows:*

Switch (B, 3, 6) ;

NAME SPACE

The name of a macro in a #define directive gets substituted for identical tokens ⇌ to the end of the file or corresponding #undef. The only tokens immune to replacement are those in comments and quoted strings.

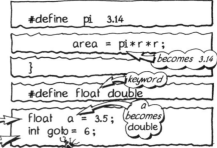

A keyword (⟮ such as float ⟯) can be replaced by the text of a macro. Otherwise keywords may be used only as keywords.

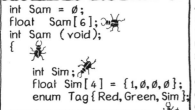

```
int Sam = ∅;
float  Sam[6];
int Sam (void);
{
      int Sim;
      float Sim[4] = {1,∅,∅,∅};
      enum Tag{Red, Green, Sim};
```

But you *may* use the same name at a different level of a block, thereby *hiding* the entity at the outer level.

An example of hidden names on Page 75 shows how you can 'unhide' a name at outer level using extern.

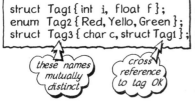

```
struct Tag1{int i, float f};
enum Tag2{Red, Yello, Green};
struct Tag3{char c, struct Tag1};
```

these names mutually distinct   *cross reference to tag OK*

The members of any one structure or union must be uniquely named, but there is no interaction between identically named members of different structures or unions.

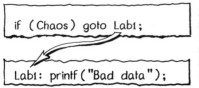

```
if (Chaos) goto Lab1;

Lab1: printf ("Bad data");
```

Among outside declarations, or at the same level of nesting in any one block, you may not give a variable the same name as an array. Furthermore, names must be unique among variables, arrays, functions, enumeration constants, and entities yet to be introduced (⟮ *viz.* defined types, structures, unions ⟯). At any one level all these share the same name space.

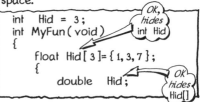

```
int  Hid = 3;
int MyFun (void)
{
      float Hid[3]={1,3,7};
      {
            double  Hid;
```

Tags are names used to identify different enumerations, structures and unions. Tags share name space and so should be mutually distinct. But you may hide one tag with another at different level in the manner already illustrated for variables.

There is no interaction between names of tags and names of other entities.

```
struct OneStruct{int i, float f};
struct TwoStruct{int i, float g};
```
OK

A goto statement specifies a name to match that of a *label* within the same function. In any one function all labels must be unique. There is no interaction between names of labels and names of any other entities in the same function.

two-d array [9] [10] — passed as two d array [ ]
pointer — 1 subscript

6

Arrays are passed by reference — its address is passed

POINTERS, ARRAYS, STRINGS

This is probably the most important chapter in the book; the art of C is handling *pointers*. Pointers are closely associated with *arrays*, and arrays with *strings*.

The chapter begins by explaining the concept of a *pointer* and defines two operators, * and &, with which to declare and manipulate pointers.

Because C works on the principle of 'call by value' you cannot return values from functions by altering the values stored in their parameters. *But you can use pointers as parameters* and make functions alter the contents of the objects they point to. This concept may appear tricky at first, but *glorious* when you can handle it confidently. The chapter spends some time on this concept.

When you add 2 to a pointer into an array, the pointer then points to the element two further along, regardless of the length of element. This is a property of *pointer arithmetic*, the subject next described in this chapter.

Most pointers point to objects, but you can make them point to functions as well. The chapter shows the correspondence between *pointers to arrays* and *pointers to functions*. You may care to skip this topic on first reading; likewise the next which analyses the structure of *complex declarations*. Complex declarations are easy to understand once you have felt the need to set up a data structure in which pointers point to other pointers.

To manipulate *strings* you need only simple pointers. The second half of this chapter explains strings and their use. Strings are simply character arrays designed to hold words and sentences. C programmers follow certain conventions in the structure of strings. These conventions are described.

POINTERS

The idea behind pointers was introduced in the context of sorting, Page 63. The following statement causes the letters to be printed in order:

```
for ( k=Ø; k < 8; ++k )
    printf ("\n%c", Letters[Pointers[k] ]);
```

But this is too clumsy for C which has special variables and operators for handling pointers. If you find the concepts confusing, persevere! They become beautifully clear when the penny drops.

	Pointers		Letters
[Ø]	1	[Ø]	G
[1]	4	[1]	B
[2]	Ø	[2]	L
[3]	7	[3]	I
[4]	3	[4]	C
[5]	2	[5]	N
[6]	6	[6]	M
[7]	5	[7]	H

✳ OPERATOR

If p names a *pointer variable*, *p denotes the object currently pointed to by p.

Terminology: When a job is advertised, the one who appoints is called the *appointer*. The successful applicant is called the *appointee*. On the same linguistic principle, let the object indicated by the *pointer* be called the *pointee*. *p denotes the *pointee* of p.

The term *p (〖 the pointee of p 〗) may be used like the name of a variable:

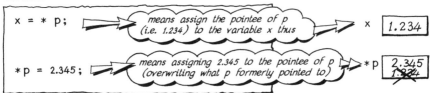

& OPERATOR

Behind the scenes, pointer and pointee are linked by *address*.

The address of an object is denoted by the object's name, preceded by ampersand, to say 'the address of ...' or 'the value of pointers to...'

the address of x is denoted &x

$\begin{array}{c} x \\ 1024 \end{array}$ [2.345]

Point to x by assigning &x ⟨ you need not know it's 1024 ⟩ to q thus:

q = &x;

q [1024] $\begin{array}{c} x \\ 1024 \end{array}$ [2.345]

Now you can access the content of x via the pointer variable as *q.

There is no further need to depict absolute addresses. Here is the picture that says it all:

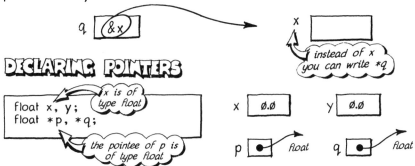
q [&x]   x [   ]

instead of x you can write *q

DECLARING POINTERS

float x, y;
float *p, *q;

x is of type float

the pointee of p is of type float

x [0.0]   y [0.0]

p [•] — float   q [•] — float

The first declaration establishes x and y as variables of type float in the usual way. The second declares 'pointer variables' named p and q, of which the pointees are of type float. In other words p and q are intended for pointing to variables of type float.

To declare a 'pointer variable' you tell the processor what type of object you intend to point to.

char *pv[6];

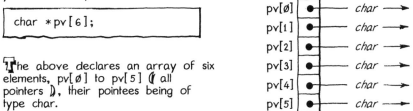
pv[0] [•] —— char →
pv[1] [•] —— char →
pv[2] [•] —— char →
pv[3] [•] —— char →
pv[4] [•] —— char →
pv[5] [•] —— char →

The above declares an array of six elements, pv[0] to pv[5] ⟨ all pointers ⟩, their pointees being of type char.

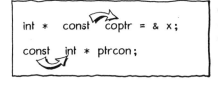
int * const coptr = &x;

const int * ptrcon;

Qualifiers apply to the nearest rightwards entity; coptr is a constant ⟨ initialized ⟩ pointer with an integer pointee; the pointee of ptrcon is a constant integer.

PARAMETERS

A common requirement in programming is the exchange of values held in a pair of variables or array elements.

Here is a block of 'in-line' code to exchange the values held in a pair of variables, i and j.

```
{
    int Temp = i;
    i = j;
    j = Temp;
}
```
in-line code

How about a *function* for swopping values?

```
void Swap ( char i, char j )
{
    int Temp = i;
    i = j;
    j = Temp;
}
```

This one is no good. Parameters in C are *called by value*. The function manipulates *copies* only.

Suppose your program had 2 stored in A, 3 stored in B. And suppose you invoked this function as:

```
Swap ( A, B );
```

The processor would enter the function, assigning a copy of the contents of A into i, a copy of the contents of B into j. It would then swop the contents of i and j, then return, leaving the contents of A and B undisturbed. No good! The trick is to employ *pointers* as parameters and swop their *pointees*.

The function on the right may be invoked as:

```
Swop ( & A, & B );
```

The processor enters the function assigning the *address* of A to i (which makes i point to A) and the *address* of B to j (which makes j point to B) The *pointees* of i and j are then exchanged.

```
void Swop ( int * i, int * j )
{
    int Temp = * i;      type of Temp
    * i = * j;           to match that
    * j = Temp;          of *i
}
```

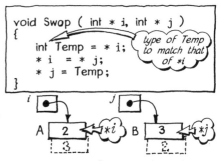

The above function may be invoked with addresses of array elements as arguments (*e.g.* Swop (&p[i], &p[j])) or you may write a swopping function that has three parameters, the first nominating the array and the other two the subscripts. This function (which exchanges elements of an array of pointers to char) might be invoked as:

```
Exch ( p, 2, 4 );
```

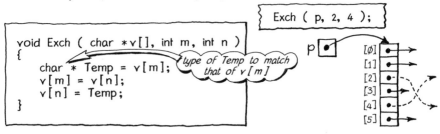

```
void Exch ( char *v[], int m, int n )
{
    char * Temp = v[m];      type of Temp to match
    v[m] = v[n];             that of v[m]
    v[n] = Temp;
}
```

ILLUSTRATING C

QUICKSORT AGAIN

PROTOTYPES, POINTERS,
POINTERS AS PARAMETERS

Here is the sorting function from Page 63 re-written with (i) prototypes to allow functions to be assembled in any order, (ii) an array of pointers ((a *pointer vector*)) instead of making do with integers, (iii) a function for exchanging the contents of array elements, (iv) a function for comparing entities. This arrangement keeps the sorting algorithm separate from the details of comparing and swopping. By writing replacement Comp () and Exch() functions you may use Qsort ((unchanged except for the type declaration)) to sort objects of any type.

```
#include < stdio.h >
void Qsort(char *[], int, int);
void Exch(char *[], int, int);        prototypes
int Comp ( char, char );
char *pv[100], Letters[100];
void main( void )
{
    int i, n, c;
    printf("\nType some letters & press Return\n");
    for (n=0; (c = getchar() ) != '\n'; ++n )
        {
            Letters [n] = c;                 stops reading
            pv [n] = & Letters [n];          chars on
        }                                    Return
    Qsort(pv, 0, n-1);
    for (i=0; i<n; ++i)
        printf(" %c ", *pv[i]);
}
```

pv   Letters

```
[0] •——→ C
[1] •——→ A
[2] •——→ E
[3] •——→ D
[4] •——→ B
```

```
[0] •  ⤬  C
[1] •  ⤬  A
[2] •  ⤬  E
[3] •——→ D
[4] •——→ B
```

≡ *ABCDE*

```
void Qsort(char * p[], int i, int j)     logic
{                                        explained
                                         on Page 62
    if (i < j)
    {
        int First=1, Last=j, Way=1, Temp;
        while (i != j)          see foot of this page for Comp
        {
            if ( Way == Comp ( * p[i], *p[j] ) )
            {                                   append function Exch()
                Exch ( p, i, j );               shown at the foot of the
                Temp = i, i = j, j = Temp;      opposite page
                Way = !Way;
            }                               in-line code
            j += (!Way - Way);              for swop
        }
        Qsort (p, First, i-1);
        Qsort (p, i+1, Last);
    }
}
```

```
int Comp ( char a, char b )     Comp () would be more complicated if it
{                               compared words rather than letters
    return a>b;
}
```

POINTER ARITHMETIC

Arrays were introduced earlier as named patterns of subscripted elements, the elements behaving like variables. Behind the scenes, however, subscripts of arrays are handled as *pointers*. Here is a fresh way to depict arrays:

```
float a[] = { 1.23, 2.34, 3.45, 4.56 };
int b[] = { 1Ø, 11, 12, 13 };
```

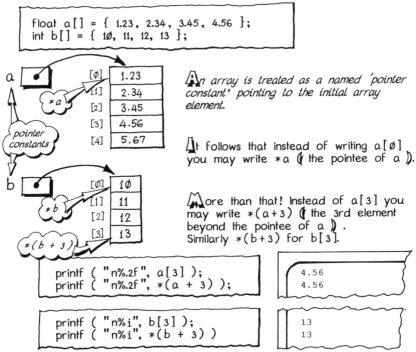

An array is treated as a named 'pointer constant' pointing to the initial array element.

It follows that instead of writing a[Ø] you may write *a (the pointee of a).

More than that! Instead of a[3] you may write *(a+3) (the 3rd element beyond the pointee of a).
Similarly *(b+3) for b[3].

```
printf ( "n%.2f", a[3] );          4.56
printf ( "n%.2f", *(a + 3) );      4.56
```

```
printf ( "n%i", b[3] );            13
printf ( "n%i", *(b + 3) )         13
```

On a typical installation an element of a[] (type float) would be twice as long as an element of b[] (type int). To locate a[3] or b[3] the processor compensates for length. In one case the '3' signifies three times the length of a float, in the other it signifies three times the length of an int.

The same applies to *(a+3) and *(b+3); the '3' signifies the third element, whatever the types of a and b.

When you work with array subscripts, or with pointers, the processor takes care of types and their lengths; &a[1] - &a[Ø] yields 1 whatever the type of a.

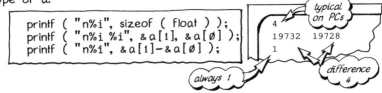

```
printf ( "n%i", sizeof ( float ) );         4
printf ( "n%i %i", &a[1], &a[Ø] );          19732   19728
printf ( "n%i", &a[1]-&a[Ø] );              1
```

typical on PCs

always 1

difference 4

A corresponding example using pointers in place of array subscripts would involve the terms $\&*a$ and $\&*(a+1)$. But the '$\&*$' says 'the address of the pointee of ...' which cancels itself out. So $\&*a$ is the same thing as a; $\&*(a+1)$ is the same thing as $a+1$. It follows that $\&*(a+1)-\&*a$ is the same thing as 1, being independent of the length of type a.

You may assign the value of a pointer-constant to a pointer-variable of compatible type:

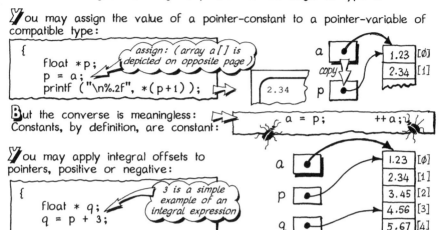

But the converse is meaningless: Constants, by definition, are constant:

You may apply integral offsets to pointers, positive or negative:

The constant $\emptyset$ ((zero)) may be assigned to a pointer-variable to signify that it is unset ((no element can have an absolute address of zero)). The header file `<stdio.h>` offers a zero constant, NULL, for indicating unset pointers.

You may subtract ((never add)) pointers that point into the same array. The result is integral and it could be large. Header file `<stddef.h>` offers the special type, ptrdiff_t for declaring variables in which to store such differences.

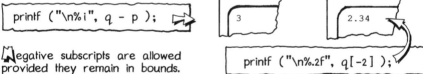

Negative subscripts are allowed provided they remain in bounds.

```
printf ("\n%.2f", q[-2] );
```

Exception: The pointer is allowed to point just one increment beyond the last element. In the following example, p ends up pointing to a non-existent element, $a[5]$. At that stage $*p$ would be undefined.

Pointers into the same array may be compared using >, >=, ==, != *etc.*

The number of elements in an array may be found from:

        sizeof *arrayname* / sizeof (*type*)

parentheses essential for types, not for objects

More neatly:

        sizeof *arrayname* / sizeof *arrayname*[$\emptyset$]

PARLOUR TRICK

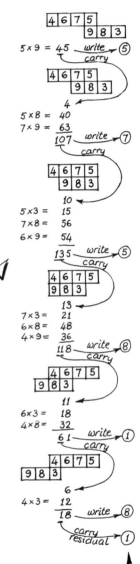

Amaze your friends. Write down a long multiplication such as this; then start writing down the answer, digit by digit, from right to left, carrying all the working in a cool head.

The trick is mentally to reverse the bottom number, mentally shunting it leftwards past the top number. At each shunt multiply only the digits lying beneath one another, summing the products. Write down the last digit of this sum and carry the rest into the next shunt. The entire process is depicted down the right of the page.

To see how it works, consider each number as a polynomial in 10. In every shunted position the products of terms lying one above the other yield the same power of 10. Furthermore these terms are the *only* terms in the same power of 10 (| but not forgetting the carry from above |).

$$4 \times 10^3 \ + \ 6 \times 10^2 \ + \ 7 \times 10^1 \ + \ 5 \times 10^0$$
$$9 \times 10^0 \ + \ 8 \times 10^1 \ + \ 3 \times 10^2$$
$$\overline{54 \times 10^2 \ + \ 56 \times 10^2 \ + \ 15 \times 10^2}$$

e.g. all the terms in 10^2

The program opposite automates the method of multiplication described above. It can cope with any reasonable length of multiplication by adjusting the constant OP (| e.g. #define OP 35 |). As set opposite, the program can multiply terms as long as 35 digits, giving a product as long as 70 digits.

To use the program type two numbers separated by an asterisk and terminated by an equals sign. Then press Return.

```
4675*389=
1818575
1111111111111111111111*20000000000000000000=
22222222222222222222220000000000000000000
```

The program offers another go. When fed up with it, hold down Ctrl and press C (| or whatever it is you do on your particular implementation to abort a run |).

```c
/* Any-length multiplication */
#include < stdio.h >
#define OP 2Ø
int Read_Op ( int *, char );

void main ( void )
{
    long int sum;
    int a[ OP ], b[ OP ], c[ OP + OP ];
    int i, j, k, m, n, ch;
    while ( 1 )
    {
        i = Read_Op ( a, '*' );
        j = Read_Op ( b, '=' );

        n = i + j;
        sum = Ø;
        for ( k=n; k >= Ø; --k )
        {
            for ( m=k; m >= Ø; --m )
                if ( m <= i && (k-m) <= j )
                    sum += a[ m ] * b[ k-m ];
            c [ n-k ] = sum % 1Ø;
            sum /= 1Ø;
        }
        if ( sum )
            c[ ++n ] = sum;
        while ( n+1 )
            printf ( "%i", c [ n-- ] );
        printf ( "\n" );
    }
}

int Read_Op ( int *p, char Xit )
{
    int r, Ch;
    for ( r=Ø; ( Ch = getchar() ) != Xit; ++r )
        if ( Ch >= 'Ø' && Ch <= '9' )
            p[r] = Ch - 'Ø';
        else
            --r;
    return --r;
}
```

Annotations (in clouds):

- set desired limit of operand
- prototype of Read-operand function
- length of product accommodates operators
- invoke function with pointer to array a[ ] then with pointer to array b[ ]
- a ▢ [Ø] [1] [2] [3] | 4 6 7 5 | 9 8 3 | [2] [1] [Ø] | b ▢
- pick off last digit
- carry sum
- final carry if not zero
- print result
- pointer to int
- invoke with '*' or '='
- accept only digits
- ignore non-digit
- return subscript of last digit

The function for reading the operands terminates on the character you specify as the second parameter. It reads the digits into the array pointed to by the first parameter. The function returns the subscript of the final digit; thus if the function reads a seven digit number (Ø through 6) the function returns 6.

POINTERS TO FUNCTIONS

YOU MAY CARE TO SKIP THIS ON FIRST READING

The demonstration program on Page 77 is reproduced below.

```
#include < stdio.h >                    double (*LibFun) ()
#include   < math.h >
double Lookup ( double LibFun ( ), double Argument )
{
    return LibFun ( Argument );
}                                      4.000000   0.999896
void main ( void )
{
    printf ("\n%f %f", Lookup ( sqrt, 16 ), Lookup ( log, 2.718 ) );
}
```

The program shows that one function (Lookup()) may have another function (LibFun()) as a parameter. When you invoke Lookup() you provide the name of an available function as an argument in place of the dummy parameter. In essence, you follow the same pattern as for numerical parameters.

But 'double LibFun()' is actually an allowable shorthand form of:

double (* LibFun) ( )

return type — double

necessary parentheses; ( ) binds tighter than * — (* LibFun)

( ) signifies 'function (which has unspecified arguments) returning ... — ( )

The parentheses around * LibFun are needed because ( ) binds tighter than *. Without parentheses this parameter would parse as double * (LibFun ( )) which says 'Function returning pointer to a double'. With parentheses as shown it reads:

'LibFun is a pointer to a function that returns a double.'

You may find the concept easier from a different point of view:

double (*LibFun)( ) The full declaration

* ▓▓▓▓▓ This shape signifies a pointee (something pointed to)

▓▓▓▓▓ This part of a pointee identifies the pointer of the pointee, in our case LibFun:
'LibFun is a pointer pointing to ...'

double ▓▓▓▓▓▓ ( ) This shape declares a function that returns a double.
'LibFun is a pointer to a function returning a double.'

So a function name (sqrt or log in the program above) is a *constant pointer*. The concept of array names is similar; an array name is a *constant pointer* to the beginning of that array; see the depictions opposite.

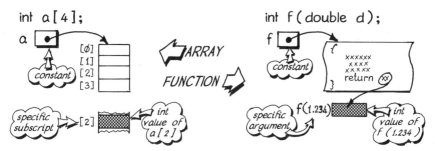

int a[4];   int f(double d);

ARRAY

FUNCTION

Here is a demonstration program to take the concept a step further. Given a number, the program prints its square root, log and anti-log. These are library functions with prototypes in <math.h>.

The data structure is depicted here. P names an array of pointers ((function names)) to library functions.

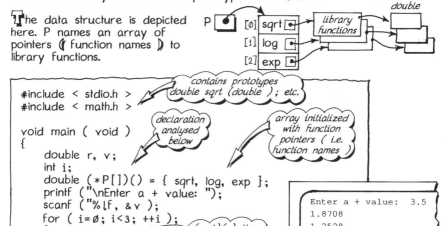

```
#include < stdio.h >                    contains prototypes
#include < math.h >                     double sqrt (double ); etc.

                          declaration              array initialized
void main ( void )        analysed                 with function
{                         below                    pointers ( i.e.
    double r, v;                                    function names )
    int i;
    double (*P[])() = { sqrt, log, exp };
    printf ("\nEnter a + value: ");          ┌──────────────────────────┐
    scanf ("%lf, & v );                      │ Enter a + value:   3.5   │
    for ( i=0; i<3; ++i );                   │ 1.8708                   │
    {                      (sqrt)(v) then    │ 1.2528                   │
        r = (*P[i]) (v);   (log)(v) then     │ 33.1155                  │
        printf ("\n%.4f", r );  (exp)(v)     └──────────────────────────┘
    }
}
```

The complicated declaration may be analysed in the manner shown opposite:

double (* P [ ]) ( )   Mind the precedence! [] binds tighter
                                    than *. Implied parentheses are shown
double (* (P [ ])) ( ) ◁ here.

┌──────────────────┐
│   P [ ]   │   This nominates an array element
└──────────────────┘

* ▨▨▨▨▨▨▨▨▨   The pointee of any element P[i] is

double ▨▨▨▨▨▨▨▨▨ ( )   ... a function that returns a double.

'P is an array of pointers, each of which points to a function ((having unspecified parameters)) that returns a double'

COMPLEX DECLARATIONS

YOU MAY CARE TO SKIP ON FIRST READING

A complex declaration is illustrated on the previous page. Here it is again, analysed as a 'parse tree':

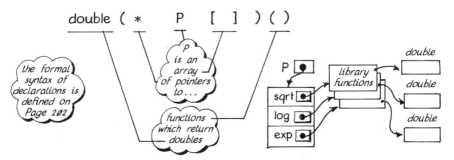

double (* P [ ]) ( )

the formal syntax of declarations is defined on Page 202

P is an array of pointers to...

functions which return doubles

Here is a data structure involving arrays of pointers to arrays:

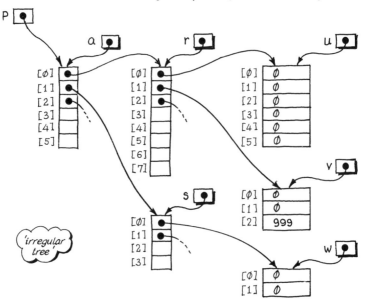

'irregular tree'

The demonstration program opposite shows how such a structure may be set up; first by declaring the arrays, then by linking pointers to addresses. The structure may be described by analogy with a tree having a root, branches and leaves.

The program shows how to access a particular leaf from each junction on the path from the root. Notice how the expressions for access suggest and reflect the array declarations.

ILLUSTRATING C

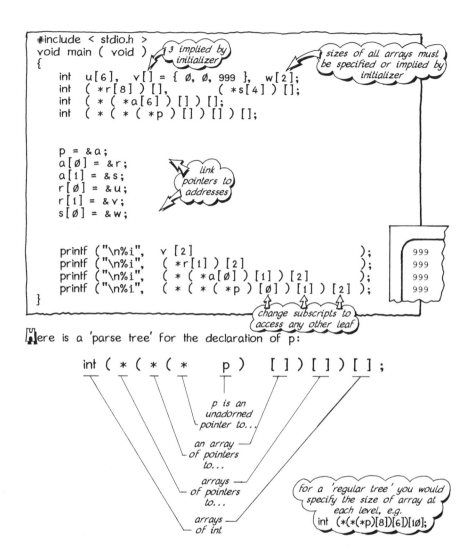

```
#include < stdio.h >
void main ( void )                    [3 implied by initializer]    [sizes of all arrays must be specified or implied by initializer]
{
    int   u[6],  v[] = { ∅, ∅, 999 },  w[2];
    int   ( *r[8] ) [],          ( *s[4] ) [];
    int   ( * ( *a[6] ) [] ) [];
    int   ( * ( * ( *p ) [] ) [] ) [];


    p = &a;
    a[∅] = &r;              [link pointers to addresses]
    a[1] = &s;
    r[∅] = &u;
    r[1] = &v;
    s[∅] = &w;


    printf ( "\n%i",  v [2]                          );     999
    printf ( "\n%i",  ( *r[1] ) [2]                  );     999
    printf ( "\n%i",  ( * ( *a[∅] ) [1] ) [2]        );     999
    printf ( "\n%i",  ( * ( * ( *p ) [∅] ) [1] ) [2] );     999
}
                                              [change subscripts to access any other leaf]
```

Here is a 'parse tree' for the declaration of p:

```
int ( * ( * ( *    p )    [ ] )  [ ] )  [ ] ;
```

p is an unadorned pointer to...

an array of pointers to...

arrays of pointers to...

arrays of int

[for a 'regular tree' you would specify the size of array at each level, e.g. int (*(*(*p)[8])[6])[10];]

In the expressions for access to the same leaf (which mirror the declarations of pointer vectors) climb back from leaf to root by replacing each local array name with the pointee from the previous level. For example, both v and r[1] point to the same place, so replace v with the pointee of r[1]. Follow this on the diagram apposite:

```
                           [replace v with (*r[1])]
                             [replace r with (*a[∅])]
    printf ( "\n%i",   v [2]    [replace a with (*p)]      );
    printf ( "\n%i",   ( *r[1] ) [2]                       );
    printf ( "\n%i",   ( * ( *a[∅] ) [1] ) [2]             );
    printf ( "\n%i",   ( * ( * ( *p ) [∅] ) [1] ) [2]      );
```

Here is an array of characters initialized from a list of character constants:

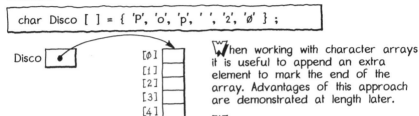

```
char Disco [ ] = { 'P', 'o', 'p', ' ', '2', 'ø' } ;
```

Disco [•] → [ø]
[1]
[2]
[3]
[4]
[5]

When working with character arrays it is useful to append an extra element to mark the end of the array. Advantages of this approach are demonstrated at length later.

What character do we use for the marker?

To appreciate the problem, consider how characters are represented inside the computer. Many implementations represent characters by their ASCII codes. (I have shown ASCII codes as decimal numbers; the computer would store them as *binary* numbers.)

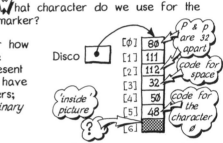

Disco [•] [ø] 80 — *P & p are 32 apart*
[1] 111
[2] 112 — *code for space*
[3] 32
[4] 50 — *code for the character ø*
'inside' picture [5] 48
? [6]

The answer is to use *zero* for the marker, not 'ø' (which has an ASCII code of 48) but an internal code of zero. Use the escape sequence \ø to represent the internal code of zero.

```
char Disco [ ] = { 'P', 'o', 'p', ' ', '2', 'ø', '\ø' } ;
```

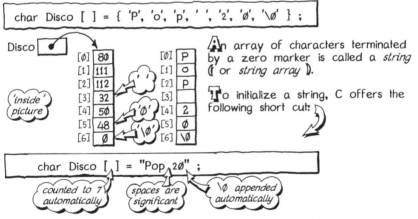

Disco [•]

'inside' picture

[ø] 80   [ø] P
[1] 111   [1] o
[2] 112   [2] P
[3] 32   [3]
[4] 50 '2' [4] 2
[5] 48 'ø' [5] ø
[6] ø '\ø' [6] \ø

An array of characters terminated by a zero marker is called a *string* (or *string array*).

To initialize a string, C offers the following short cut:

```
char Disco [ ] = "Pop 2ø" ;
```

counted to 7 automatically   *spaces are significant*   *\ø appended automatically*

The zero marker is included in the count. The same result would be got from char Disco[7] = "Pop 2ø". But char Disco[6] = "Pop 2ø" is an error, a likely result being the loss of the zero marker.
Disco[1ø] = "Pop 2ø" would create a string with zeros in the extra elements:

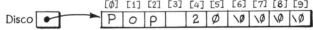

[ø] [1] [2] [3] [4] [5] [6] [7] [8] [9]
Disco [•] → P | o | p | | 2 | ø | \ø | \ø | \ø | \ø

STRING ARRAYS

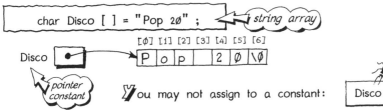

```
char Disco [ ] = "Pop 2∅" ;
```
string array

Disco → [∅] [1] [2] [3] [4] [5] [6]
P o p   2 ∅ \∅

pointer constant

You may not assign to a constant: `Disco = p ;`

But you *may* change the contents of elements in the array provided you do not try to extend it.

```
Disco [ ∅ ] = 'T';
Disco [ 1 ] += 'A' - 'a';
Disco [ 2 ] += 'A' - 'a';
```

[∅] [1] [2] [3] [4] [5] [6]
T O P   2 ∅ \∅

Programs which manipulate strings typically declare a set of string arrays, each of adequate length. An example is :

```
char r[ 81 ], s[ 81 ], t[ 81 ],
```

where the string currently in each array may grow to a length of 8∅ characters (and its terminating '\∅').

r → [∅] [1] [2] [3] [4] [5] [6]   [8∅]
T O P   2 ∅ \∅

reserved area of memory

STRING POINTERS

```
char *p, *q, *Gig = " TUNE" ;
```
string pointers

p q *p and q can point only to characters ~ they point nowhere at present*

Gig → T U N E \∅

Gig is initialized to a constant string

Although you may find it *possible* to alter a string constant (e.g. Gig[2] = 'O' to change " TUNE" to " TONE") the outcome would be undefined.

But you may freely assign pointers (including pointers to constant strings) to pointer variables:

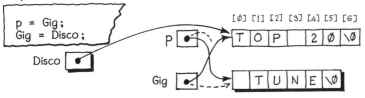

```
p = Gig ;
Gig = Disco ;
```

[∅] [1] [2] [3] [4] [5] [6]
p → T O P   2 ∅ \∅

Disco →

Gig → T U N E \∅

PRINTING STRINGS

A call to the printf ( ) function (¶ defined in <stdio.h>) takes the form:

printf (string , expression)

The *string* contains as many descriptors as there are expressions
following. So far we have met %i, %f, %c. There is also %s for the
substitution of a string defined by its pointer:

```
printf ( "%s TO %s", p, Gig );
```

⟹ TUNE TO TOP 20

All examples of printf have so far shown *string* as a *literal* string (¶ in
other words in quotes ¶). But wherever a string is demanded, you may
provide either a literal string or a *pointer* to a string. There should be a
zero marker at the end of the string.

```
printf ( Gig );
printf ( p );
```

CAREFUL!
if Gig or p contained %,
printf would look for an extra
argument to match each %

⟹ TOP 20 TUNE

RAGGED ARRAYS

*NO NEED FOR EVERY ROW
TO BE THE SAME LENGTH*

It is sometimes useful to store a set of constant strings such as names
of days of the week (¶ "Monday", "Tuesday",...¶) or error messages
addressed to the user of your program:

```
void ErrCode ( int n )
{                         ⟵ array private to ErrCode
    static char *Mess [ ] =
    {
        "Bug",
        "Should be greater than 1",
        "Too many sides",
        "Unrecognized code"
    }
    int s = sizeof Mess [ ] / sizeof Mess [ Ø ] - 1;
    n = ( n > s || n < Ø ) ? Ø : n;
    printf ("Error No. %i: %s!", n, Mess [ n ] );
}
```

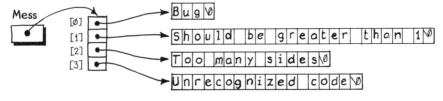

Mess

[Ø] • ⟶ |B|u|g|Ø|
[1] • ⟶ |S|h|o|u|l|d| |b|e| |g|r|e|a|t|e|r| |t|h|a|n| |1|Ø|
[2] • ⟶ |T|o|o| |m|a|n|y| |s|i|d|e|s|Ø|
[3] • ⟶ |U|n|r|e|c|o|g|n|i|z|e|d| |c|o|d|e|Ø|

COMMAND LINE

CATERING FOR OPTIONS
WHEN YOU RUN THE PROGRAM

The way to set a C program running depends on the implementation. Typically you type a *command* nominating the file in which the executable program is stored, then press Return.

MIMIC ← *command*

A program may be written that demands **(** or will accept as an option **)** extra information in the command line:

MIMIC   Caps   tabs ← *command line*

The manual that explains how to use such a program might define the allowable command line by a syntax diagram like this:

MIMIC ──── CAPS ─────────●
        └── L/C ──┘ └─TABS─┘

The options are automatically handed to function main( ) provided that you give main( ) two parameters: the first is of type int, the second is an array of pointers to char. Conventionally these are called argc and argv[ ] respectively:

```
void main ( int argc, char * argv [ ] )
{
```

The processor parses the command line into strings, recording their number **(** at least one **)** in argc, and setting up a pointer vector ∾ terminated by NULL ∾ as depicted below:

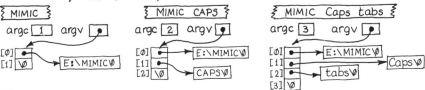

Here is a program that lists the arguments corresponding to its command-line parameters, excluding the name of the program file:

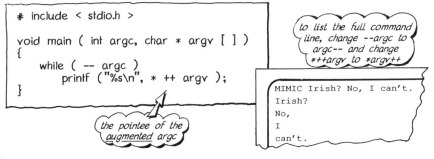

```
# include < stdio.h >

void main ( int argc, char * argv [ ] )
{
    while ( -- argc )
        printf ( "%s\n", * ++ argv );
}
```

*to list the full command line, change --argc to argc-- and change *++argv to *argv++*

the pointee of the augmented argc

```
MIMIC Irish? No, I can't.
Irish?
No,
I
can't.
```

6: POINTERS, ARRAYS, STRINGS   95

PARAMETER COUNTING , . . .)

The printf ( ) function is defined in Chapter 7 as follows:

int printf (const char *, ...);

first parameter a string

the ellipsis denotes an unspecified number of arguments

Examples of invocations (each with a different number of arguments) are:

printf ("\nThere are %i lumps weighing %f grams", n, w);

%i says the first argument will be an int

%f says the second argument will be in floating form

parameters for the two extra arguments expected

printf ("\nAnswer is %i", count);

one extra argument expected

You can write functions such as this, in which there is at least one fixed argument followed by an unspecified number of extra arguments. The header file <stdarg.h> defines a tool kit for retrieving the extra arguments. The tools are described below:

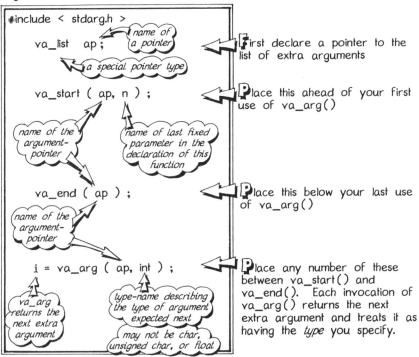

```
#include < stdarg.h >
        va_list   ap ;
```
name of a pointer

a special pointer type

First declare a pointer to the list of extra arguments

```
        va_start ( ap, n ) ;
```
Place this ahead of your first use of va_arg()

name of the argument-pointer

name of last fixed parameter in the declaration of this function

```
        va_end ( ap ) ;
```
Place this below your last use of va_arg()

name of the argument-pointer

```
        i = va_arg ( ap, int ) ;
```
Place any number of these between va_start() and va_end(). Each invocation of va_arg() returns the next extra argument and treats it as having the *type* you specify.

va_arg returns the next extra argument

type-name describing the type of argument expected next

may not be char, unsigned char, or float

ILLUSTRATING C

Here is a function to compute the arithmetic mean of its extra parameters. It has only one *fixed* parameter, and that is to convey the number of extra arguments you supply:

```
#include < stdarg.h >        ← prototypes of va_arg( ) etc.
#include < stdio.h >
double Mean ( int Count, ... )
{
    int n ;
    double Sum=∅ ;          declare ap as pointer to
    va_list ap ;              va_list
    va_start ( ap, Count );        ← make ap point to the first extra
    for ( n = ∅; n < Count; ++n )      argument ( after count )
        Sum += va_arg ( ap, double );  ← pick up each extra argument in
    va_end ( ap );           ← tidy up    turn - treating it as a double
    return  Sum / Count;
}
```

Here is a test-bed for the function. It is tested on four, two and one extra arguments respectively;

```
void main ( void )
{                      argument for
                       fixed parameter
    printf ("\n\n%f", Mean(4, 1.5, 2.4, 3.6, 2.8 ) );
    printf ("\n%f", Mean(2, 1.2, 3.6) );         2.575000
    printf ("\n%f", Mean(1, 6.7) );              2.400000
}                                                6.700000
```

By now you should have spotted a fundamental weakness in the argument-retrieval scheme: *you have to tell the function how many extra arguments to expect, and what the type of each will be.* There is no equivalent of the 'argc' and 'argv' parameters of function main( ).

There are three distinct ways of telling the function how may extra arguments to expect:

• As in the example above, use one of the fixed parameters as a *counter*; or

• Let the final extra argument act as a marker. For example, if all arguments should be positive numbers, terminate the argument list with −1 and watch for this signal when reading them with va_arg( ); or

• Use the idea found in printf( ), scanf( ), *et al.* The last fixed parameter is a string; each occurrence of % in the string signifies the expectation of a corresponding extra argument in the list that follows. Furthermore, the style code (%i, %f, %s *etc.*) tells what *type* the expected argument should be. You can handle a range of distinct types with a switch statement having a different va_arg( ) for each case.

STRING UTILITIES

Much of programming is concerned with strings. The ANSI C library offers about thirty string-handling functions that cover everything one would want to do. Here we develop a similar, but smaller, set of functions which nevertheless covers most of what one needs. Some resemble functions in the library, others are different ((particularly the one for reading strings from the keyboard)) .

READ FROM KEYBOARD

int KeyString (char *, int(), int);

This is a function for reading strings typed at the keyboard.

```
J    Janette   3.5
```

An example of a call is:

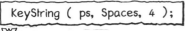

```
KeyString ( ps, Spaces, 4 );
```

Which serves to read and ignore leading spaces, then to

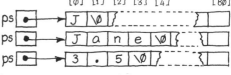

read up to four characters into the array pointed to by ps, then to read and ignore any remaining characters in that string ((e.g. 'tte' in 'Janette')) .

Strings typed at the keyboard may be terminated in the usual way ((whitespace)) or *by any other characters you care to list*. Name a function and list your selection. For example:

```
int Punctuators ( char t )
{
    return ( t == '\t' ) + ( t == ' ' ) + ( t == '\n' ) + ( t == ';' );
}
```

The above causes termination on tab, space, new line, semicolon. The function below terminates the item on reading a space or new line only.

```
int Spaces ( char t )
{
    return ( t == ' ' ) + ( t == '\n' );
}
```

The third function (below) terminates the item on reading new line only. In other words it gets the next line of input:

```
int Lines ( char t )
{
    return ( t == '\n' );
}
```
get next line

The first parameter of KeyString() points to the array into which the string from the keyboard buffer is to go, the second nominates the termination function, the third specifies the maximum number of characters to be stored in the receiving array ((the 'significant' characters)) .

```
/* READ NEXT STRING FROM KEYS */
int KeyString ( char *p, int TermFunc( char ), int length )
{
    int c;
    char *s;
    if ( length < 1 )
        return 1;
    s = p + length - 1;
    while (    TermFunc ( c = getc( stdin ) ) && c != EOF)
        ;
    ungetc( c, stdin );
    while ( ! TermFunc ( c = getc( stdin ) ) && c != EOF)
        if ( p < s )
            *p ++ = c;
    *p = '\ø';
    return (c == EOF) ? EOF : ø;
}
```

(annotations:)
- short for (*TermFunc)
- return 1 if erroneous call
- c=getc(stdin) is the same as c=getchar( )
- constant in stdio.h signals end of file
- return c to input for next getc( ) to read
- return EOF signal if end of file
- return ø if OK

Two features of this function need clarification:

- ungetc( ) causes the nominated character to be 'pushed back' on the nominated stream ⟮ in this case stdin ⟯ to be picked up by the next getc( ).

- EOF is a constant defined in < stdio.h > ⟮ in several processors it takes the value –1 ⟯. EOF is what you get if you read when there is nothing more on the input stream to be read. With every processor there is a way of sending EOF from the keyboard. With DOS systems you hold down Ctrl and press Z. Consult your particular manual on what to press.

Below is a little test bed for demonstrating the KeyString( ) function. To try the test bed, run it and type:

```
Note; This function is useful!
```

and press Return.

The screen responds:

```
Note
This
func
is
usef
```

(annotations:)
- terminated by semicolon
- specified truncation in call to KeyString

```
/* TEST BED FOR KeyString */
#include < stdio.h >
int KeyString ( char, int (*) (), int );
int Punctuators ( char );
void main ( void )
{
    int i;
    char String [ 81 ];
    while ( 1 )
    {
        i = KeyString( String, Punctuators, 4 );
        printf ("\n%s", String );
        if ( i == EOF )
            break;
    }
}
```

(annotation: append KeyString ( ), and Punctuators ( ))

Type other sentences. Finish with EOF.

WHAT KIND OF CHARACTER ?

The following two functions work for ASCII code in which letters are numbered contiguously. EBCDIC code would require some complication.

```
/* NOT FOR EBCDIC: Returns 1 if c is a capital, otherwise Ø */
int IsCap ( char c )
{
    return c >= 'A' && c <= 'Z' ;
}
```

```
/* NOT FOR EBCDIC: Returns 1 if c is a letter, otherwise Ø */
int IsLetter ( char c )
{
    return IsCap(c) || ( c >= 'a' && c <= 'z' );
}
```

The next two functions work for any code. For IsVowel() a static array is initialized at compile time and scanned on each call.

```
/* ANY CODE: Returns 1 if c is a vowel, otherwise Ø */
int IsVowel ( char c )
{
    static char v [ ] = "EeAaIiOoUu";
    char * p ;
    p = v ;                          short for *p != '\Ø'
    while ( *p && (*p != c ) )
        ++p ;
    return *p == c ;
}
```

p ☐

v ☐ → | E | e | A | a | I | i | O | o | U | u | \Ø |
      [Ø]   [1Ø]

```
/* ANY CODE: Returns 1 if c is a digit, otherwise Ø */
int IsDigit ( char c )
{
    return c >= 'Ø' && c <= '9' ;         digits are
}                                          contiguous in
                                           all codes
```

HOW LONG IS A STRING ?   *LENGTH EXCLUDING THE NULL*

To compute the length of a string, take a copy of its pointer. Then increment the pointer, stopping when its pointee is \Ø (*false*). The length of string, *excluding* the \Ø element, is 1 less than the difference between the augmented and original pointers.

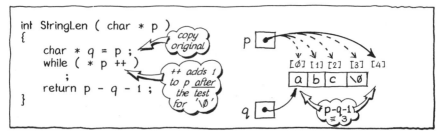

```
int StringLen ( char * p )
{                               copy
    char * q = p ;              original
    while ( * p ++ )
        ;                       ++ adds 1
    return p - q - 1 ;          to p after
}                               the test
                                for '\Ø'
```

p ☐

        [Ø] [1] [2] [3] [4]
        | a | b | c | \Ø |

q ☐   p-q-1
            ≡ 3

COPYING STRINGS

If you want q to point to the string pointed to by p, simply copy pointers thus: q = p . But sometimes copying pointers will not do; you have to copy a string, element by element, to another location. To do this, copy the pointee of p to the pointee of q, then increment both q and p, stopping when the pointee of p is '\ø'.

```
void StringCopy ( char * p, char * q )
{
    while ( * q = * p )     it loops until \ø
      ++ q, ++ p ;          is copied to *q
}
```

p ●

[ø] [1] [2] [3] 4
| a | b | c | \ø |

q ●

| a | b | c | \ø |
[ø] [1] [2] [3] 4

And here is an even more terse version: ➡

```
void StringCopy ( char * p, char * q )
{
    while ( * q ++ = * p ++ ) ;
}
```
null statement

The next function copies *part* of a string. You give the position of the starting character and the number of characters to be copied to the new location.

```
void Middle ( char * n, char * p, int Start, int Span )
{
    int L = StringLen ( p ) ;
    if ( Start >= ø && Start < L && Span > ø )       conditions to
    {                                                be met
        if ( Start + Span > L )          if Span overlaps end of
            Span = L - Start;            string, truncate it
        *( n + Span ) = '\ø' ;
        while ( Span -- )
            *( n + Span ) = *( p + Start + Span );
    }
    else
        * n = '\ø' ;
}
```

n ●→

[ø] [1] [2] [3]
| X | Y | Z | \ø |

Start = 4

p ●→

[ø] [1] [2] [3] [4] [5] [6] [7] [8]
| A | B | C | D | X | Y | Z | W | \ø |

Span = 3

The final copying utility copies two strings, locating them end to end as a new string. A typical call is Concat (N, L, R); the only overlapping allowed is Concat (L, L, R). Either original string may be empty.

```
void Concat ( char * new, char * left, char * right )
{
    if ( * left )
    {
        while ( * new ++ = * left ++ )
            ;                          step back
        new -- ;                       over \ø
    }
    while ( * new ++ = * right ++ )
        ;
}
```

left ●→ | a | b | c | \ø |

right ●→ | d | e | f | g | \ø |

new ●→ | a | b | c | d | e | f | g | \ø |

COMPARING STRINGS

When comparing strings, is "Twine" equal to "twine" ? And do we want to test for equality or for relative ordering ? The function Compare() offers parameters by which to specify both such requirements.

To make the parameters meaningful, create two *types*: enum Mode and enum Logic, by the following declarations:

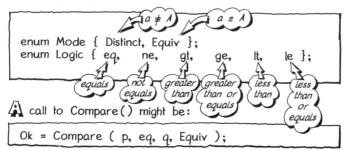

```
enum Mode { Distinct, Equiv };
enum Logic { eq,    ne,    gt,    ge,    lt,    le };
```

A call to Compare() might be:

```
Ok = Compare ( p, eq, q, Equiv );
```

Which sets Ok to 1 if strings p and q are equal on the assumption that upper and corresponding lower-case letters are equivalent:

```
Ok = Compare ( ps, gt, "Wilkins", Equiv ) ;
```

The above would set Ok to 1 if the string pointed to by ps is to be placed *above* "Wilkins" in a sorted list like a telephone directory.

The function assumes 'a' < 'b' < 'c' *etc.* and distinguishes strings on their first non-matching character. Thus "Jones" is greater than "Joan's" because 'n' > 'a'. Also, "Jo" is less than "Joan's" because '\0' < 'a'.

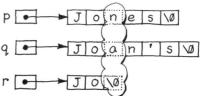

Punctuation marks and other characters are ordered according to their internal codes. In ASCII, for example, an apostrophe is less than a full stop, so "X's" precedes "X.s" in a sorted list. One would expect "Buzz9" to precede "Buzz10" but the criterion is the first non-matching character; 9 is greater than 1 so "Buzz10" precedes "Buzz9" in the sorted list (not nice).

To handle case distinction or equivalence we call on the function Uc() shown below:

```
/* NOT FOR EBCDIC: Returns upper case equivalent of c /*
/* if c is a lower case and letter and if Mode is Equiv /*

char Uc ( char c, enum Mode M )
{
    return ( M && ( c >= 'a' ) && ( c <= 'z' ) ) ? c + 'A' - 'a' : c ;
}
```

ILLUSTRATING C

```
/* Compare two strings for equality (∅), non-equality (1), etc.  */
/* with Equiv case (∅) or Distinct case (1)                      */

int Compare (char *p, enum Logic L, char *q, enum Mode M)
{
    L %= 6;        ⟵ ensures range 1 to 5            Distinct or Equiv ⟶
    while (*p && *q && (Uc(*p,M) == Uc(*q,M)) )
        p++, q++;
    switch(L)
    {
        case ∅: return *p == *q;                   ⟵ eq    ⟵ ne
        case 1: return *p != *q;
        case 2: return Uc(*p, M) >  Uc(*q, M);      ⟵ gt    ⟵ ge
        case 3: return Uc(*p, M) >= Uc(*q, M);
        case 4: return Uc(*p, M) <  Uc(*q, M);      ⟵ lt    ⟵ le
        case 5: return Uc(*p, M) <= Uc(*q, M);
    }
    return ∅;
}
```

The second comparing function finds the first occurrence of a short string in a long string. If a match is found, the function returns a pointer to the starting character of the matching portion in the long string.

If no match is found the function returns a NULL pointer. NULL is defined in \<stdio.h >.

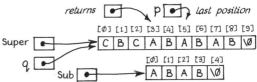

The mode of comparison (❨ cases Distinct or cases Equiv ❩) may be specified as for the Compare() function.

```
/* Finds first occurrence of substring in superstring      */
/* Returns pointer to substring in superstring, or NULL    */

char * Instr(char *Super, char *Sub, enum Mode M)
{
    char *p, *q;
    int i;
    q = Super;
    p = q + StringLen(q) - StringLen(Sub);
    if (p >= q)
    {
        while ( q <= p )
        {
            for(i=∅; *(Sub+i && Uc(*(q+i),M) ==
                                  Uc(*(Sub+i),M); ++i)
                ;
            if ( ! *(Sub+i) ) return q;             ⟵ match
            ++q;
        }                     ⟵ no match
    }
    return NULL;
}
```

Isthay isay Ackslangbay! Ancay ouyay eadray itay? Erhapspay otnay atay irstfay.

Backslang is a secret language spoken in boarding schools. It is suitably incomprehensible when heard for the first time but easy to master once you know the grammatical rules. There are probably many dialects of Backslang ((also called *pig Latin*)); this one is remembered from school days. Each English word is folded about its first vowel and *ay* is appended ((*tea → eatay, tomato → omatotay*)). If a word begins with a vowel, the second vowel becomes the pivot ((*item → emitay*)) unless there is no second vowel, in which case there is no fold ((*itch → itchay*)). A diphthong at the beginning of a word is treated as a single vowel ((*oil → oilay* not *iloay*; *earwig → igearway* not *arwigeay*)).

A capital letter at the beginning of a word has to be transformed ((*Godfather → Odfathergay* not *odfatherGay*)). The *u* after *q* demands special treatment ((*Queen → Eenquay* not *ueenQay*)). A trailing punctuation mark has to remain trailing ((*Crumbs! → Umbscray!* not *Umbs!cray*)).

Opposite is a header file and main program for encoding a sentence into Backslang.

When you run the program it waits for you to type a sentence and press Return. Type:

```
This is Backslang! Can you read it? Perhaps not at first.
```

The program encodes and responds with:

```
Isthay isay Ackslangbay! Ancay ouyay eadray itay?  Erhapspay
otnay atay irstfay.
```

Type another sentence and press Return until fed up with it. Stop ((after *space* or *new line*)) by holding down Ctrl and pressing Z ((or whatever you do to send EOF from your keyboard)) then press Return.

There are checks this program fails to make. Numbers are not respected at all: 356 comes out as 35ay6 ((can you see why?)). Punctuation marks are catered for only at the end of a word ((Backslang! comes out as Ackslangbay!)); a punctuation mark in front of or inside a word is treated as if it were a consonant (("Think" becomes ink"Thay" and Joan's becomes Oans'jay)). And a sentence can only be as long as the keyboard buffer.

Nevertheless this small program does illustrate string manipulation using a 'library' of simple home-made functions ≋ and it's more fun than the usual examples in text books, like counting lines and occurrences of words.

```
/* Header file, STRINGY.H,  declaring string facilities */
#include < stdio.h >
enum Mode { Distinct, Equiv };
enum Logic { eq, ne, gt, ge, lt, le };
void Middle ( char *, char *, int, int );
char Uc ( char, enum Mode );
int Compare ( char *, enum Logic, char *, enum Mode );
void Concat ( char *, char *, char * );
int StringLen ( char * );
char * Instr ( char *, char *, enum Mode );
int KeyString ( char *, int (*) (), int );
int Lines ( char );
int Spaces ( char );
int Punctuators ( char );
void StrCopy ( char *, char * );
int IsDigit ( char );
int IsVowel ( char );
int IsCap ( char );
int IsLetter ( char );
```

this is a header file containing all the string utilities described.
#include "STRINGY.H" to make them available

Backslang encoder

```
/* Enigma encoder, English >>> Backslang */
#include "STRINGY.H"
void main ( void )
{
    char p[20], fore[40], aft[40], PuncMk, * Qu;
    int Cap, Length, i ;

    while (KeyString ( p, Punctuators, 15 ) != EOF )
    {
        Length = StringLen ( p );
        if ( Length <= 2 )
            Concat ( p, p, "ay" );
        else
        {
            if ( Cap = IsCap ( *p ) )
                *p += 'a' - 'A';
            PuncMk = *( p + Length -1 );
            if ( ! IsLetter ( PuncMk ) )
                *( p + --Length) = NULL;
            if ( Qu = Instr ( p, "qu", Equiv ) )
                *( Qu + 1 ) = '#';
            i = IsVowel ( *p ) ? 2: 1;
            for (   ; ! IsVowel ( *(p+i) ) && i < Length; ++i )
                ;
            if ( Qu )
                *( Qu + 1 ) = 'u';
            Middle ( fore, p, i, Length - i );
            Middle ( aft, p, 0, i );
            Concat ( p, fore, aft );
            Concat ( p, p, "ay" );
            if (!IsLetter ( PuncMk ) )
                Concat ( p, p, &PuncMk );
            if (Cap && IsLetter ( *p ) )
                *p += 'A' - 'a';
        }
        printf ("%s ", p );
    }
}
```

for short words, simply append "ay"

if first letter is capital, mark Cap true, set letter to lower case

pick up last character

if it is not a letter, shorten string by 1

if string contains "qu" replace by "q#"

initial i▲ "antelope"

"buck"

move i to first vowel beyond ▲

replace "q#" by "qu"

copy last part and first part and concatenate

append "ay"

if the original word ended in something other than a letter, append it now

if the original word was capitalized, convert 1st letter to a capital

space

EXERCISES

1 When the price of an article includes value-added tax, book keepers have to break down the price into net cost and amount of tax. Write a function having four arguments: inclusive price, percentage rate of tax, pointer to location for storing net cost, pointer to location for storing amount of tax. The function should return Ø if successful, otherwise a non-zero value. An example call might be: n = VAT (23.95, 17.5, &Cost, &Tax)

2 Convert the sorting program on Page 83 so that it sorts *words* rather than single letters. This exercise involves handling strings. To read the words, use KeyString() defined on Page 99. Set up a two-dimensional array of characters for storing the words by rows, each row terminated with Ø. To compare words, use Compare() (defined on page 1Ø3) with Mode set to Equiv.

3 An exercise with pointers to functions. Recast the areas program on Page 55 to comprise a main program and three functions, each of which returns an area. Function Rectangle() reads two values from the keyboard, Triangle() reads three, Circle() reads only one. The main program reads a letter, R, T or C. It then calls the associated function and displays the value returned. Don't use a switch statement; set up an array of pointers to functions as shown on Page 89.

4 The declaration int * x() declares a function returning a pointer to int. The declaration double (*(*z)[])[] declares a pointer to an array of pointers to arrays of double. What does the declaration long int (*(*z[])[])() declare?

Tackle it verbally, or draw a parse tree, or depict the data structure with boxes and arrows. (In the second edition of Kernighan & Ritchie ≈ see Bibliography ≈ are functions for constructing and unraveling complex declarations *automatically*.)

5 Page 1Ø4 lists some deficiencies of the Backslang program. Improve the program accordingly, making it respect numbers and all usual punctuation marks.

7

INPUT, OUTPUT

This chapter explains how to handle input and output, both on the standard streams ((stdin, stdout, stderr)) and on streams connected to files. The chapter explains how to open such streams and create files on the disk.

The chapter begins with the input and output of single characters using library functions already introduced ((getc( ), ungetc( ), putc( ))). Related functions are described ((fgetc( ), fputc( ) and getchar( ), putchar( ))).

The mysterious format strings used in scanf( ) and printf( ) are at last fully described.

Streams are explained, and how to open and close them. Also how to *rewind*, *remove* and *rename* files. These techniques are illustrated by an example of a simple utility for concatenating files under keyboard control.

The use of temporary files is explained.

Finally, *binary files* are introduced and *random access* explained. These subjects are illustrated by an example of a rudimentary data base.

ONE CHARACTER

Input and output of a single character has already been introduced informally. The most common library functions are explained on this double page. All are defined and summarized in Chapter 10.

GET

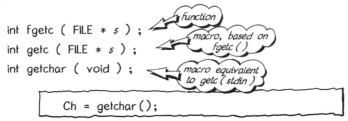

```
int fgetc ( FILE * s ) ;          function
int getc ( FILE * s ) ;           macro, based on
                                  fgetc ( )
int getchar ( void ) ;            macro equivalent
                                  to getc ( stdin )
```

```
Ch = getchar ( );
```

Each of these 'get' functions returns the code value of the next character waiting in the stream buffer, or EOF if the buffer is empty.

A typical *stream* is stdin. This stream is automatically connected to the keyboard buffer. You may, however, nominate any input stream that has been created and connected to a file as described on Page 116. For example:

```
FILE * MyStream ;
MyStream = fopen ("MYFILE", "r" ) ;
i = fgetc ( MyStream ) ;
```

The return value, i, is of type int as shown by the prototypes above. The following *coerces* the return value to type char:

```
char c ;
c = fgetc ( stdin ) ;
```

But this may cause trouble. Suppose your implementation treats type char as a one-byte signed integer. A variable of this kind can store any ASCII character (value ∅ to 127) but cannot properly handle characters with values $-128 \rightarrow +127$

sign bit → [diagram with bits 0 1 2 3 4 5 6 7]

128 to 255 because these would demand a 1 as bit ∅. This is the sign bit; setting it to 1 would make the variable *negative*.

Some C compilers offer a global 'switch' by which to change the interpretation of type char to a one-byte *unsigned* integer, allowing correct interpretation of character values in the range ∅ to 255 (typical of a personal computer). But for the sake of portability it is wise to leave this switch alone and to treat characters as type int in all input operations.

ANSI C has facilities for handling characters that need more than eight bits to encode them. They are called 'multi-byte characters'. The Kanji alphabet illustrates a typical requirement for multi-byte characters. This book does not deal specifically with them.

PUT

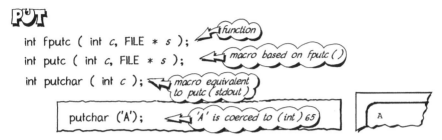

```
int fputc ( int c, FILE * s );          ← function
int putc ( int c, FILE * s );           ← macro based on fputc ( )
int putchar ( int c );                  ← macro equivalent to putc ( stdout )
```

```
putchar ('A');    ← 'A' is coerced to (int) 65
```

A

Each of these 'put' functions places the character corresponding to code c onto the nominated stream. Each function returns c if successful, otherwise EOF.

Typical *streams* are stdout or stderr. Other streams may be nominated and connected to files as described on Page 116. For example:

```
FILE * YrStream;
YrStream = fopen ( "YRFILE", "w" );
```

The first parameter is of type int, implying that if you provide a value of type char, the value will be promoted to type int before transmission.

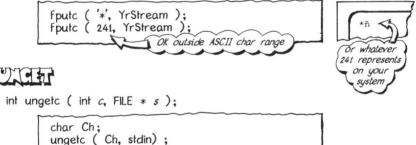

```
fputc ( '*', YrStream );
fputc ( 241, YrStream );
              ← OK outside ASCII char range
```

*n̄

Or whatever 241 represents on your system

UNGET

```
int ungetc ( int c, FILE * s );
```

```
char Ch;
ungetc ( Ch, stdin) ;
```

The function puts any character c on the front of the nominated input stream such that the next fgetc() (or getc()) to nominate the same stream will pick up character c.

This function is intended for use in cases where you cannot know if you have finished reading one item until you have read the first character of the next. You can then 'push back' this character, making the keyboard buffer appear as though the character had never been read from its stream. See the example on Page 99.

Don't try to 'push' any more than *one* character on the front of a stream. The function returns EOF if unsuccessful.

PRINT FORMAT

int fprintf (FILE *, const char *, ...);

This double page defines fprintf() which sends formatted output to a nominated stream. The 'specifiers' needed are common to all library functions having the letters 'printf' in their name: printf(), sprintf() *etc.*

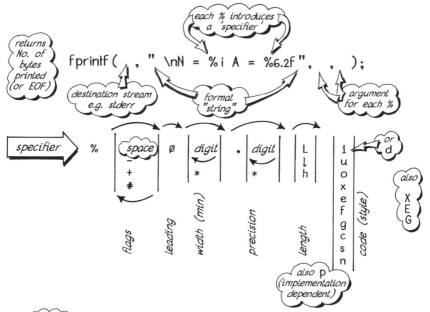

Flags

(space) Ignore if + is also present, otherwise precede a negative number with a minus sign, a non-negative number with a space.

  – Left justify, then pad rightwards with spaces (absence of a minus sign means right justify and pad to the left)

  + Precede the number with + or –

  # Print values coded e, f, g with at least one decimal place (e.g. 10.0) Prefix 0x to values coded as style x; prefix 0 to values coded as style o.

leading Print a leading zero (but ignore this flag if a minus flag is also present)

width Minimum field width expressed as digits, e.g. 12 (wider values are not constrained to this width)

  * Signifies that width is specified by an int argument preceding the argument that provides the value to be printed. The following program displays one cycle of a sine curve:

ILLUSTRATING C

```
#include < stdio.h >
#include < math.h >
void main ( void )
{
    int i;
    double rad = 3.141593 / 180;
    for ( i=0; i<= 360; i+= 20 )
        fprintf ( stdout, "\n%*c", (int)( sin( i*rad )*35 + 40 ), '+' );
}
```

"\n%*c"

scaled sine

'+'

precision   Number of places after the decimal point expressed as digits; *e.g.* 2. In the case of a string, *precision* expresses the maximum number of characters to be printed. The asterisk works in the same way for *precision* as it does for *width*.

length   The type of each numerical argument must be compatible with its associated style code, optionally modified by h, l or L, as defined in the following table. *e.g.* Le signifies a long double to be printed in scientific format.

code (style)	unmodified	h	l	L
d, i, n e, f, g	int double	short int –	long int –	– long double
o, u, x	int	unsigned short int	unsigned long int	–

<table>
<tr><td>i, d</td><td>Decimal integer e.g. –123</td></tr>
<tr><td>u</td><td>Decimal integer, unsigned e.g. 123</td></tr>
<tr><td>o</td><td>Octal integer, unsigned e.g. 777 ❲ 175 decimal ❳</td></tr>
<tr><td>x</td><td>Hex integer, unsigned e.g. 1a ❲ 26 decimal ❳</td></tr>
<tr><td>e</td><td>Scientific format e.g. –1.23e002</td></tr>
<tr><td>f</td><td>Decimal number e.g. –123.05</td></tr>
<tr><td>g</td><td>In style e or f, whichever is the shorter</td></tr>
<tr><td>X,E,G</td><td>These specify the same forms as x, e, g respectively, but any letters involved are printed in capitals ❲ if code x produced ff2a, code X would produce FF2A ❳</td></tr>
<tr><td>c</td><td>Single character</td></tr>
<tr><td>s</td><td>The associated argument points to a string. Print the entire string, extending field width ❲ if necessary ❳ to accommodate.</td></tr>
<tr><td>n</td><td>The associated argument points to an int variable to which the current count of printed characters is sent:</td></tr>
</table>

code (style)

```
int m;
fprintf ( stdout, "123456%n", &m );
fprintf ( stdout, "=%i", m );
```
⟹ 123456=6

The sequence of arguments must match precisely the sequence of specifiers in the string. When the type of an argument fails to match its associated specifier the result is either crazy or non-existent.

SCAN FORMAT

char * gets (char *) ;
int sscanf (const char *, const char *, ...) ;

Examples in this book show input from the keyboard via scanf(). That is not a practical way to read data. If the item you type on the keyboard does not match precisely what scanf() has been told to expect, scanf() evokes mayhem by *ignoring* the item. So if you really need the extensive scanning facilities offered by scanf() it pays to use them under control of sscanf() (*string* scan format) as described below. Do not use scanf() for practical programs.

To use sscanf() with keyboard data, first input a line as a string. The easiest way to do this is by gets() (get *string*). Use fflush(stdin) to flush the keyboard buffer. Its prototype is in <stdio.h>.

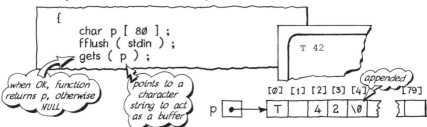

Function gets(), when called, reads from the keyboard buffer into the string pointed to by the nominated pointer (p in the example shown). Reading terminates on new line, but the new-line character itself is *not* stored with the string. '\0' is automatically appended.

It is up to you to make the string buffer long enough (typically 80).

Now scan the string using sscanf(). If things go wrong you can scan again and again.

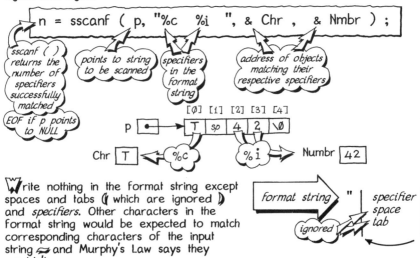

Write nothing in the format string except spaces and tabs (which are ignored) and *specifiers*. Other characters in the format string would be expected to match corresponding characters of the input string ⇆ and Murphy's Law says they wouldn't.

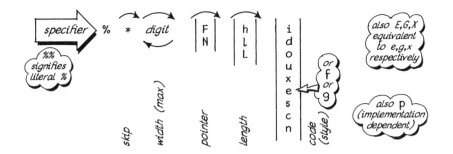

skip
: The characters associated with a 'skip' specifier are read from the keyboard buffer, interpreted according to the specifier, then discarded (《 %*i as the first specifier would cause the first item from the keyboard to be treated as an integer, then skipped 》)

width (max)
: You may specify a field width beyond which the next specifier takes over (《 456 processed by %2i would be int 45, leaving 6 to be resolved by the next specifier in the string 》).

pointer
: The F or N signifies a 'Far' or 'Near' pointer to override the default format. (《 This is a matter of particular implementations and is beyond the scope of this book. 》)

length
: The input string is encoded according to its associated letter, optionally modified by h, l or L, and coerced to the type of the receiving variable as tabulated below (《 e.g. hi ≡ short int 》):

basic code	length modifier			
	unmodified	h	l	L
d,i,n	int	short int	long int	–
e,f,g	float	–	double	long double
o,u,x	unsigned int	unsigned int	unsigned long	–

code (style)

d
: Decimal integer *e.g.* −78

i
: Integer: decimal *e.g.* −78; octal *e.g.* Ø77; hex *e.g.* Øx1a

e,f,g
: Decimal number *e.g.* Ø, −12.3, +1.2E−6

u,o,x
: Unsigned decimal, octal, hex integer respectively

c
: %6c reads next 6 characters (《 including whitespace 》) and stores them as an array from the given address. '\ø' is *not* appended. %c implies %1c.

s
: %7s reads non-whitespace characters sequentially and stores them as a string from the given address. The string is terminated by '\ø' on meeting a whitespace character or achieving the count, whichever happens first. %s implies %*big*s where *big* is a large number, implementation dependent.

n
: Integer count of successfully read characters prior to meeting %n.

EASIER INPUT

Using gets( ) and scanf( ) is a clumsy way to handle keyboard input if your need is to read only simple numbers and words. How often do you need to read numbers in scientific format? Or in octal or hex? If the answer is 'Often!' use sscanf( ). Otherwise read on.

Decide what characters are to behave as terminators. Typically these are *space*, *tab* and *new line*, but you might wish to add *comma*, *colon*, *semicolon*. It depends on the kind of program you are writing. Specify your chosen terminators in a function having the form described on Page 98. Assume the one called Punctuators( ) for the example opposite.

In your program, get the next item by a call to GetNext( ). It does not matter what sort of value you *expect*; the person at the keyboard may have typed it wrongly anyway; you simply cannot know what you may get and have to deal with.

Now *consult the return value of GetNext*. This value tells you what was found in the keyboard buffer as far as the next terminator:

Ø: neither number nor name   1: a whole number
2: a decimal number   3: a name

A 'name' is here defined as a string of letters (and optionally digits) that starts with a letter. *Underscore* is not included; modify IsLetter( ) on Page 100 if you want it to be.

A numerical result is stored in a variable of type double.

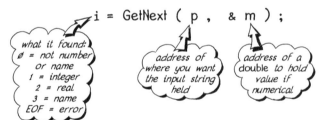

i = GetNext (p , & m) ;

what it found:
Ø = not number
or name
1 = integer
2 = real
3 = name
EOF = error

address of
where you want
the input string
held

address of a
double *to hold*
value if
numerical

Assuming *comma* and *space* to be terminators, five calls to this line would produce results as follows:

    -1234, -1234.0, H2SO4 Me4$, 2B||!2B

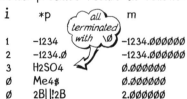

i	*p	_all terminated with_ Ø	m
1	-1234		-1234.000000
2	-1234.Ø		-1234.000000
3	H2SO4		0.000000
Ø	Me4$		0.000000
Ø	2B||!2B		2.000000

A call to GetNext( ) says:

'Get the next item from the keyboard and show me what kind of item it is'

```
int GetNext ( char *p, double *n )
{
    int Status;
    double Frac = Ø;
    char Sign, *r;
    enum { string, integer, decimal, name };        the four possible
    Status = KeyString ( p, Punctuators, 15);       values of Status
    if ( Status != EOF )                            ignore characters after
    {                                               the 15th
        Sign = (*p == '+' || *p == '-') ? *p: NULL;
        *n = Ø.Ø;                                   point to char after ±
        for ( r = Sign ? p+1: p; IsDigit(*r); ++r )
            *n = *n * 1Ø + (*r - 'Ø');              digits before decimal
        if ( *r == '.' )
            for ( ++r , Frac=1; IsDigit ( *r ); ++r )
                *n += ( *r - 'Ø') / ( Frac *= 1Ø );
        if ( Sign == '-' )                          digits after decimal
            (*n) *= -1.Ø;
        if ( !*r )                                  if whole string has
            Status = Frac ? decimal : integer;      been read
        else
        {                                    if it starts with letter and comprises
            if ( IsLetter (*p) )                    only letters & digits
                while ( IsLetter(*p) || IsDigit (*p) )
                    ++p ;
            Status = !*p ? name : string;
        }
    }
    return Status;
}
```

Below is a driving program with which to test GetNext().

```
#include "STRINGY.H"        listed on Page 1Ø5
void main(void)                             simple driver to
{                                           demonstrate
    char w[8Ø];                             GetNext ()
    double m;
    int i;
    while (1)        infinite loop; enter EOF to get out
    {
        i = GetNext( w, &m );
        if ( i == EOF ) break;
        puts ( w );                 echo to screen as a string
        switch( i )
        {
            case 4:  printf ("     Name     "); break;
            case Ø:  printf ("     String   "); break;
            case 1:  printf ("     Integer  "); break;
            case 2:  printf ("     Decimal  "); break;
            default: printf ("     Chaos    ");
        }
        printf ("    Value =%lf\n", m );     try this with the input
    }                                        line shown opposite
}
```

STREAMS AND FILES

The standard 'streams' are:

- stdin   standard input stream ((from keyboard))
- stdout   standard output stream ((to screen))
- stderr   standard error stream ((to screen))

You may define any number of other streams connected to various devices ((such as printers and plotters)) and to 'files' on disk. This book deals only with disk files. The means of attaching other devices depends on the implementation, but the concept of a 'stream' remains independent of the implementation; it should be possible to direct an input stream from any input device, an output stream to any output device.

OPENING

```
FILE * fopen ( const char *, const char * ) ;
FILE * freopen (const char *, const char *, FILE * ) ;
```

A stream may be opened and connected to a file using fopen ().

NULL if opening fails

```
stream = fopen ( filename, mode );

freopen ( filename, mode, stream );
```

redirect from stream to filename
e.g. freopen ("PRNFILE.DOC", "w", stdout)

stream → name

This name nominates a stream in the same manner as stdin nominates a stream. The name must have been declared as a pointer to FILE, where FILE is a *type* ((just as int is a type)) defined by C. For example:

```
FILE * MyStream
```

filename → "name"

The allowable syntax of *name* depends on the implementation. In DOS, for example, lower case and corresponding upper case letters are equivalent and the path is punctuated by backslash. Examples are: "MYFILE.DOC" and "C:\\MYDIR\\MYFLE2.DOC" ((where \\ is an escape sequence to represent a single \ )).

You may express *filename* as a pointer to a string. For example, in a DOS environment:

```
char *p = "C:\\MYDIR\\MYFILE.DOC";
MyStream = fopen ( p, "w" ) ;
```

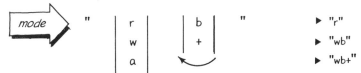

mode	"	r	b	"	▶ "r"
		w	+		▶ "wb"
		a			▶ "wb+"

You may express *mode* as a pointer to a string:

```
char * q = " w + b " ;
MyStream = fopen ( "MYFILE", q ) ;
```

mode symbol	⇌ significance of mode symbols ⇌	
	if nominated file exists	*if file doesn't exist*
r	open file for reading	*error* : return NULL
w	open file for writing	create file, and open it for writing
a	open file for appending (writing on the end)	
b	declares file to be 'binary' ⇌ as handled by fread() and fwrite(). The absence of b implies a formatted text file	
+	permits both reading and writing ⇌ using fseek() and ftell(), or using fgetpos() and fsetpos(). Or just by rewind()	

CLOSING   int fclose (FILE *) ;

When you have finished with a file you should close it. The exit() function demonstrated overleaf serves to close all open files when obeyed; in such a case you do not need fclose(). The function returns Ø if successful, otherwise EOF.

```
i = fclose ( stream ) ;
```

REWINDING   void rewind (FILE *) ;

When a file has been written, or added to, it must be rewound before it can be read. This can be achieved by resetting the file pointer, as explained later, or by rewind().

```
rewind ( stream ) ;
```

The rewind function automatically clears error indicators (see later).

REMOVING   int remove (const char *) ;

You may remove (delete) an existing file, but not while the file is open. Close it first. The function returns Ø if successful, otherwise EOF.

```
i = remove ( "MYFILE.DOC" );
```

RENAMING

int rename (const char *, const char *) ;

Any file, open or closed, may be *renamed*.

i = rename ("ELDERLY", "SENIOR") ;

returns ø if OK   *old name*   *new name*

Because a file name may define a path, rename() may be used to 'move' a file from one directory to another. The following rudimentary utility achieves this in a general way:

store this file as MOVER.C

```
#include < stdio.h >
void main ( void )
{
    char old[80], new[80];
    printf ( "Enter existing path\n> " );
    gets ( old );
    printf ( "Enter new path\n> ");
    gets ( new );
    if ! rename ( old, new ) )
        printf ( "Success!\n" );
    else
        printf ( "Try again!\n" );
}
```

```
Mover
Enter existing path
> C:\MINE\LETTER.DOC
Enter new path
>C:\YOURS\LETTER.DOC
Success !
```

ERRORS

int ferror(FILE *); int feof(FILE *); clearerr(FILE *):

Every file stream has two *indicators*, initially clear (| zero |):

* error indicator
* end-of-file indicator

If something goes wrong during an attempted read or write, the error indicator for that stream becomes non-zero and stays non-zero until specifically cleared by clearerr() or rewind(). An attempt to read beyond the end of a file causes the end-of-file indicator to be set non-zero, but this indicator clears itself before every attempt at reading.

You can interrogate either indicator, and re-set both to zero, using the following functions:

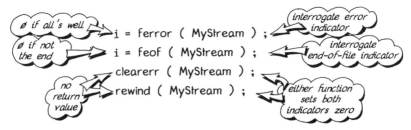

ø if all's well → i = ferror (MyStream) ; ← *interrogate error indicator*

ø if not the end → i = feof (MyStream) ; ← *interrogate end-of-file indicator*

clearerr (MyStream) ;

no return value → rewind (MyStream) ; ← *either function sets both indicators zero*

CATS

This program is a rudimentary utility. To run it, type CATS, then nominate the file you want to be the concatenated file, then nominate the files to be copied into the concatenated file. For the concatenated file you may nominate a new file (and let the utility create it) or an existing file (and let the utility wipe out its current contents).

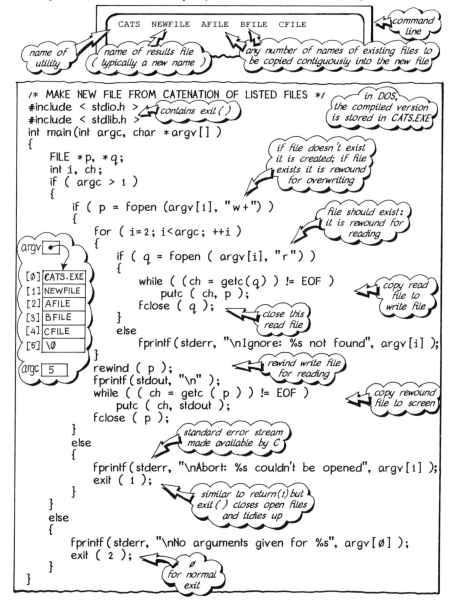

```c
/* MAKE NEW FILE FROM CATENATION OF LISTED FILES */
#include < stdio.h >
#include < stdlib.h >          /* contains exit ( ) */
int main (int argc, char *argv[] )
{
    FILE *p, *q;
    int i, ch;
    if ( argc > 1 )
    {
        if ( p = fopen (argv[1], "w+") )
        {
            for ( i=2; i<argc; ++i )
            {
                if ( q = fopen ( argv[i], "r") )
                {
                    while ( ( ch = getc(q) ) != EOF )
                        putc ( ch, p );
                    fclose ( q );
                }
                else
                    fprintf (stderr, "\nIgnore: %s not found", argv[i] );
            }
            rewind ( p );
            fprintf (stdout, "\n" );
            while ( ( ch = getc ( p ) ) != EOF )
                putc ( ch, stdout );
            fclose ( p );
        }
        else
        {
            fprintf (stderr, "\nAbort: %s couldn't be opened", argv[1] );
            exit ( 1 );
        }
    }
    else
    {
        fprintf (stderr, "\nNo arguments given for %s", argv[0] );
        exit ( 2 );
    }
}
```

in DOS, the compiled version is stored in CATS.EXE

if file doesn't exist it is created; if file exists it is rewound for overwriting

file should exist: it is rewound for reading

copy read file to write file

close this read file

rewind write file for reading

copy rewound file to screen

standard error stream made available by C

similar to return(1) but exit ( ) closes open files and tidies up

0 for normal exit

argv
[0] CATS.EXE
[1] NEWFILE
[2] AFILE
[3] BFILE
[4] CFILE
[5] \0

argc 5

TEMPORARY FILES

You can create a temporary file which has no *filename*; just a name to identify its stream. The mode of opening is "wb+" ⇌ in other words you may write to the temporary file and read from it in 'binary' form. Binary form is explained opposite.

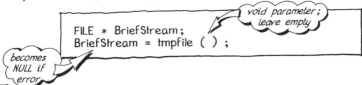

void parameter; leave empty

```
FILE * BriefStream;
BriefStream = tmpfile ( );
```

becomes NULL if error

The nameless file is automatically removed when you close its stream:

```
fclose ( BriefStream );
```

also removes temporary file

If you need a temporary *name* for a file, function tmpnam() will provide a string guaranteed not to clash with the name of any other file. You may give tmpnam() a parameter pointing to an adequately long array in which to put the unique string. The minimal length to allow for this string is given by the constant L_tmpnam, defined in < stdio.h >.

```
#include < stdio.h >
void main ( void )
{
    char RumpleStiltskin [ L_tmpnam ];
    tmpnam ( RumpleStiltskin );
    printf ("My name is %s\n", Rumplestiltskin );
}
```

My name is TN ??

If you omit its argument, tmpnam() returns a pointer to a static array created internally.

MayFly ???

```
char * MayFly = tmpnam ();
MyStream = fopen ( MayFly, "w+b" );
```

```
fclose ( MyStream );
remove ( MayFly );
```

it is your responsibility to remove the named file

The name returned by tmpnam() may be associated with a new file using fopen(). When the stream to that file is eventually closed, the file itself remains in the file directory. If you want to get rid of it, use remove(). The only files to be removed automatically on closure of the stream are the nameless files created by tmpfile().

BINARY I/O

```
size_t fwrite ( const void *, size_t, size_t, FILE * );
size_t fread ( void *, size_t, size_t, FILE * );
```

All streams so far illustrated are streams of characters, or text. A text stream comprises *lines*, each line having zero or more characters terminated by a *new line* character. No matter how the local hardware treats such a file, the C programmer may use library functions ((getc(), scanf(), printf() *etc.*)) on the assumption that the file is modelled as just described.

If you need to store a great many numbers in a file, and subsequently read them back for further processing, it would be wasted effort converting, say, the binary integer Ø1111111111111111111111111111111 to its decimal equivalent of 2147483647 for filing, then subsequently converting 2147483647 back to Ø1111111111111111111111111111111 for processing in memory. In doing this you might drop or pick up bits wherever binary numbers do not have precise decimal equivalents. So the C library provides functions for writing and reading a stream of bytes regardless of what they represent. As long as you remember what you wrote to file you can read it back without conversion, precisely as it was.

Binary streams are especially useful for filing data structures such as the personnel records defined on Page 127. The size of any such structure is given by sizeof(*type*) where *type* is the type of the structure ((*e.g.* sizeof (struct MyStruct))).

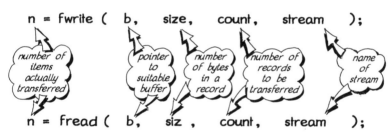

```
n = fwrite ( b, size, count, stream );
```

- number of items actually transferred
- pointer to suitable buffer
- number of bytes in a record
- number of records to be transferred
- name of stream

```
n = fread ( b, siz, count, stream );
```

```
#include < stdio.h >
/* JUST A DEMONSTRATION */
void main ( void )
{
    FILE * BinStream = tmpfile ();
    char PrintBuf [ 40 ];
    char Record [ ] = "You'll never guess where I've been!\n";
    int Size = 36 + 1;

    fwrite ( Record, Size, 1, BinStream );
    rewind ( BinStream );
    fread ( PrintBuf, Size, 1, BinStream );
    printf ( "%s\n", PrintBuf );
    fclose ( BinStream );
}
```

- open a stream to a temporary file
- record with 36 visible characters
- add 1 for the '\Ø'
- write 1 Record out to BinStream
- read BinStream into print buffer
- print the print buffer

RANDOM ACCESS

int fseek (FILE *, long, int) ;
long ftell (FILE *) ;

In the previous examples the files that have been written are *rewound* before being read. But access to a file can be more selective; you can locate a conceptual 'file pointer' at any point in a file, then read the record it points to, or write a record on the file starting at that position. The pointer is located by the function fseek( ) and you can discover its current position using ftell( ). (Functions fsetpos( ) and fgetpos( ) serve a similar purpose.)

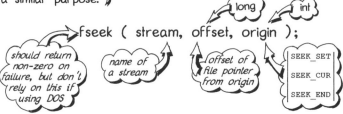

fseek (stream, offset, origin);

should return non-zero on failure, but don't rely on this if using DOS

name of a stream

offset of file pointer from origin

```
SEEK_SET
SEEK_CUR
SEEK_END
```

The origin may be located at the start of the file (at its first byte) by SEEK_SET, or at the end of the file (one past its last byte) by SEEK_END. The origin may be located at the current position of the file pointer by SEEK_CUR. These three constants are defined in < stdio.h > as an enumeration:

enum { SEEK_SET, SEEK_CUR, SEEK_END };

You may use equivalent integers or provide a less clumsy enumeration such as enum { start, current, end };

The offset locates the file pointer relative to the origin. The offset is expressed as a number of bytes and may be positive or negative: fseek (MyStream, 13, 0) is depicted below:

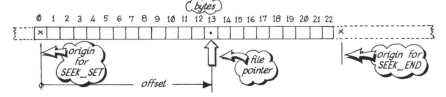

The next fwrite( ) or fread( ) starts with the byte at the file pointer.

The offset for a text stream should be given either as zero or as a value returned by ftell( ). The value returned by ftell( ) is the number of bytes from the start of the file to the file pointer.

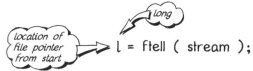

location of file pointer from start

l = ftell (stream);

ILLUSTRATING C

DATABASE

TO ILLUSTRATE fwrite ( ), fread ( ), fseek ( )
(BINARY I / O WITH RANDOM ACCESS FILE)

The following is a primitive database for names and addresses. The program asks for a surname, then an address, then another name and address, and so on until you enter EOF (Ctrl + Z in DOS). The program then asks for a surname. When you enter one, the program searches the database it has created and prints a name and address. If records have the same surname, *all* associated addresses are printed. To stop the program asking for names, enter EOF from the keyboard.

```c
/* PRIMITIVE DATABASE */
#include < stdio.h >
#include "STRINGY.H"            prototypes for
                                utilities listed
                                on Page 105
void main ( void )
{
                                              creates a file
    char p[20], q[60], r[20];                 called DBASE.BIN
    long i, Point;                            and retains it
    FILE * Dbase = fopen ( "DBASE.BIN", "w+" );

    /* PART ONE: INPUT DATA */
    for ( Point=0;        ; Point += 80 )          Name?
    {                                              > Benson
        printf ( "Name?\n> " );                    Address?
        KeyString ( p, 19 );                       > Mr. A.J. 2 Kingfisher Drive
        if ( feof ( stdin ) )                      Name?
            break;                                 > Williams
        printf ( "Address?\n> " );                 Address?
        KeyString ( q, 59 );                       > Mrs. T.E., 7 The Cottages
        fwrite ( p, 20, 1, Dbase );                Name?
        fwrite ( q, 60, 1, Dbase );
    }

    /* PART TWO: INTERROGATE */               Who?
    for ( ; ; )                               >Benson
    {                                         Mr. A.J. 2 Kingfisher Drive
        printf ( "Who?\n> " );                Ms. P. 97 Wentworth Avenue
        KeyString ( r, 19 );                  Who?
        if ( feof ( stdin ) )
            break;                         offsets jump
        for ( i=0; i<Point ; i+= 80 )      in 80s
        {
            fseek ( Dbase, i, SEEK_SET );      offset at
            fread ( p, 20, 1, Dbase );         start
            if ( Compare ( r, eq, p, Equiv ) )
            {
                fread ( q, 60, 1, Dbase );
                printf ( "%s\n", q );
            }
        }
    }
}
```

EOF

EOF

name 20   address 60   name 20   etc.

i   +80   +80

EXERCISES

1 Write a function, with fprintf() at its heart, to tabulate numbers. Let its prototype be:
void Tabulate (double Value, int Line, int Field, int Places);

Value identifies the next value to be printed
Line is set 0 if printing on the same line, 1 if on the next line
Field is the number of character positions in the complete field
Places is the number of places after the decimal (zero signifying none, and no point).
Tabulate (234, 0, 10, 3) would print the result on the same line as the previous number, in the form *sss*234.000 (where *s* represents a space) . Tabulate (234, 0, 10, 3) would display *sssssss*234 as an integer.

With this simple function you can produce complex and elegant tabulations.

2 Convert one of your C programs that employs scanf() to using gets() followed by sscanf(). Consult the return value on each call to sscanf(). Display an error message if the number of matching specifiers is wrong; arrange for a remedial line to be input by gets().

3 Convert another C program to using function GetNext() (defined on Page 115) . You should find error conditions much easier to handle than with gets() and sscanf().

4 The concatenation utility on Page 119 is badly designed. If you nominate an existing file to receive the information, you lose the current contents of that file without further warning. Rectify this deficiency. Make the utility ask if you really intend to lose the current contents of the nominated file; offer the chance to retract.

5 Improve the database program on Page 123. The possibilities are endless; man-years of effort are expended in producing saleable address-book programs, but attempt the following minimal improvements. Make it possible to keep names and addresses in a disk file on leaving the program, and make it possible to add names and addresses in subsequent runs. Make it possible to delete and modify names and addresses.

8

STRUCTURES, UNIONS

This chapter explains the concept of a *structure* as a collection of variables, this collection including nested structures if desired.

A structure can be handled in much the same way as a variable; you can copy a structure, assign to a structure, take the address of a structure with &, access the *members* of a structure. You may declare arrays of structures. You can nominate a structure as a parameter of a function or write a function that returns a structure.

This chapter introduces structures by analogy with arrays. The operators for accessing members are defined and their use explained. Concepts are illustrated by an example of a library list in which to search for a book if you know its title or can remember only part of its title.

Unions and bitfields are introduced ((a union is a structure in which members share storage space)).

Having described structures and unions it is possible to define, fully, the syntax terms *type* and *declaration*. The allowable syntax of *declaration* differs according to context, so a separate diagram is drawn for each context.

Finally the chapter explains the idea of *stacks* and gives an example of their use in converting simple algebraic expressions to reverse Polish notation.

INTRODUCING STRUCTURES

Much of information handling is about updating and sorting lists of names and addresses. With each name and address may come other information: an amount of money owing, a list of diseases survived, a code indicating the subject's purchasing power or likelihood of signing an order. In short, information comes as large sets of structured sub-sets.

For a list of names and addresses you *could* define an array of two-dimensional arrays ((in other words a three-dimensional array)) as depicted below:

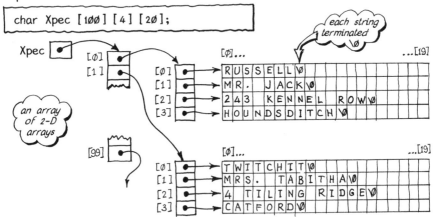

```
char Xpec [100] [4] [20];
```

You could use this scheme to sort names and addresses on various keys ((surname, town *etc.*)). You might display the complete list of names and addresses as follows:

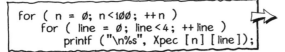

```
for ( n = 0; n<100; ++n )
    for ( line = 0; line<4; ++line )
        printf ("\n%s", Xpec [n] [line]);
```

```
RUSSELL
MR. JACK
243 KENNEL ROW
HOUNDSDITCH
TWITCHIT
MRS. TABITHA
4 TILING RIDGE
CATFORD
```

But this scheme has deficiencies. Arrays are too uniform; every item ((surname, forename, house and street, town)) must have the same amount of storage allocated to it. And numbers, and sums of money, have to be stored as character strings instead of integers, hence cannot by used directly as sorting keys.

These deficiencies can be overcome using a *structure* instead of a two-dimensional array. You may define a *shape* to suit any particular collection of entities to be stored. A structure may incorporate any type of variable. It may also incorporate other structures ((nested structures)).

The address book above is re-defined as an array of *structures* opposite.

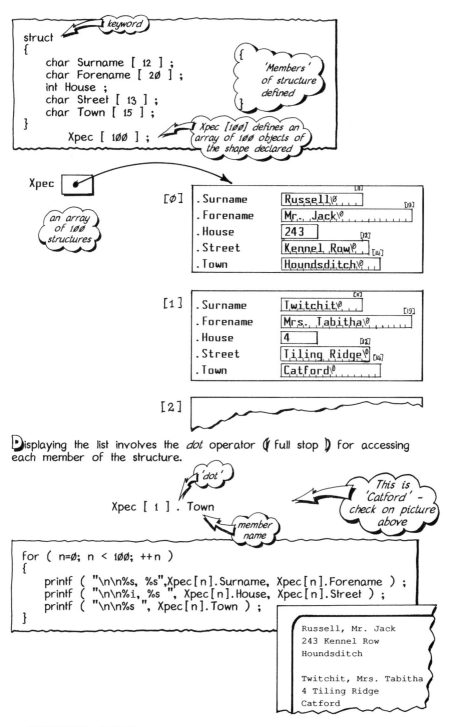

```
struct
{
    char Surname [ 12 ] ;
    char Forename [ 20 ] ;
    int House ;
    char Street [ 13 ] ;
    char Town [ 15 ] ;
}
        Xpec [ 100 ] ;
```

keyword

'Members' of structure defined

Xpec [100] defines an array of 100 objects of the shape declared

Xpec

an array of 100 structures

[∅] .Surname   Russell\∅
     .Forename   Mr. Jack\∅
     .House   243
     .Street   Kennel Row\∅
     .Town   Houndsditch\∅

[1] .Surname   Twitchit\∅
     .Forename   Mrs. Tabitha\∅
     .House   4
     .Street   Tiling Ridge\∅
     .Town   Catford\∅

[2]

Displaying the list involves the *dot* operator (full stop) for accessing each member of the structure.

'dot'

Xpec [1] . Town

member name

This is 'Catford' - check on picture above

```
for ( n=0; n < 100; ++n )
{
    printf ( "\n\n%s, %s",Xpec[n].Surname, Xpec[n].Forename ) ;
    printf ( "\n\n%i, %s ", Xpec[n].House, Xpec[n].Street ) ;
    printf ( "\n\n%s ", Xpec[n].Town ) ;
}
```

```
Russell, Mr. Jack
243 Kennel Row
Houndsditch

Twitchit, Mrs. Tabitha
4 Tiling Ridge
Catford
```

USAGE OF STRUCTURES

Here is a declaration of a typical shape of structure along with the definition of two objects, S1 and S2, of the shape declared.

```
struct
{
    char Name [ 20 ];
    int Number ;
}
    S1, S2 ;
```

S1 . Name [   ]
    . Number [   ]

S2 . Name [   ]
    . Number [   ]

Objects S1 and S2 may be handled in some respects like scalar variables and arrays. You may do the following:

- Initialize the members of structures in the manner of initialized arrays

- Declare structures static, extern, auto, as described on Pages 136 to 137. An auto structure may be initialized by assignment.

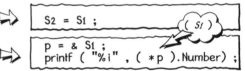

```
struct
{
    char Name [ 20 ] ;
    int Number ;
}
    S1 = { "Mo Niker", 123 },
    S2 = { "Pat Ronymic", 987 };
```

size must be declared

- Access the members of a structure in much the same manner as variables

```
n = S1.Number ;
S1.Number = S2.Number ;
S2.Number = n ;
```

- Copy or assign an entire structure as a unit

```
S2 = S1 ;
```
(S1)

- Take the address of a structure

```
p = & S1 ;
printf ( "%i" , ( *p ).Number) ;
```

- Define functions that have structures as parameters (**this** depicts the invocation)

```
n = Fun ( S1 ) ;
```

- Define functions that return a complete structure (**this** depicts the invocation)

```
S1 = OtherFun ( "Jones" , 33 ) ;
```

You may *not* compare structures logically

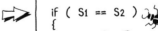

```
if ( S1 == S2 )
{
```

The above rules apply to *unions* as well as to *structures*.

ACCESS OPERATORS  ○ AND ▭❯

Use of the dot operator for access to a member is demonstrated by an earlier example, part of it reproduced below:

```
for ( n=0; n < 100; ++n )
{
    printf ( "\n\n%s, %s", Xpec[n].Surname, Xpec[n].Forename ) ;
    printf ( "\n\n%i, %s ", Xpec[n].House, Xpec[n].Street ) ;
    printf ( "\n\n%s ", Xpec[n].Town ) ;
}
```

Russell, Mr. Jack
243 Kennel Row
Houndsditch

The essential shape of each access expression is:

Instead of writing Xpec[n] as the reference to the structure we may write:

$$* (Xpec + n)$$

This demonstrates pointer notation as an alternative to array notation as described on Page 84. So the access expression may be written:

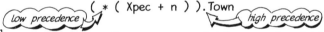

The outermost parentheses are essential because the dot binds more tightly 《 has higher precedence 》 than the asterisk. Without the outermost parentheses the expression would be treated as *((Xpec + n).Town) which signifies a pointer to a member of an impossible object.

To avoid the clumsiness of the dot expression, C provides the arrow operator -> 《 minus sign followed by greater than 》. p->a is short for (*p).a   So the access expression may be written:

where the parentheses are needed because -> binds more tightly than + 《 without them it would say Xpec + (n -> Town) 》 .

The fragment of program at the top of the page may be re-written as:

```
for ( n=0; n < 100; ++n )
{
    printf ( "\n\n%s, %s",(Xpec+n)->Surname, (Xpec+n)->Forename ) ;
    printf ( "\n\n%i, %s ", (Xpec+n)->House, (Xpec+n)->Street ) ;
    printf ( "\n\n%s ", (Xpec+n)->Town ) ;
}
```

STYLE OF DECLARATION

The full syntax for declaring an 'aggregate' (⟨ structure, union, enumeration ⟩) is defined on pages 136 and 137. It is possible to arrange such a declaration in several ways, three of which are illustrated below.

1.
```
struct MyTag { int Ego; char Sweet[16]; } ;
struct MyTag a, b;
```
make tag & define shape

quote tag & declare objects

In the above arrangement a *type* of structure is defined and given a tag. Subsequently (⟨ not necessarily on the next line ⟩) objects of the same type may be declared by reference to the tag. These objects may then be used much like variables: initialized, copied, pointed to, used as arguments of functions and returned by functions.

Terminology: Excessive use of the word 'type' causes confusion. I use the synonym 'shape' to avoid ambiguity where 'type' applies to a structure or union. Thus: 'A structure of such and such a *shape* comprises objects of such and such *types*.'

2.
```
struct { int Id; char Ripe[35]; } c, d;
```
define shape & declare objects

The second arrangement is shorter than the first, and establishes the shape of objects c, d in the same manner as a, b. But with the first arrangement you may subsequently declare more objects of the same shape:

```
struct MyTag  e, f[6], *g;
```
struct followed by a tag constitutes a shape (in other words a type)

It is impossible to do likewise with c, d in the second arrangement because there is no tag, hence no shape, to which to refer.

You can declare an *alias* (⟨ synonym ⟩) for a shape using the keyword typedef:

3.
```
typedef  struct MyTag  MyType
```
'MyType' is now an alias for 'struct MyTag'

or more imaginatively:

```
typedef { int Id; char Ripe[35]; } YourType ;
```

after which you may declare objects as follows:

```
MyType   r, s[6], *t ;
YourType   u, v[3], *w ;
```

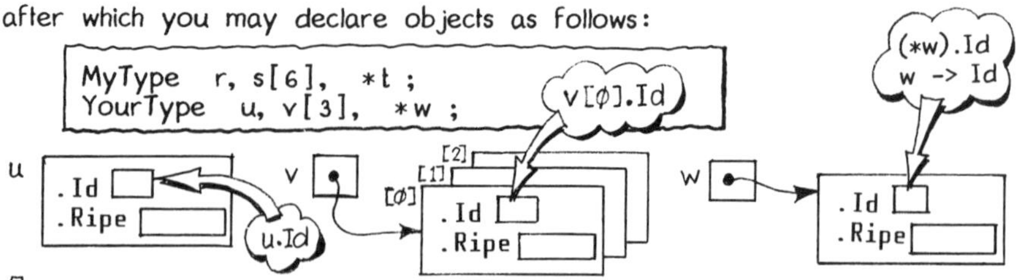

`v[0].Id`

`(*w).Id`
`w -> Id`

```
u  .Id
   .Ripe
```
`u.Id`

```
v      [2]
       [1]
   [0]
       .Id
       .Ripe
```

```
w      .Id
       .Ripe
```

An *alias* (⟨ via typedef ⟩) is neat and avoids the need for a tag.

ILLUSTRATING C

BOOKLIST

SEARCH FOR A BOOK, OR SET OF BOOKS,
IF YOU REMEMBER ONLY PART OF A TITLE

```c
#include "STRINGY.H"         STRINGY.H is listed on Page 105
typedef struct
{
    char  Title[ 40 ];
    char  Author[ 30 ];              Search on fragment: fortr
    char  Publisher[ 30 ];
    int   Year;                      Title:            Illustrating Fortran
}     Record_Shape;                  Author:           Donald Alcock
                                     Publisher:   Cambridge University Press, 1982

static Record_Shape List[ ] =
{                                    Search on fragment:
    { "Illustrating BASIC", "Donald Alcock",
        "Cambridge University Press", 1977 },
    { "Illustrating Computers", "Colin Day & Donald Alcock",
        "Pan Information", 1982 },
    { "Illustrating Fortran", "Donald Alcock",         List
        "Cambridge University Press", 1982 },
    { "Illustrating Super-BASIC", "Donald Alcock",
        "Cambridge University Press", 1985 },              [2]
    { "Illustrating BBC-BASIC", "Donald Alcock",        [1]
        "Cambridge University Press", 1986 },          [0]
    { "Illustrating Pascal", "Donald Alcock",               •Title
        "Cambridge University Press", 1987 },               •Author
    { "Illustrating C", "Donald Alcock",                    • Publisher
        "Cambridge University Press", 1992 },               •Year
};                                                                    Record_Shape
static int Num_Books = sizeof List / sizeof ( Record_Shape );

int main ( void )
{
    char Buffer[ 40 ];
    Record_Shape * p;
    enum { Distinct, Equiv };

    printf ("\nDatabase: Type any part of a book title to\n"        display
            "initiate a search for a book or books.\n"            instruction to
            " (Ctrl+Z to end the session)" );                         user
    while ( 1 )
    {
        printf ("\nSearch on fragment: ");                  read the
        fflush ( stdin );                                 search string
        if ( KeyString ( Buffer, 40 ) != EOF )
        {                                                   seek occurrence of
            for ( p = List; (p-List)<Num_Books; ++p )       search string in
            {                                                  each title
                if ( Instr ( &(p - Title ), Buffer, Equiv ) )
                {                                              Equiv:
                    printf ("\nTitle:    %s", p->Title );    lets Illus ≡ ILLUS
                    printf ("\nAuthor:   %s", p->Author );
                    printf ("\nPublisher: %s, %i\n", p->Publisher, p->Year);
                }
            }                           return on
        }                              reading EOF
        else
            return 0;
    }
}
```

8: STRUCTURES, UNIONS   131

A union is an aggregate similar to a structure, the difference being that all its fields share the same storage space. Like the married couple ⚭ factory workers ⚭ who shared the same narrow bed but never slept together because he was on night shift and she on days. When you use a union you have to remember who is currently in bed.

```
union Factory
{
    char Him [ 6 ] ;
    double Her ;            shape
    int Fido ;              (type)
}
union Factory  Worker ;
enum { He, She, It }  Tab;
```

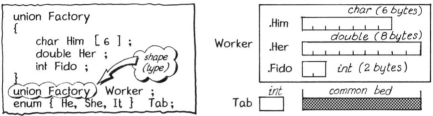

In this example there are three fields sharing storage space. The processor reserves enough space to accommodate the longest; in this example the double.

The idea of 'Tab' is to keep tabs on the current type. If you assign to Worker.Him, write Tab=He; if you assign to Worker.Her, write Tab=She; and so on. Check when you 'fetch' from a union: use a statement such as 'if (Tab==She) i = Worker.Her; else exit( );'

You may initialize a union, but *only* with reference to its first field. An example, using the shape defined above, is:

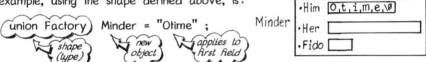

```
union Factory   Minder = "Otime" ;
       shape            new        applies to
       (type)          object      first field
```

A union may be nested inside a structure. In the example shown here you could refer to the fields of the union named Nested_Object, which lies inside the structure named Demo_Object, as:
Demo_Object.Nested_Object.Him[1],   Demo_Object.Nested_Object.Her *etc.*

```
struct Composite_Type
{
    char Title [ 40 ] ;
    union                   no tag
    {
        char  Him [ 6 ] ;
        double Her ;
        int  Fido ;
    }      Nested_Object ;
}
struct Composite_Type Demo_Object ;
```

Unions are useful for handling large sets of entities of different sizes (some int, some double, some pointers). By expressing each as a union you may make all entities the same size, thereby simplifying the handling functions (filing, chaining). The cost of this expedient is wasted space in unions that contain the smaller members.

 **BIT FIELDS**

Here is an array of 52 structures representing a deck of blank playing cards:

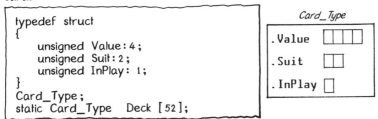

```
typedef struct
{
    unsigned Value: 4;
    unsigned Suit: 2;
    unsigned InPlay: 1;
}
Card_Type;
static Card_Type    Deck [52];
```

Card_Type

.Value
.Suit
.InPlay

The colon denotes a 'bit field'. The integer after the colon specifies the number of bits ❨ binary digits ❩ in the field. The four-bit field can represent Ace ❨ 1 ❩ through to King ❨ 13 ❩ leaving Ø, 14, 15 unused. The two-bit field represents Spades, Hearts, Diamonds or Clubs ❨ Ø, 1, 2 or 3❩. The one-bit field is for representing the state 'not in play' or ' in play' ❨ Ø or 1 ❩.

Initializing the deck would be possible but laborious. The following fragment ❨ in which i, s, v are of type int ❩ does it dynamically:

```
for ( i=s=Ø ; s < 4 ; ++s )
    for ( v=1 ; v < 14 ; ++v )
    {
        Deck [ i ] . Suit = s ;
        Deck [ i ] . Value = v ;
        Deck [ i ] . InPlay = Ø ;
    }
```

bit fields addressed just like ordinary members

How does the processor arrange the storage of bit fields? In the above example, common sense would suggest that the processor would pack each seven-bit record into an eight-bit byte, wasting one bit per record. Possible. But you cannot know; the method of storage depends on the whim of the processor.

You can, however, declare *unnamed* bit fields to create boundaries where computers like them best ⇌ at powers of 2:

```
typedef struct
{
    unsigned Value: 4;
    unsigned Suit: 2;
    unsigned InPlay: 1;
    unsigned : 1;
}
```

bring the total to 8 bits

Bit fields are useful to programmers who work at low level ⇌ close to the machine ⇌ and best left alone by the rest of us. If you want to play card games there are more appropriate facilities in C than bit fields.

 **SYNTAX**

TYPE OR SHAPE

The syntax of scalar *type* is defined in Chapter 4 as :

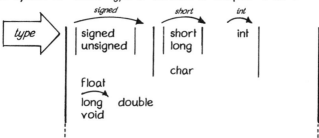

The concept of *type* is now extended to structures, unions and enumerations. These are collectively termed 'aggregates.' We extend the *type* diagram to include aggregates. But to make subsequent explanations clearer we use the term *shape* for the extended part of *type*:

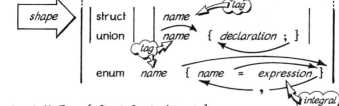

▶ struct MyTag { float f, double d }
▶ struct MyTag
▶ struct { int *p, struct MyTag }   ◁ *nested*
▶ union { long l, float f }
▶ enum Boolean { True = 1, False = ∅ }

ALIAS

Examples of *type* or *shape* can be more complicated than those shown. To prevent complexity getting out of hand, C provides the typedef facility for declaring an *alias* (in other words a synonym) that may be used instead of a complicated phrase:

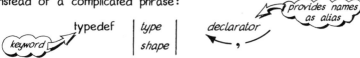

▶ typedef unsigned long int Lengthy;   ◁ *alias for 'unsigned long int'*
  Lengthy   a, b, c ;   ◁ *a, b, c declared unsigned long int*

▶ typedef   struct { double r, theta }   Polar, *PolePt ;
  Polar   c, d, e ;   ◁ *c, d, e have the shape*
  PolePt   p, q ;   ◁ *p, q may point to Polar shapes*

ILLUSTRATING C

DECLARATORS

A *declaration* comprises three parts: an optional storage class specifier, a *type* (| or *shape* |), a list of *declarators*. For example:

static int   i, Colour [3], Fun (float), *p;

list of declarators

Each declarator provides a unique name. In this example the names in the list of declarators are: i, Colour, Fun, p.

The syntax of *declarator* is formally defined as follows:

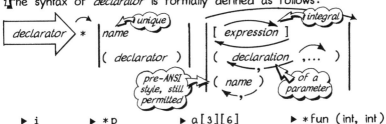

▶ i   ▶ *p   ▶ a[3][6]   ▶ *fun (int, int)

In some contexts a declarator appears without a name. An example is the prototype declaration 'double Sine(double);' where the name of the parameter has been omitted. (| Omission is optional in this case, the prototype may be written 'double Sine(double Angle);' where Angle is no more than commentary. |) But in type casts, and in sizeof() when finding the size of a *type* (| *shape* |), it is essential to omit the name. A declarator that omits the name is called an 'abstract declarator' (| *abstractor* for short |) and is defined as follows:

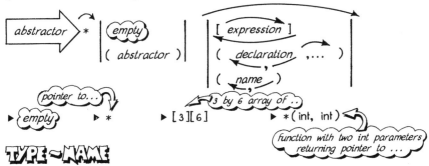

TYPE~NAME

In sizeof(*type-name*), and optionally as parameters in a prototype, the entity denoted *type-name* combines *type* and *abstractor* as follows:

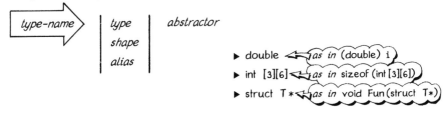

A function definition and the declaration of a structure employ different symbols. The declaration of a parameter shows by its form and content whether the function is being defined or whether it is being declared as a prototype. So although it is *possible* to draw a single diagram defining the syntax of all declarations, it is not *helpful* to do so. For a particular context the general definition would not show which paths through the diagram were permitted and which forbidden.

Here are seven separate diagrams, each defining *declaration* in a different context.

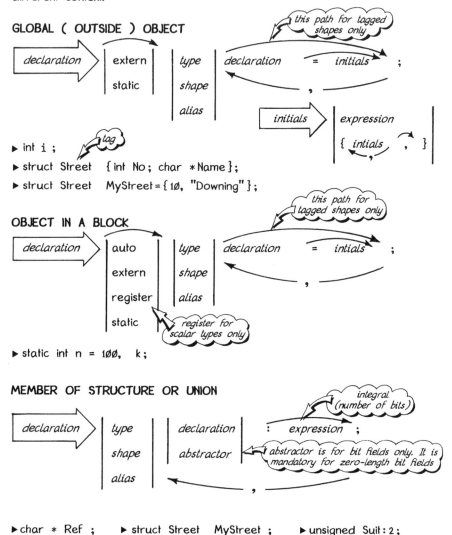

GLOBAL (OUTSIDE) OBJECT

▶ int i ;
▶ struct Street { int No ; char ∗ Name };
▶ struct Street MyStreet = { 10, "Downing" };

OBJECT IN A BLOCK

▶ static int n = 100, k ;

MEMBER OF STRUCTURE OR UNION

▶ char ∗ Ref ;   ▶ struct Street   MyStreet ;   ▶ unsigned Suit : 2 ;

FUNCTION DEFINITION (ALWAYS GLOBAL)

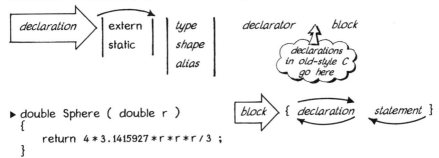

```
▶ double Sphere ( double r )
  {
       return 4 * 3.1415927 * r * r * r / 3 ;
  }
```

PARAMETERS OF A FUNCTION DEFINITION

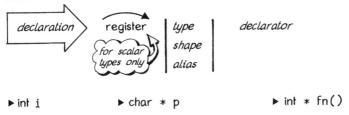

▶ int i   ▶ char * p   ▶ int * fn( )

PROTOTYPE DECLARATION

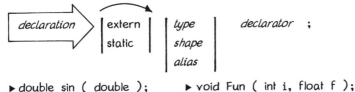

▶ double sin (double);   ▶ void Fun (int i, float f);

PARAMETERS OF A PROTOTYPE DECLARATION

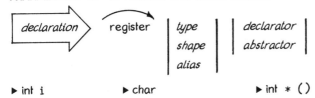

▶ int i   ▶ char   ▶ int * ( )

SIMPLIFICATION   *const AND volatile EXCLUDED*

These definitions exclude the qualifiers const and volatile. Including them would complicate the syntax diagrams out of all proportion to their worth. Placement ((to the left of the entity qualified)) is depicted for const at the foot of Page 81. The effect of volatile depends on the implementation.

STACKS

A programmer's *stack* is a simple concept with wide application. Stacks can be found in all kinds of program, at system level and in every field of application. To maintain the analogy of a physical stack ((of bricks or trays)) we draw the programmer's stack ((of numbers, characters or structures)) upside down.

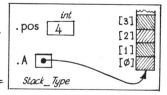

A stack may be created, as depicted, from an array of stackable objects and an integer variable for storing the number of objects currently stacked.

Three functions are all we need to manage such a stack:

Push   Place a new object on the top of the stack

Pop   Take a copy of the object at the top of the stack, then remove the top object

Peep   Take a copy of the object at the top of the stack without removing it. Send a signal if the stack was empty.

Below is the type definition of the shape depicted above, setting it up to stack characters. On the right of the page are compatible function definitions of Push, Pop and Peep. For typical invocations of these, see the program on Page 141.

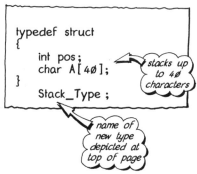

```
typedef struct
{
    int pos;
    char A[40];
}
    Stack_Type;
```

stacks up to 40 characters

name of new type depicted at top of page

The next chapter explains how to avoid arrays ((for which you have to specify a maximum height of stack)) by using *dynamic storage*.

```
void Push (Stack-Type *q, char c)
{
    if ( q -> pos < 40 )
        q -> A[ q -> pos ++ ] = c;
}
```

```
char Pop ( Stack_Type *q )
{
    if ( q -> pos > 0 )
        return q -> A[--q -> pos];
    else
        return NULL;
}
```

```
char Peep ( Stack_Type *q )
{
    if ( q -> pos > 0 )
        return q -> A[q -> pos - 1];
    else
        return NULL;
}
```

REVERSE POLISH NOTATION
ILLUSTRATING THE USE OF STACKS

Algebraic expressions in conventional form may be expressed in reverse Polish notation which has no parentheses (('Polish' because the notation was devised by the Polish logician Jan Lukaciewicz which only Poles can pronounce; 'Reverse' because his original order of operators and operands has been reversed)). As an example of reverse Polish notation:

A + (B - C) * D - F / (G + H) transforms to A B C - D * + F G H + / -

The reverse Polish expression is easier to evaluate than might appear. For example let A = 6, B = 4, C = 1, D = 2, F = 3, G = 7, H = 5. With these values the expression to be evaluated is:

6   4   1   -   2   *   +   3   7   5   +   /   -

Work from left to right taking each item in turn. Whenever you come to an operator, *apply it to the previous two terms*, reducing two terms to one:

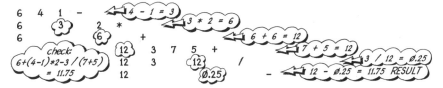

The above should demonstrate that reverse Polish notation would be useful for evaluating expressions by computer. So how do you transform an expression such as A + (B - C) * D - F / (G + H) in the first place? The process employs two stacks; the steps are explained below:

A + (B - C) * D - F / (G + H) =

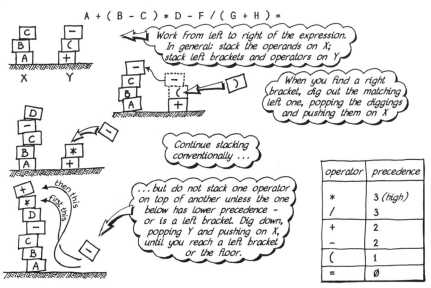

operator	precedence
*	3 (high)
/	3
+	2
-	2
(	1
=	Ø

Notice that the left bracket is included in the precedence table and allocated low precedence. This is a trick to avoid having to treat explicitly the condition *...or is a left bracket*. Clever.

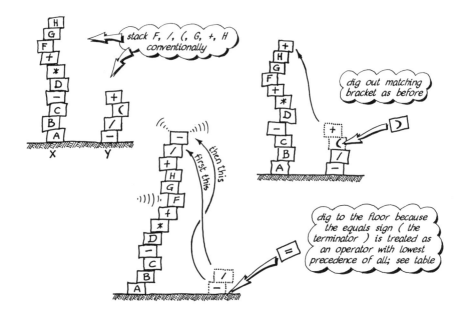

In addition to the functions Push() and Pop() a function is needed to return the precedence of an operator. The function shown below is given a character as its parameter and returns the corresponding integer from the little table.

```
int Prec ( char c )
{
    switch ( c )
    {
        case '=' :   return 0 ;
        case '(' :   return 1 ;
        case '+' :   case '-' : return 2 ;
        case '*' :   case '/' : return 3 ;
        default : printf ("\nChaos") ;
    }
}
```

operator	precedence
*	3 (high)
/	3
+	2
–	2
(	1
=	0

On the next page is a program to transform conventional expressions to reverse Polish. To use the program type the expression and terminate with an equals sign:

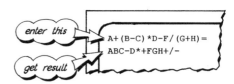

ILLUSTRATING C

```
#include < stdio.h >
typedef struct
    {
        int pos;
        char A[40];
    }
    Stack_Type;

void Push ( Stack_Type *, char );
char Pop ( Stack_Type * );
char Peep ( Stack_Type * );
int Prec ( char );

void main ( void )
{
    Stack_Type X = { 0 }, Y = { 0 };
    char ch;
    int i;
    do
    {
        ch = getchar ();
        switch ( ch )
        {
            case '(':
                Push ( &Y, ch );
                break;
            case ')':
                while ( Peep (&Y) != '(' )
                    Push ( &X, Pop (&Y) );
                ch = Pop (&Y);
                break;
            case '+': case '-': case '*': case '/': case '=':
                while( Peep(&Y)!=NULL && Prec(ch)<=Prec(Peep(&Y)))
                    Push ( &X, Pop (&Y) );
                Push ( &Y, ch );
                break;
            default:
                if ( ch >= 'A' && ch <= 'Z' )
                    Push ( &X, ch );
        }
    }
    while ( ch != '=' );

    for ( i=0; i< X.pos; ++i )
        printf ("%c", X.A[i] );
    printf ("\n");
}
```

.pos [0]   Stack_Type

       [0] [1] [2] [3]   [39]
.A [| | | | ~ |]

prototypes

define stacks
X & Y
initialize pos
to zero in each

print stack X
as an array
(bottom up)

place here: Push ( ), Pop ( ), Peep ( ), Prec ( )

EXERCISES

1 What is one third times seven eighths? Answer: Seven twenty-fourths precisely. By contrast, 0.3333 times 0.875 gives an approximate answer. Write a set of functions to add, subtract, multiply and divide pure fractions and produce pure fractions. Base the work on a special shape defined to contain fractions:

```
typedef struct
{
      unsigned int .Numerator;
      unsigned int .Denominator;
      int .Sign;
}           Fraction_Shape
```

Use HCF(), defined on Page 24, to convert vulgar fractions to simpler form (1470/693, for example, reduces to 70/33 when numerator and denominator are divided by their highest common factor of 21) .

Devise a test program for reading two fractions (as two pairs of integers), selecting an operation (add, multiply, *etc.*) and printing the resulting fraction.

2 Adapt the book list program on Page 131 for looking up other books or other kinds of information particular to your own field. There is no reason to confine the search to the first member; let the user of the program specify any of the members and provide a fragment of text for the search. In the case of numerical members, adopt a suitable convention ⤳ such as a match wherever a date falls within a year of the search date.

3 The program on Page 141 transforms an algebraic expression from one notation to another. Change the program so that it reads a numerical expression instead of an algebraic one ⤳ and produces a single numerical result.

The left stack should be made to contain numbers instead of letters. Whenever you are about to place an operator on the left stack, pop two numbers, apply the operator, then push the result back on the left stack. When you meet the equals sign you should be left with a single number on the left stack; that is the result of the expression. Try your program with
6 + (4 - 1) * 2 - 3 / (7 + 5) =
and the answer should be 11.75.

9

DYNAMIC STORAGE

This chapter explains the shortcomings of arrays having pre-determined length and the consequent need for dynamic storage. The use of library functions for allocating and freeing memory is then explained.

The concept of a linked list is introduced with particular reference to stacks. The concept is then extended to cover rings and binary trees.

Examples in this chapter include a program for demonstrating ring structures and a program for finding the shortest route through a road network. Finally there is a sorting program based on the *monkey puzzle* technique.

MEMORY ALLOCATION

The trouble with arrays is that the processor has to be told what space to allocate to each of them before execution starts. There are many applications for which it is impossible to know the detailed memory requirements in advance. What we need is a scheme in which the processor allocates memory during execution and on demand. A program written to use such a scheme fails only if demands on *total* memory exceed supply, not if one of many individual arrays exceeds its bounds.

The scheme is called '*dynamic storage.*' For practical purposes it is based on structures. When the program needs a new structure it creates one from a 'heap' of unstructured memory. When a program has finished with a structure it frees the memory from which that structure was built, tossing it back on the heap. With good luck and management the heap should retain enough memory to meet all demands throughout execution.

Dynamic storage involves linking structures of identical shape. We use a library function for allocating these structures.

To create structures of identical shape it is meaningless to define a member that has the same shape as its parent structure:

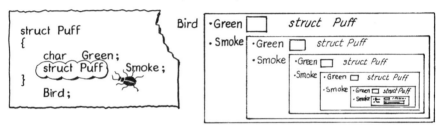

But you *can* declare a member that *points* to a structure of the same shape:

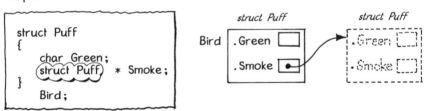

To create the structure being pointed to we must allocate space for it. To allocate space, use the library function malloc() (⟨ memory allocator ⟩) whose prototype may be found in the header file < stdlib.h >. This function returns a pointer to a region of storage of a size specified by the argument of the function.

The prototype of malloc() is shown opposite, embellished with explanatory remarks. The prototype of free(), which returns storage to the heap, is: void free(); where p must have been established using malloc() (⟨ or one of its derivatives, calloc() or realloc() ⟩).

prototype:

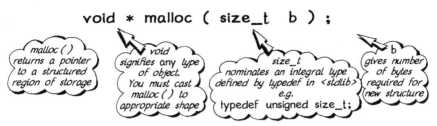

void * malloc (size_t b) ;

- *malloc ( ) returns a pointer to a structured region of storage*
- *void signifies any type of object. You must cast malloc ( ) to appropriate shape*
- *size_t nominates an integral type defined by typedef in <stdlib> e.g.* typedef unsigned size_t;
- *b gives number of bytes required for new structure*

In the example opposite, the shape of object pointed to is struct Puff. The size of object is sizeof (struct Puff) where the value returned by sizeof () is of the shape demanded by malloc () (namely the type: size_t). The library defines an appropriate 'size_t' for your particular implementation and 'model' (tiny, huge, *etc.*) .

If you declare a pointer, p, pointing to objects of shape struct Puff:

```
struct Puff  *p;
```

you may create a pointee thus:

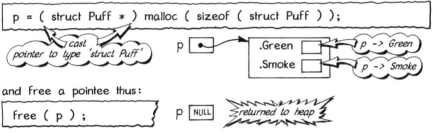

```
p = ( struct Puff * ) malloc ( sizeof ( struct Puff ) );
```

cast pointer to type 'struct Puff'

p → .Green | *p -> Green*
.Smoke | *p -> Smoke*

and free a pointee thus:

```
free ( p ) ;
```

p | NULL | *returned to heap*

More usefully, you may link structures in the form of a *chain*:

```
Bird.Smoke = ( struct Puff * ) malloc ( sizeof( struct Puff ) );
```

Add another link:

```
Bird.Smoke->Smoke = (struct Puff * ) malloc ( sizeof( struct Puff ) );
Bird.Smoke -> Smoke -> Smoke = NULL ;
```

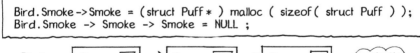

Bird | .Green | .Green | .Green | *make the last link NULL*
.Smoke | .Smoke | .Smoke | NULL

And so on: Bird.Smoke -> Smoke -> Smoke ->   ...

STACKS

In the previous chapter, stacks are based on arrays and have the shape depicted on the right. A new shape of stack is introduced below; it is based on dynamic storage rather than an array.

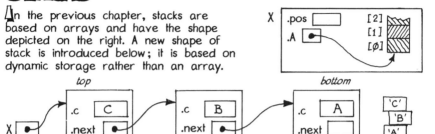

Here is the definition of the shape of each element:

```
typedef struct Element
        {
            char c;
            struct Element   * next;
        }
        Element_Type, * Pointer_Type;
```

alias for 'struct Element'

alias for 'pointer to objects of type struct Element'

'List processing' is the art of diverting pointers by copying addresses from one pointer variable to another. To depict such operations we use the notation shown here. The fat arrow depicts a simple copying of contents in the direction of the arrow. The ordinal number (1st, 2nd, *etc.*) shows the order of operations needed to avoid overwriting.

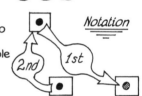

Notation

Here is the definition of Push(). The copy operations are depicted opposite, together with sketches of the linkage before and after the copy operations:

pointer to objects of type Pointer_Type

```
void Push ( Pointer_Type * q, char ch )
{
    Pointer_Type p;
    p = ( Pointer_Type ) malloc ( sizeof ( Element_Type ) ) ;
    p -> c = ch ;
    p -> next = * q ;
    * q = p ;
}
```

enter data into new element

1st

2nd

An invocation of Push() demands two arguments of which the first nominates a pointer. For example, Push(&X, 'A') to push 'A' onto stack X.

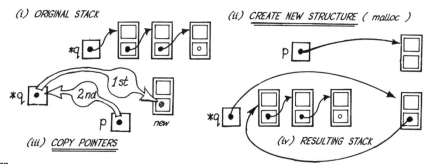

(i) ORIGINAL STACK   *(ii) CREATE NEW STRUCTURE (malloc)*

(iii) COPY POINTERS   *(iv) RESULTING STACK*

Here is the definition of Pop(). The copy operations are depicted under the definition together with sketches of the linkage before and after the copy operations.

```
char Pop ( Pointer-Type * q )
{
    char ch ;
    Pointer_Type p ;          pointer to objects of type
    p = * q ;          1st        'Pointer_Type'
    if ( * q != NULL ) ;
    {
        ch = p -> c ;
        * q = p -> next ;    2nd
        free ( p ) ;
        return ch ;
    }
    else
        return NULL ;
}
```

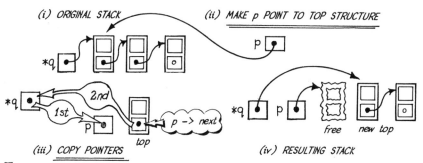

(i) ORIGINAL STACK   *(ii) MAKE p POINT TO TOP STRUCTURE*

(iii) COPY POINTERS   *(iv) RESULTING STACK*

Finally, here is the definition of Peep(). No pointers are disturbed.

```
char Peep ( Pointer_Type * q )
{
    if ( * q != NULL )
        return ( * q ) -> c ;        necessary parentheses
    else                                because ->
        return NULL ;                 binds tighter than *
}
```

POLISH AGAIN

THIS TIME WITH DYNAMIC STACKS

A program for transforming algebraic expressions into reverse Polish form is given below. The main loop from 'do' to 'while(ch != '=');' is identical to that on Page 141. Function Prec() is also identical. Functions Push(), Pop(), Peep() are replaced by the dynamic versions defined on the previous double page, but their prototypes are the same as before.

```
/* POLISH WITH DYNAMIC STACKS */
#include < stdio.h >
typedef struct Element
    {
        char c;
        struct Element * next;
    }
    Element_Type, * Pointer_Type;
void Push ( Pointer_Type *, char );
char Pop ( Pointer_Type * );
char Peep ( Pointer_Type * );
int Prec ( char );

void main (void)
{
    char ch;
    Pointer_Type X = NULL, Y = NULL;
    do
    {
        ch = getchar ();
        switch (ch)
        {
            case '(':
                Push ( &Y, ch );
                break;
            case ')':
                while ( Peep (&Y) != '(' )
                    Push ( &X, Pop (&Y) );
                ch = Pop (&Y);
                break;
            case '+': case '-': case '*': case '/': case '=':
                while (Peep(&Y) != NULL && Prec(ch) <= Prec(Peep(&Y)) )
                    Push ( &X, Pop (&Y) );
                Push ( &Y, ch );
                break;
            default: if ( ch >= 'A' && ch <= 'Z' )
                    Push ( &X, ch );
        }
    }
    while ( ch != '=' );      /* end of do-while loop */

    while ( Pop(&Y) != NULL )         flush Y
        ;
    while ( Peep(&X) )                pop from X into Y
        Push(&Y, Pop(&X) );          thus reversing order
    while ( Peep (&Y) )
        printf ("%c", Pop( &Y) );    pop and print entire Y
    printf ("\n");
}
```

these as before

two stacks
X [0] Y [0]

this loop as before

Element_Type
.c [ ]
.next [•]
[•] Pointer_Type

place here: Push( ), Pop( ), Peep( ), Prec( )

148   ILLUSTRATING C

SIMPLE CHAINING

A *chain* is demonstrated on earlier pages in the particular form of a *stack*. In general, chains are more flexible than this; they have many applications. The example which follows this introduction illustrates an algorithm for finding the shortest route through a road network.

For demonstrating the techniques introduced below, we adopt the same structure (I type Element_Type) as that employed on the opposite page for stacks. Assume the following chain already set up;

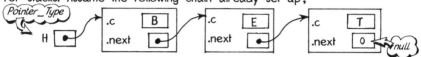

Traversal means referring sequentially to the elements of a chain. In this demonstration, 'referring to' involves printing the content of an element ≋ the content being just a single character.

```
Pointer_Type p, n;                        declare two
/* TRAVERSAL - NON RECURSIVE */          working pointers
p = H;              copy head
while ( p )         of chain                       linkage:
{                                                        before
                              refer             - - - - - >  after
    printf ("\n%c", p -> c );    to
    p = p -> next;               data
}
                        point to next
                        element
```

Insertion:

```
/* INSERT 'R' AFTER 'E' */       traverse to
p = H ;                          find 'E'
while ( p -> c != 'E' )
    p = p -> next;               create new
n = (Pointer_Type)               element
      malloc ( sizeof ( Element_Type ));
n -> c = 'R';          1st copy
n -> next = p -> next;
p -> next = n;              2nd copy
```

Deletion:

```
/* DELETE 'E' LEAVING GARBAGE */
if ( H -> c == 'E' )
    H = H -> next ;         α
else
{
    p = H ;
    while ( p -> next -> c != 'E' )
        p = p -> next ;
    p -> next = p -> next -> next ;
}                                 β
```

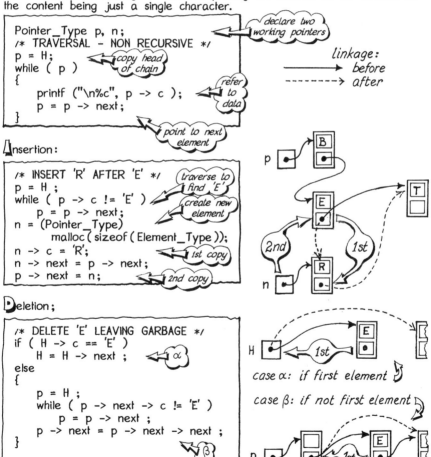

case α: if first element

case β: if not first element

SHORTEST ROUTE

Finding the shortest (or longest) route through a network is a problem that crops up in various disciplines ⇌ one of which is *critical path scheduling* for the control and monitoring of construction projects. Given a network such as that below, the problem is to find the shortest route from the node marked *START* to that marked *END*. The journey must follow the direction of the arrow. The number against each arrow shows the journey time.

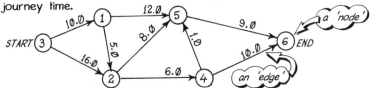

The data structure needed for a shortest-route program is depicted below. There is a record for each *node*, and a chain runs from each such record. Each chain comprises *edge* records which store data describing all the edges which run *out* of that node.

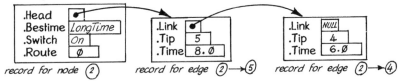

Records for all nodes are held in an array named *NodeFacts*. The record for node 2 is annotated more fully below. In the component named *Bestime* is the value *LongTime* (a constant set to 10^{20}). In the component named *Switch* is a Boolean value, initially switched to *On*. Uses of these items are explained later.

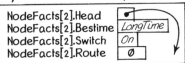

NodeFacts[2].Head	
NodeFacts[2].Bestime	*LongTime*
NodeFacts[2].Switch	*On*
NodeFacts[2].Route	∅

The records for edges running out of a node are created dynamically. Each record has a component for storing the link, another for storing the node number at the tip, another for storing the journey time along the particular edge. This example is for edge 2 to 5.

NodeFacts[2].Head.Link	
NodeFacts[2].Head.Tip	5
NodeFacts[2].Head.Time	8·∅

The shortest route is found by an iterative process. Before the process can start the chains must be formed ⇌ and initial values placed in the components that will eventually hold changing values. The component named *Bestime* is to hold the best time so far achieved to this node by different trial routes; the initial time in this component is set so high that the first feasible route, however slow, has to be an improvement. An exception is the starting node: the best time to the starting node is, by definition, nothing.

All switches are turned *On* initially. A switch that is *On* implies that the edges leading out of that node must be explored (or re-explored) .

The iterative process starts at the starting node, then cycles the array of node records until terminated. The process terminates on detection of all switches being *Off*.

At each node the chain of edge records is traversed. For each edge in the chain, the time to reach its tip is found by taking the best time so far achieved at the tail and adding it to the journey time for that edge. The result is compared with the best time so far recorded in the *node record* for the tip. If the new time is better, several things must be recorded. These are depicted below:

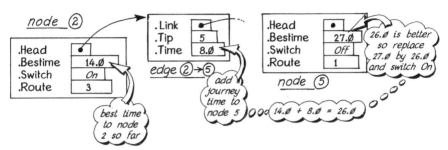

Whenever a better route to a node is found, the faster time is substituted and the node switched *On*, as depicted for node 5 above. To be able to trace this improved route subsequently, the *Route* component is made to contain the number of the node through which the route came. So the outcome of dealing with the edge from 2 to 5 is as shown here:

node ⑤

```
.Head      •        better time
.Bestime   26.0
.Switch    On       On
.Route     2
                    came via
                    node 2
```

After traversing the chain of edges from node 2, the *Switch* at node 2 is turned off. However, the action at node 2 included turning *On* the switch at node 5, so the iteration is not yet finished. The process continues until all switches are off ⇔ in other words until a complete cycle through the nodes fails to make a single improvement to the route.

The node records are assembled as an array rather than being created dynamically and linked as a chain. The array structure was chosen because node records are accessed in a 'random' way (*e.g.* when dealing with node 2 you have to refer to nodes 5 and 4) . Using an array, such references are resolved quickly by a simple change of subscript.

Tried with the network sketched opposite, data and results would be as shown here.

```
No.nodes No.edges Startnode Endnode
6        9        3         6
3    1   10.0
3    2   16.0
1    2   5.0
1    5   12.0                data
2    4   6.0
2    5   8.0
5    6   9.0
4    6   10.0
4    5   1.0
Route from 6 to 3
   6...4...2...1...3          results
Time taken is 31.0
```

SHORTEST ROUTE

```
/*   SHORTEST ROUTE PROGRAM */

#include < stdio.h >
#include < stdlib.h >


/* ROUTE PROGRAM BEGINS */

typedef struct Edge
    {
        struct Edge     *          Link ;
        int                        Tip ;
        double                     Time ;
    }
    Edge_Type, * Ptr_Edgetype ;


typedef struct Node
    {
        Ptr_Edgetype               Head ;
        double                     Bestime ;
        int                        Switch ;
        int                        Route ;
    }
    Node_Type, * Ptr_Nodetype ;

int main ( void )
{
    enum                      { Off, On };          ⟵ Boolean switch
    double  const             Nothing = 0.0 ;
    double  const             LongTime = 1E20 ;     ⟵ impracticably high
    double                    Try, Best ;
    int                       Nodes, Edges, StartNode, EndNode,
                              Tail, Cycles, i, j, n ;
    Ptr_Edgetype              Edge = NULL, p = NULL ;

    Node_Type                 NodeFacts [ 30 ] ;    ⟵ array of node records

    printf ("\nNo.Nodes, No.Edges, Startnode, Endnode\n");
    scanf ("%i %i %i %i", & Nodes, & Edges, & StartNode, & EndNode );

    for ( i=1; i <= Nodes; ++i)                     ⟵ input 4 counters
    {
        NodeFacts[i].Head = NULL ;
        NodeFacts[i].Bestime = LongTime ;           ⟵ initialize all
        NodeFacts[i].Switch = On ;                     node records
        NodeFacts[i].Route = 0 ;
    }
    NodeFacts [ StartNode ] . Bestime = Nothing ;   ⟵ replace time
                                                      at start node
```

```
for ( j=1; j<=Edges; ++j)
{
    p = (Ptr_Edgetype) malloc ( sizeof (Edge_Type) );
    scanf ("%i %i %1f", & Tail, & p->Tip, & p -> Time );
    p -> Link = NodeFacts [ Tail ] . Head;
    NodeFacts [ Tail ] . Head = p;
}
```

chain each edge to the node it leads out of

```
Cycles = Ø;
n = StartNode - 1;
while ( Cycles < 2 )
{
    Cycles += 1;
    n = n % Nodes + 1;
    if ( NodeFacts [ n ] . Switch == On )
    {
        Cycles = Ø;
        Edge = NodeFacts [ n ] . Head;
        while ( Edge != NULL )
        {
            Try = NodeFacts [ n ].Bestime + Edge -> Time;
            if ( Try < NodeFacts[ Edge->Tip ].Bestime )
            {
                NodeFacts [ Edge->Tip ].Bestime = Try;
                NodeFacts [ Edge->Tip ].Route = n;
                NodeFacts [ Edge->Tip ].Switch = On;
            }
            Edge = Edge -> Link;
        }
        NodeFacts [ n ] . Switch = Off;
    }
}
Best = NodeFacts [ EndNode ] . Bestime;
if ( Best != LongTime && Best != Nothing )
{
    printf ("\nRoute from %i to %i\n", EndNode, StartNode );
    n = EndNode;
    while ( n )
    {
        printf ("%i", n);
        n = NodeFacts [ n ] . Route;
        if ( n ) printf ("...");
    }
    printf ("\n\nTime taken is %.2f", Best);
}
else
    printf ("\nNo way through, or going nowhere");
return Ø;
}
```

n is augmented by 1 before use, hence -1 in preparation

INTRODUCING RINGS

The fundamental record of a doubly linked ring has pointers pointing fore and aft thus:

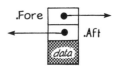

Access to records in a ring is simplified by employing one record as a dummy head as illustrated below. This device makes it unnecessary to check whether the record to be added or deleted is next to the fixed head, and, if so, to take special action. Very messy.

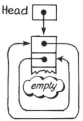

A ring is depicted above with four records; it is also depicted empty.

Here is the definition of a shape suitable for constructing a ring. To keep everything simple, this shape is made capable of storing just a single character.

```
typedef struct Petal
    {
        struct Petal * Fore ;
        struct Petal * Aft ;
        char Data ;
    }
Ring_Type, * P_Type ;
```

In the main program an empty ring may be set up as follows:

```
p = ( P_Type ) malloc ( sizeof ( Ring_Type ) ) ;
```

A new record may be inserted before *or* after the record currently pointed to. Procedures for both these operations are given below:

```
void In_After ( P_Type Old, P_Type Young )
{
    Young -> Fore = Old -> Fore ;
    Young -> Aft = Old;
    Old -> Fore -> Aft = Young ;
    Old -> Fore = Young ;
}
```

*pointers
initially* ⟶

finally
‑ ‑ ‑ ‑ ‑►

*INSERT Young
AFTER Old*

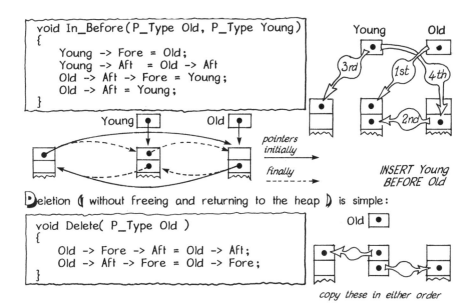

```
void In_Before( P_Type Old, P_Type Young )
{
    Young -> Fore = Old;
    Young -> Aft  = Old -> Aft
    Old -> Aft -> Fore = Young;
    Old -> Aft = Young;
}
```

pointers
initially

finally

INSERT Young
BEFORE Old

Deletion (without freeing and returning to the heap) is simple:

```
void Delete( P_Type Old )
{
    Old -> Fore -> Aft = Old -> Aft;
    Old -> Aft -> Fore = Old -> Fore;
}
```

Old

copy these in either order

Traversal is simple in either direction, the only difficulty is stopping. If the aim is to traverse the ring precisely once, start by pointing to the first record and arrange to stop as soon as the pointer points to the dummy head (before trying to refer to data in the dummy head).

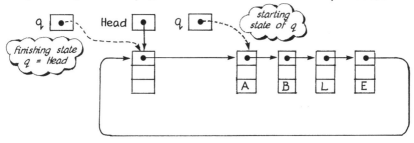

finishing state
q = Head

starting state of q

```
q = Head -> Fore ;
while ( q != Head )
{
    printf ("%c", q -> Data ) ;
    q = q -> Fore ;
}
printf ("\n") ;
```

ABLE

If both occurrences of Fore were changed to Aft, the result of the above piece of program would be ELBA rather than ABLE.

Overleaf is a demonstration program designed to exercise the principles and procedures introduced on this double page.

**A PROGRAM TO DEMONSTRATE THE
PRINCIPLES OF A DOUBLY-LINKED RING**

The following program maintains a doubly-linked ring organized alphabetically. To introduce a letter, enter +L (or + other letter) . To remove a letter, enter –L (or – whatever the letter) . To display the stored data in alphabetical order, enter > at the start of a line. To display in reverse order enter <. To stop, abort the run (e.g. in DOS, hold down Ctrl and press C) .

```
/* RING A RING OF ROSES */

#include < stdio.h >

typedef struct Petal
    {
        struct Petal *   Fore;
        struct Petal *   Aft;
        char   Data;
    }
    Ring_Type, * P_Type;

void In_Before( P_Type Old, P_Type Young ) ;
void Delete( P_Type Old ) ;

/* MAIN PROGRAM */

void main( void )
{
    char        Choice, Letter;
    P_Type      Head, p, q;
    char        w[ 80 ];

    Head = ( P_Type ) malloc ( sizeof ( Ring_Type ) );

    Head -> Fore = Head;
    Head -> Aft  = Head;
    Head -> Data = NULL;

    printf ( "\nEnter +L ( or + any letter ) to add letter to the ring"
             "\nEnter -L ( or - any existing letter ) to remove letter"
             "\nEnter > to list alphabetically, or < to list in reverse\n" );
```

struct Petal
. Fore
. Aft
. Data
P_Type
Ring_Type

prototypes

input buffer for sscanf( )

set up Head

Head

```
Enter +L (or + any letter) to add letter to the ring
Enter -L (or - any existing letter) to remove letter
Enter ) to list alphabetically, or ( to list in reverse
+ C
+F
+A
)
ACF
 -  C
(
FA
```

156   ILLUSTRATING C

```
while ( 1 )
{
    Choice = Letter = Ø;
    fflush ( stdin );
    sscanf ( gets(w), " %c %c ", & Choice, & Letter );
    if ( Letter == Ø || ( Letter >= 'A' && Letter <= 'Z') )
    {
        switch ( Choice )
        {
            case '+':
                p = ( P_Type ) malloc ( sizeof ( Ring_Type ));
                p -> Data = Letter;
                q = Head -> Fore;
                while ( q != Head && q -> Data < Letter )
                    q = q -> Fore;
                In_Before ( q, p );
                break;

            case '-' :
                q = Head -> Fore;
                while ( q != Head && q -> Data != Letter )
                    q = q -> Fore;
                if ( q != Head )
                    Delete ( q );
                break;

            case '>' :
                q = Head -> Fore;
                while ( q != Head )
                {
                    printf ("%c", q -> Data );
                    q = q -> Fore;
                }
                printf ("\n");
                break;

            case '<' :
                q = Head -> Aft;
                while ( q != Head )
                {
                    printf ("%c", q -> Data );
                    q = q -> Aft;
                }
                printf ("\n");
        }
    }
}
```

add a
letter

remove
a letter

list
alphabetically

list in
reverse order

insert functions In_Before ( ) and Delete ( ) here

An application such as a book index (a secondary sorted list under each entry) can be handled as a *ring* of rings.

BINARY TREES

Take some letters to sort:

D, Z, B, E, A, F, C

Bring the first letter, D, to the root of a *tree* and store it as a *node*. (Trees grow upside down as do several metaphors in computer science.)

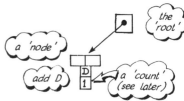

the 'root'

a 'node'

add D

a 'count' (see later)

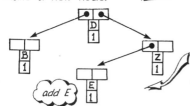

add Z

Now take the next letter, Z, and bring it to the root node. It is 'bigger' than D so go *right* and make a new node to contain Z as shown here.

Now the third letter, B. It is smaller than D so go *left* and make a new node.

add B

The next letter, E, is bigger than D so go *right*. It is smaller than Z so go *left*. Then make a new node to contain E as shown here.

add E

In general, bring the next letter to the root node and compare. If the new letter is smaller go *left*, if bigger go *right*. Do the same thing as you reach the next node, and the next and the next. Eventually you will find no node for comparison. At that stage make a new node and store the new letter in it.

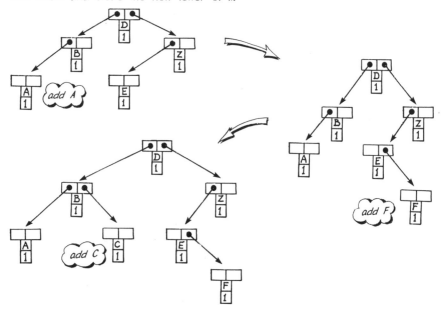

add A

add C

add F

At any stage the tree may be traversed (or *stripped*) as shown below. Notice that the arrow runs through the letters in alphabetical order.

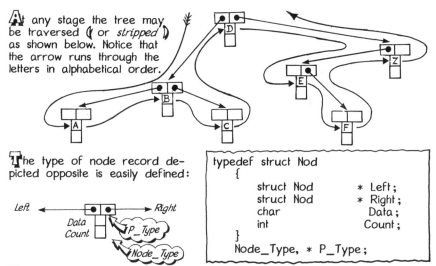

The type of node record depicted opposite is easily defined:

Left ←———•• ——→ *Right*
Data
Count   P_Type
           Node_Type

```
typedef struct Nod
    {
        struct Nod      * Left;
        struct Nod      * Right;
        char            Data;
        int             Count;
    }
Node_Type, * P_Type;
```

Hanging letters on a tree ⌇ depicted in stages opposite ⌇ is best done recursively. If the current node is NULL make a new node to contain the new letter; otherwise invoke Add_Item with the parameter specifying the left or right pointer according to how the new letter compares with that pointed to:

```
P_Type   Add_Item ( P_Type p,   char Letter )
{
    if ( p == NULL )
        p = Create_Node ( Letter, 1 );        create new
    else                                      node with null
        if ( Letter < p -> Data )             pointers
            p -> Left = Add_Item ( p -> Left, Letter );
        else
            if ( Letter > p -> Data )
                p -> Right = Add_Item ( p -> Right, Letter );
            else
                p -> Count ++;         don't store twice, just
    return p;                          add 1 to the count
}
```

The function for creating a node involves the malloc() function whose prototype is in <stdlib.h>:

```
P_Type Create_Node (char D, int C)
{
    P_Type p;
    p = (P_Type) malloc ( sizeof ( Node_Type ) );
    p -> Left  = NULL;
    p -> Right = NULL;
    p -> Data  = D;
    p -> Count = C;
    return p;
}
```

p •   L ☐☐ R
                D
                C

The tree may be traversed recursively:

```
void Strip ( P_Type p )
{
    if ( p != NULL )
    {
        Strip ( p -> Left  );
        Print ( p -> Count, p -> Data );
        Strip ( p -> Right );
    }
}
```

recursive call to strip left tree

access the data - in this case just print a letter

recursive call to strip right tree

where the Print() function is as follows:

```
void Print ( int i, char c )
{
    while ( i-- )
        printf ("%c", c);
}
```

print the letter as many times as Count dictates

The order of stripping shown above is called 'in order' stripping. Two other orders are useful to programmers:

```
'pre order'   D BAC ZEF

Print ( p -> Count, p -> Data );
Strip ( p -> Left  );
Strip ( p -> Right );
```

```
'post order'  ACB FEZ D

Strip ( p -> Left  );
Strip ( p -> Right );
Print ( p -> Count, p -> Data );
```

Adding to the tree is simple, as demonstrated by the elegant brevity of Add_Item, but true deletion is not simple because it requires re-arrangement of the tree. The following function finds the letter specified, then decrement its count of occurrences. The Print() function ignores letters that have a zero count, so Lose_Item effectively deletes letters.

```
void Lose_Item ( P_Type p, char Letter )
{
    if ( p != NULL )
    {
        if ( Letter   p -> Data )
            Lose_Item ( p -> Left, Letter );
        else
            if ( Letter   p -> Data )
                Lose_Item ( p -> Right, Letter );
            else
                if ( p -> Count   Ø )
                    p -> Count -- ;
    }
}
```

node not found

recursive calls

node found and decremented if positive

ILLUSTRATING C

MONKEY-PUZZLE

ANOTHER NAME FOR THE
BINARY TREE SORT

```c
/* MONKEY PUZZLE SORTING */
#include <stdio.h>
#include <stdlib.h>
typedef struct Nod
    {
        struct Nod      * Left;
        struct Nod      * Right;
        char            Data;
        int             Count;
    }
    Node_Type, * P_Type;

P_Type              Create_Node ( char, int );
P_Type              Add_Item ( P_Type, char );
void                Lose_Item ( P_Type, char );
void                Strip ( P_Type );
void                Print ( int, char );
```

```
+B
+A
+B
+O
+O
+N
>
ABBNOO
−B
>
ABNOO
```

prototypes

```c
void main ( void )
{
    P_Type              Root;
    char                Choice, Letter, w[80];

    printf ("\nEnter +L ( or + any letter ) to add letter to tree"
            "\nEnter -L ( or - any existing letter ) to remove it"
            "\nEnter      to list alphabetically\n" );

    Root = NULL;
    while (1)
    {
        Choice = Letter = 0;
        fflush (stdin);
        sscanf ( gets (w), " %c %c ", & Choice, & Letter );
        if ( Letter == 0 || ( Letter >= 'A' && Letter <= 'Z' ))
        {
            switch ( Choice )
            {
                case '+':
                    Root = Add_Item ( Root, Letter);
                    break;

                case '-': case '_':
                    Lose_Item ( Root, Letter );
                    break;

                case '>':
                    Strip ( Root );
                    printf ("\n");
            }
        }
    }
}
```

to leave the loop, abort the program

flush keyboard buffer

make underscore a synonym for a minus sign

place here the functions whose prototypes are listed above

161

EXERCISES

1 Implement the program on Page 148; it employs dynamic stacks. Change the program so that it reads a numerical expression instead of an algebraic one ≈ and produces a single numerical result. The way to go about it is explained on Page 142, exercise 3.

2 Implement the shortest route program on Page 152. Contrive a network in which there is more than one 'shortest' route. Which does the program choose and why? Modify the program so that it detects multiple shortest routes and warns the user of their existence.

3 Modify program ROSES such that it stores *words* in alphabetical order rather than just letters.

As a challenge, develop the program as a tool for book indexing. The structure on the ring should contain a pointer to a chain of integers representing page numbers. Each structure on the main ring should also contain a nested structure ((of similar shape)) defining a sub-ring to enable an entry in the book index to look something like this:

        cats, 172ff
                care of, 172-4
                habits of, 176-7
                in literature, 178-81

in which the sub-entries for 'cats' are in alphabetical order.

4 Implement the monkey puzzle program on Page 161. Extend its scope so that entering < from the keyboard makes the list of letters appear in reverse order. ((The scope of binary trees is only touched on in this book.))

LIBRARY

This chapter presents the functions of the ANSI C library.

Each function is described by name of function, name of header file in which it is defined, its prototype, a brief description of the function, and an example of its usage. Functions are grouped according to application; use the summary in Chapter 11 for alphabetical reference.

Functions concerned with multi-byte characters and foreign locales are not fully described in this book. For full details see ANSI X 3.195 which also explains why such functions were included in the standard library.

INPUT, OUTPUT, FILES

Functions for dealing with input, output and file management are described under the following subheadings:

- Low-level input & output
- Single character input & output
- File management
- Random access
- String input & output
- Formats for input & output
- Temporary files
- Buffering

fwrite, fread

■   #include < stdio.h >
      size_t fwrite (const void * *buf*, size_t *b*, size_t *c*, FILE * *s*);
      size_t fread (void * *buf*, size_t *b*, size_t *c*, FILE * *s*);

Low level functions for writing from buffer to file and reading from file to buffer. Both functions return the number of items successfully transferred. size_t is a special type defined by typedef in stdio.h.

```
Nr_Out = fwrite ( P_out, sizeof ( char ), 80, OutStream );
Nr_In  = fread ( P_in, sizeof ( char ), 80, InStream );
```

fputc, putc, putchar

■   #include < stdio.h >
      int fputc (int *c*, FILE * *s*);

Output a single character to stream *s*.

■   #include < stdio.h >
      int putc (int *c*, FILE * *s*);
      int putchar (int *c*);

macros: putc( ) is equivalent to fputc( ), so avoid arguments that have side effects; putchar( ) is equivalent to putc(int *c*, stdout);

```
fputc ( Ch, stdout );
```

fgetc, getc, getchar

■   #include < stdio.h >
      int fgetc (FILE * *s*);

Input and return a single character from stream *s*.

- ```
  #include <stdio.h>
  int getc ( FILE * s );
  int getchar ( void );
  ```

macros: getc( ) is equivalent to fgetc( ), so avoid arguments that have side effects; getchar( ) is equivalent to getc(stdin).

```
Ch = fgetc ( stdin );
```

ungetc

- ```
  #include <stdio.h>
  int ungetc ( int c, FILE * s );
  ```

Causes the next fgetc( ) ((or other 'get' function)) on this stream to pick up the character 'ungot'. If a second character is 'ungot' before the first has been picked up, the first is lost. Returns the code of the character 'ungot', or EOF if unsuccessful.

```
ungetc ( Ch, stdin );
```

FILE MANAGEMENT

fflush

- ```
  #include <stdio.h>
  int fflush ( FILE * s );
  ```

Flush input buffer on stream *s*. Return Ø if successful.

```
fflush ( stdin );
```

fopen, freopen, fclose

```
#include <stdio.h>
FILE * fopen ( const char * file, const char * mode );
FILE * freopen ( const char * file, const char * mode, FILE * s );
```

Function fopen( ) opens a file in the mode specified and returns a pointer to the associated stream. Returns NULL if unsuccessful. The composition of *mode is defined on Page 117.

Function freopen( ) is similar to fopen( ), but points to stream *s*, thereby redirecting input or output from stream *s* to the nominated file.

- ```
  #include <stdio.h>
  FILE * fclose ( FILE * s );
  ```

Closes an open stream, flushing the output buffer if writing. Returns Ø if successful, otherwise NULL.

```
char *p = "C:\\MYDIR\\MYFILE.ME";
MyStream = fopen ( p, "w+" );
freopen ( "PRNTFILE.TXT", "w", stdout );
fclose ( YourStream );
```

remove, rename, rewind

■   #include <stdio.h>
     int remove (const char * *file*);

Deletes a file, currently closed, and returns Ø if successful.

■   #include <stdio.h>
     int rename (const char * *old*, const char * *new*);

Renames a file, whether it is open or closed, returning Ø if successful.

■   #include <stdio.h>
     void rewind (FILE * *s*);

Clears end of file and error flags for stream *s*. Locates the file pointer such that the next read will pick up the first item.

```
printf ( "%s\n", remove( "MYFILE.DOC") ? "Error": "OK" );
printf ( "%s\n", rename ( "HER.SUR", "HIS.SUR") ? "Error" : "OK" );
rewind ( MyStream );
```

clearerr, feof, ferror

■   #include <stdio.h>
     void clearerr (FILE * *s*);

Resets the error indicator and end-of-file indicator without rewinding.

■   #include <stdio.h>
     int feof (FILE * s);
     int ferror (FILE * *s*);

Returns non-zero if there has been an attempt to read the stream beyond its end-of-file indicator, or the error indicator has become set. Returns zero if all's well. Each function clears its associated indicator. See page 118 for fuller description.

RANDOM ACCESS

fseek, ftell

■   #include <stdio.h>
     int fseek (FILE * *s*, long *offset*, int *origin*);

Locates the file pointer:

- at the start of stream *s* if *origin* specifies Ø,
- one byte past the end of the file if *origin* specifies 2,
- at *offset* bytes from the start of the file if *origin* is 1.

For clarity: enum { SEEK_SET, SEEK_CUR, SEEK_END }
is defined in stdio.h as constants for Ø, 1 and 2.

The function returns Ø if successful, but under MS DOS may return Ø
after an unsuccessful attempt.

■   #include < stdio.h >
       long ftell (FILE * *s*);

Returns the position of the file pointer. If the return is used as *offset* in
fseek( ), *origin* must be zero (⟨ SEEK_SET ⟩) .

```
fseek ( MyStream, Ø, SEEK_SET );
ftell ( YrStream );
```

Fsetpos, Fgetpos
■   #include < stdio.h >
       int fsetpos (FILE * *s*, const fpos_t * *p*);

Sets the file pointer for stream *s* to the value pointed to by *p*. If
successful, the function clears the end-of-file flag for stream *s* and
returns Ø. If unsuccessful, the function sets the global variable errno and
returns a non-zero value. fpos_t is a special type defined by typedef in
stdio.h.

■   #include < stdio.h >
       int fgetpos (FILE * *s*, fpos_t * *c*);

Saves the position of the file pointer on stream *s* at the location pointed
to by *c*. If successful, the function returns Ø, otherwise it sets the global
variable **errno** and returns a non-zero value.

```
fpos_t * PosPoint;
fgetpos ( MyStream, PosPoint );
fsetpos ( MyStream, PosPoint );
```

Fgets, gets, Fputs, puts
■   #include < stdio.h >
       char * fgets (char * *b*, int *n*, FILE * *s*);

From stream *s* the function reads as many as *n*-1 characters to buffer *b[ ]*.
It stops reading if it meets \n (⟨ which it RETAINS ⟩) or EOF. It appends
NULL to the character string. The function returns a pointer to buffer *b*,
or NULL if the operation fails.

- #include <stdio.h>
  char * gets (char * b);

Reads characters from stdin until meeting \n ((which it DROPS)) or EOF. It appends NULL to the character string. The function returns a pointer to buffer b, or NULL if the operation fails.

- #include <stdio.h>
  int fputs (const char * b, FILE * s);

Sends the character string in buffer b ((which must be NULL terminated)) to stream s. Returns ∅ if the operation fails.

- #include <stdio.h>
  int puts (const char * b);

Sends the character string in buffer b ((which must be NULL terminated)) to stream stdout. The function returns ∅ if the operation fails.

```
char w [ 8∅ ], v [ 8∅ ];
fgets ( w, 8∅, stdin );
gets ( v );
fputs ( w, stdout );
puts ( v );
```

FORMATS FOR I/O

fprintf, printf, sprintf

- #include <stdio.h>
  int fprintf (FILE * s, const char * fmt, ...);

Prints on stream s as many items as there are single percentage signs in fmt that have matching arguments in the ... list. Pages 11∅ and 111 describe the composition of the format string. The function returns the number of items actually printed.

- #include <stdio.h>
  int printf (const char * fmt, ...);

As fprintf( ) but with stdout implied for stream s.

- #include <stdio.h>
  int sprintf (char * p, const char * fmt, ...);

As fprintf( ) but with string p in place of stream s.

```
char fmat [ ] = "First %i, then %6.2f then %c then %s\n";
char sink [ 80 ];
fprintf ( stdout, fmat, 1, 1.25, 'A', "OK" );
printf ( fmat, 1, 1.25, 'A', "OK" );
sprintf ( sink, fmat, 1, 1.25, 'A', "OK" );
printf ( "%s", sink );
```

```
First 1 then 1.25 then A then OK
First 1 then 1.25 then A then OK
First 1 then 1.25 then A then OK
```

vfprintf, vprintf, vsprintf

■   #include <stdio.h>
    #include <stdarg.h>

```
int vfprintf ( FILE * s, const char * fmt, va_list ap );
int vprintf (const char * fmt, va_list ap );
int vsprintf ( char * p, const char * fmt, va_list ap );
```

These functions correspond to fprintf, printf, sprintf respectively, but
instead of having a list of arguments they have a pointer of type va_list
pointing to the 'next' argument retrievable by va_arg(). Page 96 explains
the use of va_arg(). va_list is a special type defined by typedef in
stdarg.h.

```
for ( n=0; n<Count; ++n)
  vprintf ( "%f", va_arg ( ap, double ) );
```

fscanf, scanf, sscanf

■   #include <stdio.h>
    int fscanf (FILE * s, const char * fmt, ...);

The function reads from stream s as many items as there are
percentage signs in fmt for which there are corresponding pointers in the
... list. White space in fmt is ignored. The function returns the number of
items actually read; if excess arguments are provided they are ignored.
Pages 112 and 113 describe the composition of the format string.

■   #include <stdio.h>
    int scanf (const char * fmt, ...);

As fscanf() with stdin implied for stream s.

■   #include <stdio.h>
    int sscanf (const char * b, const char * fmt, ...);

As fscanf() but with string b in place of stream s.

```
fscanf ( stdin, "%i", &n );
scanf ( "%i", &n );
```

```
char w [ 80 ];
gets ( w );
sscanf ( w, "%i %f %lf", &n, &x, &y );
```

tmpfile, tmpnam

■ #include < stdio.h >
   FILE * tmpfile (void);

Opens a nameless, temporary file in mode "wb+" and returns the
associated stream. Mode is defined on Page 117. The function returns NULL
if opening fails. The nameless file is automatically deleted on closure of
the stream.

■ #include < stdio.h >
   char * tmpnam (char * *nam*);

Generates a unique name and returns a pointer to it. The argument
points to the array in which you want the name stored. The minimum
length of array is given by L_tmpnam, the maximum number of names
by TMP_MAX, these constants being defined in stdio.h. Absence of an
argument implies storage in the form of a constant. See Page 120 for
clarification.

```
FILE * BriefStream;
BriefStream = tmpfile ( );        points to nameless file

fclose ( BriefStream );
```

```
char R[L_tmpnam];                 name stored in R[ ]
tmpnam ( R );
```

```
FILE * S;
char * M = tmpnam ( );            name stored as a constant
S = fopen ( M, "w+b" );

fclose ( S );
remove ( M );
```

setvbuf, setbuf

■ #include < stdio.h >
   int setvbuf (FILE * *s*, char * *b*, int *mode*, size_t *sz*);

Changes the buffer for stream *s* from that allocated by the system to
that specified by *b*. The *mode* of buffering should be specified as:

* _IOFBF for full buffering,
* _IOLBF for buffering a line at a time,
* _IONBF for no buffering.

Buffer size is specified by *sz*. The *mode* constants, and the special type size_t, are defined in stdio.h.

■   #include < stdio.h >
    void setbuf (FILE * *s*, char * *b*);

As setvbuf( ) but with *mode* set to _IOFBF and *sz* set to BUFSIZ. The constants are defined in stdio.h.

```
setvbuf ( MyStream, MyBuf, _IOFBF, 2048 );
setbuf ( YrStream, YrBuf );
```

PROCESS CONTROL

Functions for process control are described under the separate subheadings:

• Termination
• Environment
• Locale
• Error recovery
• Signals & exceptions

TERMINATION

The following functions are concerned with terminating a program, printing explanatory messages and tidying up at exit. Three libraries are involved.

exit, abort, assert
■   #include < stdlib.h >
    void exit (int *status*);

Call exit( ) to exit a program normally. The function flushes file buffers, closes files left open. If you registered a set of functions using atexit( ), these are now invoked in the reverse order of their registration.

Constants EXIT_SUCCESS and EXIT_FAILURE are defined in stdlib.h for use as an argument. EXIT_SUCCESS has the value zero.

- #include <stdlib.h>
  void abort (void);

Call abort( ) to exit a program abnormally. The function does not flush file buffers or call functions set up using atexit( ).

- #include <assert.h>
  void assert (int *expression*);

A macro intended for program development. If *expression* evaluates as zero, certain diagnostics are sent to stderr, then abort( ) is invoked. You can disable assert( ) using macro NDEBUG in the preprocessor.

```
if ( Chaos ) abort( );
if ( ! Chaos ) exit (ø);
assert ( Nodes > Edges );
```

perror
- #include <stdio.h>
  void perror (const char * *mess*);

Prints on stream stderr the message you give as argument. Precedes the message with the error number currently held by the global variable **errno**.

```
perror ( "out of memory" );
exit (2);
```

atexit
- #include <stdlib.h>
  int atexit (void (* *fun*)(void));

When atexit( ) is invoked it 'registers' the function pointed to by *fun* as a function to be invoked by exit( ). The exit( ) function invokes all registered functions in the reverse order of their registration. You may register as many as 32, possibly more, see local manual for the number permitted. Registered functions should be simple ones that cause no side affects.

```
atexit ( Second_Func( ) );
atexit ( First_Func( ) );
```

The following functions are concerned with a program's environment. Environment strings may be interrogated and commands to the operating system executed from inside the program.

getenv

■ #include <stdlib.h>
   char * getenv (const char * *Name*);

The name used as an argument is matched against the list of 'environment names' held by the system; for example "PATH" or "MYFILE2". If a match is found the function returns a pointer to the corresponding data object, otherwise it returns NULL. Do not attempt to change the static object pointed to.

```
p = getenv ( "PATH" );
```

system

■ #include <stdlib.h>
   int system (const char * *command*);

Executes, from inside a program, a command addressed to the computer's operating system. The command should be encoded as a string. Given NULL as the argument, the function returns non-zero to indicate the presence of a command processor, zero to indicate absence.

```
system ( "DIR" );
```

Monetary values in different countries are printed in diverse styles; for example $5.95 versus £3-15. Separators and groupings of digits vary, also the usage of commas and periods. A set of such conventions may be set up in a C program as a named structure, and these may be picked up for use in any 'international' functions you may write. A locale has categories ((accessed by the constants LC_NUMERIC, LC_TIME, LC_MONETARY *etc.*)) which may be independently changed.

By default, the structure named C specifies only the use of a period as a decimal point. *No function in the C library refers to any locale convention save that of the decimal point.*

The prototypes shown below declare functions for setting conventions for a locale and interrogating the structure. See ANSI X3.159 for further information.

setlocale, localeconv

- #include <locale.h>
  char setlocale (int *category*, const char * *locale*);
  struct lconv * localeconv (void);

```
setlocale ( LC_ALL, "C" );
printf ( "Out, damned %s, out I say!\n", localeconv ( ) -> decimal_point );
```

ERROR RECOVERY

The 'goto' statement, which causes a jump to a label in the same function, can be useful for error recovery but is limited in scope. The facilities, longjmp( ) and setjmp( ), are designed to serve a similar purpose as the 'goto' and the label respectively, but their use is not constrained to the scope of a single function.

A macro, setjmp( ), is defined in <setjmp.h>. Also defined is an array type named jmp_buf. On invocation, setjmp( ) saves its calling environment in the nominated buffer for use by the next invocation of longjmp( ). The location of setjmp( ) serves as the 'label'.

The macro returns ∅ if successful.

When a subsequent longjmp( ) is executed, control returns to setjmp( ). The second argument of longjmp( ) provides an error code which setjmp( ) then returns. The program behaves as though there had been no interruption to its flow.

To avoid unwanted interaction, calls to longjmp( ) should be made only in simple contexts. A definition of the four allowable contexts, referred to above as 'simple', may be found in 4.6.1.1 of ANSI X3.159.

setjmp, longjmp

- #include <setjmp.h>
  int setjmp (jmp_buf *saver*);
  void longjmp (jmp_buf *saver*, int *value*);

```
if ( ErNo = setjmp(MyBuf)==∅ )
    { normal program }
else
    { handle errors: switch (ErNo) }

if ( Chaos )
    longjmp ( MyBuf, 1 );
```

The signal.h header file provides tools for handling failures, errors and interruptions, described collectively as 'exceptions'. When an exception occurs during execution the processor raises a corresponding 'signal'.

The header file defines the following macros for processing signals:

- SIG_DFL   default treatment, depends on implementation
- SIG_IGN   ignore
- SIG_ERR   the value returned by signal( ) if signal fails.

The header file defines the following signals:

- SIGABRT   abnormal termination, as with abort( )
- SIGFPE   arithmetic error (such as division by zero)
- SIGILL   illegal instruction
- SIGINT   interrupt (typically Ctrl+C from keyboard)
- SIGSEGV   attempted access outside memory range
- SIGTERM   request for termination received by program.

Signals are objects of type sig_atomic_t, a type defined in the header file. When an exception arises, the corresponding signal is automatically raised, and 'handled' as specified in the function (which you may write) nominated as the second parameter of signal( ). This function may, itself, invoke signal( ) in various ways, and may be designed to abort the run or return to the place where the signal was raised.

Instead of writing a handling function you may call one of the standard macros SIG_IGN or SIG_DFL for ignoring the signal or treating it in the default manner. After ignoring a signal, control reverts to where the signal was raised. The 'default manner' depends on the implementation.

In addition to handling signals you may raise them. A signal is raised by means of the raise( ) function.

signal, raise

■   #include <signal.h>
       void (* signal (int *sig*, void (* *hndlr*)(int))) (int);
       int raise (int *sig*);

The first argument of signal( ) should be one of the six listed. The second argument may be the name of a function you have written for handling the exception, or it may be SIG_DFL or SIG_IGN. When the nominated exception arises, the associated function or macro is called. If the signal( ) function fails it returns SIG-ERR.

If you write a handling function it should have a single int argument for the signal to be handled and return a value of like type.

```
if ( signal ( SIGINT, MyHandler ) == SIG_ERR );
    perror (" signal failure"), exit(1);
signal ( SIGFPE, SIG_IGN );
raise ( SIGSEGV );
```

VARIABLE ARGUMENT LIST

Functions may be defined with an argument list comprising at least one argument always present followed by a variable number of 'extra' arguments. <stdarg.h> provides tools for picking up the extra arguments. The pointer must have the special type, va_list, defined in the header file.

va_start, va_arg, va_end

■   #include <stdarg.h>
     void va_start (va_list p, *name*);

Place function at start of extraction sequence. The first argument declares the pointer, the second is the name of the last fixed argument in the function.

     #include <stdarg.h>
     type va_arg (va_list p, *type*);

This is obeyed once for each argument extracted. *type* will be int, float, double, *etc.* according to the type of argument to be extracted in each case.

■   #include <stdarg.h>
     void va_end (va_list p);

Place function at end of extraction sequence. See Page 96 for clarification.

```
va_list ap;
va_start ( ap, Count );
va_end ( ap );
```

MEMORY ALLOCATION

When one structure points to another of the same type, memory has to be allocated for the structure pointed to. Memory is allocated from a 'heap' maintained by the processor. Allocation functions specify the number of bytes required.

If a pointer to a structure is made to point elsewhere, the structure formerly pointed to becomes 'garbage', which may be 'freed' and returned to the heap.

malloc, calloc, realloc, free

- #include < stdlib.h >
  void * malloc (size_t *bytes*);

The function returns a pointer to a buffer comprising storage of the specified size. The type of pointer may be indicated by a cast. Size is measured as a total number of bytes, usually by sizeof( ) which returns a value of the required type.

- #include < stdlib.h >
  void * calloc (size_t *NumElts*, size_t *EltSiz*);

The function returns a pointer to a buffer for an array having *NumElts* elements, each of *EltSiz* bytes. The type of pointer may be indicated by a cast. The size of element is usually given via sizeof( ) which returns a value of the required type.

- #include < stdlib.h >
  void * realloc (void * *p*, size_t *newsiz*);

Changes the size of an allocated section of memory, pointed to by *p*, to the new size of *newsiz* bytes. If the new size is smaller than the previous size, the new content will remain the same as far as it goes. The pointer should have been established by malloc( ), calloc( ) or realloc( ) — or it may be NULL, in which case realloc( ) behaves like malloc( ).

- #include < stdlib.h >
  void free (void * *p*);

Frees the section of memory previously allocated, and pointed to by *p*, returning it to the heap. See Chapter 9 for clarification.

```
p = (Ptr_to_Edgetype) malloc ( sizeof ( Edge_Type ) );
q = ( int * ) calloc ( 1000, sizeof ( int ) );
```

STRING TO NUMBER

The functions described below are for converting values expressed in character form to values in numerical form and *vice versa.*

atoi

- #include < stdlib.h >
  int atoi (const char * *s*);

Returns the decimal int value represented by the argument. Equivalent to the call: (int) strtol (*s*, (**char) NULL, 10).

```
printf ( "%i\n", atoi ( " -987" ) );
```

                                                                    -987

atol

■ #include <stdlib.h>
  long atol (const char * *s*);

Returns the decimal long int value represented by the argument.
Equivalent to the call: strtol (*s*, (char**) NULL, 1Ø);

```
printf ("%li\n", atoi (" -98765") );
```
-98765

atof

■ #include <stdlib.h>
  double atof (const char * *s*);

Returns the double value represented by the argument. Equivalent to the
call: strtod (*s*, (char**) NULL);

```
printf ( "%f\n", atof ( " -98.765" ) );
```
-98.765000

strtod

■ #include <stdlib.h>
  double strtod (const char * *s*, char * * *p*);

Short for 'string to double'. The form of string is expected to be the
following:

>   *wsp sign digits.digits exp sign digits excess*

• *wsp* means optional white space

• *sign* means an optional + or –

• *digits* means an optional sequence of decimal digits; at least one
  digit must follow the decimal point if there is no digit before it

• *exp* is E, e, D or d to signify 'times ten to the power...'

• *excess* signifies any trailing, non–conforming string such as "ABC" in
  "-4.5e6ABC".

The function returns the value represented by the string. It leaves *p*
NULL, or pointing to the start of the trailing string if such exists. If the
converted value is too big for its type, the function returns the value of
the constant HUGE_VAL and sets errno.

```
char String [] = "-4.5e6ABC";
printf ("%lf", strtod (String, & p ) );
printf (" %s\n", p );
```
-4500000.000000 ABC

strtol, strtoul

■ #include < stdlib.h >
long strtol (const char * *s*, char * * *p*, int *base*);
unsigned long strtoul (const char * *s*, char * * *p*, int *radix*);

Short for 'string to long' and 'string to unsigned long'. The form of string is expected to be:

wsp sign ∅ x digits

- *wsp* means optional white space
- *sign* means an optional + or –
- *x* means an optional x or X
- *digits* means a sequence of octal, decimal or hex digits.
- *excess* signifies any trailing, non-conforming string.

The function returns the value represented by string *s*, leaving *p* NULL, or pointing to the trailing string if such exists. If the value is too big for its type, strtol( ) returns the value of the constant LONG_MAX or LONG_MIN according to the sign given in *s*, and sets errno; strtoul( ) returns ULONG_MAX and sets errno.

The argument, *base*, which specifies the number base, may be set from 2 to 36 or to zero. If set zero the base is deduced from the initial characters of *s* by the following rules: first character ∅, next ∅ to 7, implies base 8 (octal); first character ∅, next x or X, implies base 16 (hex); first character 1 to 9 implies base 1∅ (decimal).

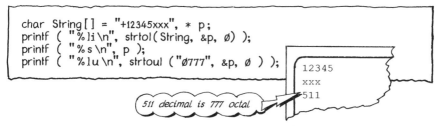

```
char String[ ] = "+12345xxx", * p;
printf ( "%li\n", strtol(String, &p, ∅) );
printf ( "%s\n", p );
printf ( "%lu\n", strtoul ("∅777", &p, ∅ ) );
```

```
12345
xxx
511
```

511 decimal is 777 octal

MATHEMATICS

The mathematical functions are described below under the headings:

- Arithmetical
- Trigonometrical
- Hyperbolics
- Random numbers
- Modular division
- Logarithms & exponentials

$\stackrel{M}{\triangle}$ost of the mathematical functions and macros are defined in the math.h header but a few are to be found in stdlib.h. These are functions concerned with:

- absolute values ((abs, fabs, labs))
- pseudo-random numbers ((rand, srand))
- modular divisions ((div, ldiv)) .

If an argument supplied to a function is outside the domain over which the function is defined, the global variable, errno, is set to the value returned by macro EDOM. If the value computed by a function cannot be represented by type double, errno is set to the value returned by macro ERANGE. In either case the value returned by the function then depends on the implementation. The value returned by macro HUGE_VAL may be employed. Check local manuals about domain and range errors.

abs, fabs, labs

■   #include <stdlib.h >
       int abs (int *n*);
       long labs (long *w*);
■   #include <math.h >
       double fabs (double *d*);

Absolute ((positive)) value of the argument.

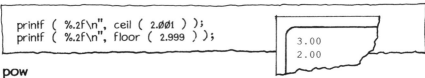

```
printf ("%i %i %i\n", abs(-2), abs(∅), abs(2) );
printf ("% li \n", labs(-2);
printf ("%.4f\n", fabs(-.∅∅2) );
```

```
2   0   2
2
0.0020
```

ceil, floor

■   #include <math.h >
       double ceil (double *d*);
       double floor (double *d*);

The nearest whole number above the value of the argument, and the nearest whole number below the value of the argument respectively.

```
printf ( %.2f\n", ceil ( 2.∅∅1 ) );
printf ( %.2f\n", floor ( 2.999 ) );
```

```
3.00
2.00
```

pow

■   #include <math.h >
       double pow (double *x*, double *y*);

The result of x raised to the power y. A domain error if x is negative and y non-integral. A range error occurs if the computed value is too big.

```
printf ( "%.2f %.2f\n", pow (2,3 ), pow (2.5, 3.5 ));
```
```
8.00   24.71
```

sqrt

■   #include < math.h >
     double sqrt (double *a*);

The square root of an argument that must be positive. Domain error if the argument is negative.

```
printf ( "%.2f %.2f\n", sqrt (Ø), sqrt (13.45) );
```
```
0.00   3.67
```

TRIGONOMETRICAL

sin, cos, tan

■   #include < math.h >
     double sin (double *ar*);
     double cos (double *ar*);
     double tan (double *ar*);

The sine, cosine, tangent ⟪ respectively ⟫ of an angle measured in radians.

```
const double pi = 3.1415926;
printf ( "%.3f %.3f\n", sin ( pi/6 ), sin ( Ø ) );
printf ( "%.3f %.3f\n", cos ( -pi/6 ), cos ( pi ));
printf ( "%.3f\n", tan ( pi/4 ) );
```
```
0.500   0.000
0.866  -1.000
1.000
```

asin, acos

■   #include < math.h >
     double asin (double *a*);
     double acos (double *a*);

The arc sine ⟪ the angle whose sine is... ⟫ , and arc cosine ⟪ the angle whose cosine is... ⟫ . The value returned is measured in radians. For asin() the range is [-π/2, +π/2], for acos() the range is [Ø, π]. Domain error if the argument falls outside the range -1 to +1.

```
printf ( "%.3f %.3f\n", asin( Ø.5), acos( sqrt( 3 )/2) );
```
```
0.524   0.524
```
π / 6

atan, atan2

- ```
  #include <math.h>
  double atan ( double a );
  double atan2 ( double y, double x );
  ```

The arc tangent ((the angle whose tangent is...)). The argument of atan( ) specifies the ratio of y to x; arguments of atan2( ) specify the same ratio but with y and x independently signed. The value returned is measured in radians. For atan( ) the range is $[-\pi/2, +\pi/2]$; for atan2( ) it is $[-\pi, +\pi]$.

```
printf ( "%.3f %.3f\n", atan(1), atan2(-1, -1) );
```
```
0.785   -2.356
```

sinh, cosh, tanh

- ```
  #include <math.h>
  double sinh ( double x );
  double cosh ( double x );
  double tanh ( double x );
  ```

The hyperbolic sine, hyperbolic cosine, hyperbolic tangent respectively. A range error occurs with sinh( ) or cosh( ) if the computed value is too big.

```
const double d = 7.6009025;
printf ( "%.3f %.3f %.3f", sinh(d), cosh(d), tanh(d) );
```
```
1000.000   1000.000   1.000
```

rand, srand

- ```
  #include <stdlib.h>
  int rand (void);
  ```

Returns a pseudo random number having a value between zero and the constant RAND_MAX which is defined in stdlib.h. The starting value ((the seed)) may be set by a call to function srand( ).

- ```
  #include <stdlib.h>
  void srand ( unsigned int seed );
  ```

When called, the function sets a seed for the rand( ) function. The seed is based on the argument given to srand( ); if a program is re-run with identical seeds, rand( ) will generate an identical sequence of numbers. In the absence of any srand( ) function, srand(1) is implied.

for example

```
srand ( 10 );
printf ( "%i %i %i\n", rand(),rand(),rand() );
```
```
10345   30957   3463
```

div, ldiv

■ #include < stdlib.h >
    div_t div (int *num*, int *denom*);

The arguments specify the numerator and denominator of a division
operation. The function returns the quotient and remainder of that
operation in a structure of type div_t. This structure is defined in stdlib.h
as:

```
typedef struct
{
        int quot;
        int rem;
} div_t;
```

■ #include < stdlib.h >
    ldiv_t ldiv (long *num*, long *denom*);

The function works as described above, but involves long integers. The
structure returned is defined in stdlib.h as:

```
typedef struct
{
        long quot;
        long rem;
} ldiv_t;
```

```
div_t shorty;
shorty = div ( 37, 8 );
printf ( "%i %i\n", shorty.quot, shorty.rem );
```

```
4   5
```

fmod

■ #include < math.h >
    double fmod (double *x*, double *y*);

Returns the remainder of a floating point division, where the division
operation is designed to stop when the quotient reaches the highest
possible integral value, positive or negative.

```
printf ( " %.2f %.2f\n", fmod(36.4, 6.3), fmod(36.4, -6.3) );
```

```
4.90   4.90
```

modf

- #include <math.h>
  double modf (double *d*, double * *p*);

Returns the fractional part of a floating point number, *d*, leaving *p* pointing to a whole number expressed in floating point form. If *d* is negative, both parts are taken as negative.

```
double Frac, Int;
Frac = modf(-12.34, & Int);
printf ( "%.2f %.2f\n", Int, Frac );
```
```
-12.00   -0.34
```

log, log10, exp

- #include <math.h>
  double log (double *a*);
  double log10 (double *a*);
  double exp (double *a*);

The natural logarithm ((base e)) of the argument, the base 10 logarithm of the argument, the natural anti-logarithm of the argument — in other words e raised to the power of the argument.

```
const double e = 2.718282;
printf ( "%.2f %.2f %.2f\n", log(1), log(e), log10(1000));
printf ( "%.2f %.2f %.2f\n", exp(0), exp(1), exp(log(123)));
```
```
0.00   1.00   3.00
1.00   2.72   123.00
```

frexp, ldexp

- #include <math.h>
  double frexp (double *x*, int * *p*);

The composition of binary floating point number *x* is *m* times 2 to the integral power *n*, where *m* is the 'mantissa'. Function frexp( ) returns the mantissa of *x* and leaves *p* pointing to the integral exponent.

- #include <math.h>
  double ldexp (double *x*, int *n*);

Function ldexp( ) returns the product of *x* times 2 to the power *n*.

```
double Man;
int Exp;
Man = frexp ( 6.3, & Exp );
printf ( "%.4f %i\n", Man, Exp );
printf ( "%.2f\n", ldexp( Man, Exp ) );
```
```
0.7875   3
6.30
```

CHARACTERS

Functions for identifying characters ('is it an integer?' *etc.*) are defined in header file ctype.h. Functions for converting values from character representation to numerical representation, and *vice versa*, are defined in header file stdlib.h.

isalnum, isalpha, isdigit, isxdigit

■
```
#include <ctype.h>
int isalnum ( int c );
int isalpha ( int c );
int isdigit ( int c );
int isxdigit ( int c );
```

These functions return a non-zero value (true) if the test passes, otherwise Ø (false). The tests are respectively for:

- isalnum( ), an alphanumeric character, letter or digit
- isalpha( ), a letter
- isdigit( ), a digit from Ø to 9
- isxdigit( ), a hex digit, Ø to F (or f)

```
printf ("%i %i %i %i\n", isalnum('*'), isalpha('G'), isdigit('b'), isxdigit('b') );
```

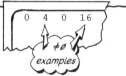

isgraph, isprint

■
```
#include <ctype.h>
int isgraph ( int c );
int isprint ( int c );
```

These functions return a non-zero value (true) if the test passes, otherwise Ø (false). The tests are respectively for:

- isgraph( ), a printable character excluding a space character
- isprint( ), a printable character including a space character

```
printf ("%i %i %i\n", isprint('*'), isprint(' '), isgraph(' ') );
```

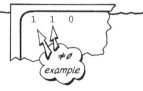

islower, isupper

■
```
#include <ctype.h>
int islower ( int c );
int isupper ( int c );
```

These functions return a non-zero value (true) if the test passes, otherwise Ø (false). The tests are respectively for:

- islower( ), a letter from a to z
- isupper( ), a letter from A to Z

```
printf ("%i %i\n", islower('n'), isupper('n') );
```

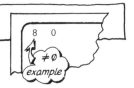

iscntrl, ispunct, isspace

■ #include <ctype.h>
  int iscntrl (int c);
  int ispunct (int c);
  int isspace (int c);

These functions return a non-zero value (true) if the test passes, otherwise Ø (false). The tests are respectively for:

- iscntrl( ), a control character such as that sent from the keyboard by holding down Ctrl and pressing C.
- ispunct( ), a punctuation mark such as ; or : or .
- isspace( ), one of the white space characters ' ', \f, \n, \r, \t, \v

```
printf ("%i %i %i\n", iscntrl(' '), ispunct('*'), isspace(';') );
```

tolower, toupper

■ #include <ctype.h>
  int tolower (int c);
  int toupper (int c);

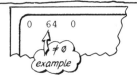

Returns the lower case or upper case equivalent of the argument respectively. If there is no such equivalent, the function returns the same value as its argument, treated as type int.

```
printf ("%c %c\n", tolower('A'), toupper('*') );
```

STRINGS

Most of the following functions are defined in string.h, a few in <stdlib.h>. They concern character arrays and their manipultation. In the explanations that follow, the phrase 'string s' is used as a short way of saying 'the array pointed to by s'.

The functions are described under the following subheadings:

- String length
- String copy & concatenate
- String comparison & search
- Miscellaneous strings

strlen

■   #include <string.h>
     size_t   strlen (const char * s);

Returns the number of bytes in the null-terminated string pointed to by s, *NOT* counting the null terminator.

```
printf ( "%i\n", strlen ( "ABC" ) );
```
```
3
```

The library offers several string copying functions, all subtly different in behaviour.

strcpy, strncpy

■   #include <string.h>
     char * strcpy (char * s1, const char * s2);
     char * strncpy (char * s1, const char * s2, size_t n);

Function strcpy( ) copies string s1, including its terminating null, to s2. strncpy( ) does a similar job, but copies only n characters. If a terminator in s2 is met before all n characters have been copied, the target string is padded with null characters to the full count of n. The functions return a pointer to the copied string. For neither function should the strings overlap.

```
char S[6];
strncpy ( S, "ABCDE", 8);
```

memcpy, memmove

- ```
  #include <string.h>
  void * memcpy ( void * b1, const void * b2, size_t n );
  void * memmove ( void * b1, const void * b2, size_t n );
  ```

The objects copied by these two functions are not limited to null-terminated strings. memcpy() copies *n* characters from buffer *b2* to buffer *b1*, returning pointer *b1*. The objects should not overlap. memmove() does a similar job to memcpy() but behaves as though the *n* characters were first copied from *b2* to a private buffer, then copied from the buffer to *b1*, thus tolerating overlap.

```
char S[3];
memcpy ( S, "ABCD", 3 );
```

strcat, strncat

- ```
  #include <string.h>
  char * strcat ( char * s1, const char * s2 );
  char * strncat ( char * s1, const char * s2, size_t n );
  ```

Function strcat() copies *s2* onto the end of *s1*, overwriting the terminating null of *s1* with the first character of *s2*. The copied string is not disturbed. The return value is *s1*. strncat() does a similar job, but appends only the first *n* characters of *s2*, then adds a null terminator. For neither function should the strings overlap.

```
char S[6] = "XY";
strncat ( S, "ABC", 2 );
```

strcmp, strncmp, memcmp

- ```
  #include <string.h>
  int strcmp ( const char * s1, const char * s2 );
  int strncmp ( const char * s1, const void * s2, size_t n );
  int memcmp ( const void * s1, const void * s2, size_t n );
  ```

Function strcmp() compares *s1* and *s2*, character by character, until it reaches the end of both strings or encounters a difference. If it reaches the end, the function returns zero; if it encounters a difference it returns a positive or negative value. The value returned is positive if the first non-matching character in *s1* is greater ((treated as unsigned char)) than the corresponding character in *s2*, otherwise the value returned is negative. strncmp() does a similar job, but considers only the first *n* characters — fewer if a null terminator is met early. memcmp() is similar to strncmp() but not constrained to work with null-terminated strings.

```
printf ( "%i\n", strcmp( "ABCDeFG", "ABCDEFG" ) );
```

ILLUSTRATING C
```

strchr, strrchr, memchr

■
```
#include <string.h>
char * strchr ( const char * s, int c );
char * strrchr ( const char * s, int c );
void * memchr ( const void * b, int c, size_t n );
```

Function strchr( ) returns a pointer to the first occurrence of c in s, or
NULL if it fails to find one. strrchr( ) is similar to strchr( ) but returns the
last occurrence instead of the first. In both these functions, '\ø' is
included as one of the characters of the string. memchr( ) does a similar
job to strchr( ) but is not constrained to work with null-terminated strings
and considers only the first n characters of buffer b.

```
printf ("%s %s\n", strchr( "abba", 'b'), strrchr("abba", 'b') );
```

```
bba   ba
```

strcspn, strpbrk, strspn, strstr

■
```
#include <string.h>
size_t strcspn ( const char * s1, const char * s2 );
char * strpbrk ( const char * s1, const char * s2 );
size_t strspn ( const char * s1, const char * s2 );
char * strstr ( const char * s1, const char * s2 );
```

Function strcspn( ) returns the number of characters in s1 encountered
before meeting any of the characters in s2. strpbrk( ) returns a pointer
to the first character encountered in s1 that matches any of the
characters in s2. strspn( ) returns the number of characters in s1
encountered before meeting one that is outside the list in s2. Function
strstr( ) finds the location of sub-string s2 in s1 and returns a pointer to
its leading character. Returns NULL if there is no match.

```
printf ( "%i leading consonants\n", strcspn("Phrygian", "aeiou") );
printf ( "%s\n", strpbrk ("Phrygian", "aeiou") );
printf ( "%i leading digits\n", strspn( "1984 JULY 23", "ø123456789") );
printf ( "%s\n", strstr( "Mares eat oats", "at") );
```

```
5 leading consonants
ian
4 leading digits
at oats
```

strtok

■
```
#include <string.h>
char * strtok ( const char * s1, const char * s2 );
```

The function returns pointers to successive tokens constituting the string s1.
Characters deemed to separate the tokens are listed in s2. On the first
call to strtok( ) the first argument should identify the string full of tokens;
on subsequent calls the first argument should be NULL to signify the same
string as before; the terminators may be different on each call. The
function returns NULL when there are no more tokens to deal with. The
original string is overwritten with undefined information.

```
char * p, Line[] = "Para 37.6 :   drs = x1 / 12.73";
printf ( "%s", p=strtok (Line, ":") );
while (p)
    printf (" %s", p=strtok( NULL, " /.=") );
printf ("\n");
```

```
Para 37.6 drs,x1,12,73,(null),
```

strerror

■   #include <string.h>
    char * strerror (int *n*);

Returns a pointer to a system message corresponding to the error
number given as the argument. The argument is typically the value of the
global variable errno. The content of the message depends on the
implementation.

```
printf ( "%s\n", strerror( errno ) );
```

```
Invalid data
```

example

memset

■   #include <string.h>
    void * memset (void * *b*, int *c*, size_t *n*);

The function sets the first *n* characters of buffer *b* to the value *c* and
returns the pointer you give as the first argument. Make sure *b* has at
least *n* characters.

```
memset ( MyBuffer, '\0', 2048 );
```

strcoll, strxfrm

Functions for comparing the strings employed in particular locales. strcoll( )
is designed for use where few comparisons are expected; strxfrm( ) is
for transforming strings such that their transformed versions can be
compared rapidly by strcmp( ). See ANSI X3.159 for details.

mblen, mbstowcs, mbtowc, wctomb, wcstombs

The ANSI C library defines a set of functions that work with multi-byte
and 'wide' characters such as those in the character sets of Asian
languages. See ANSI X3.159 for details.

SORT, SEARCH

The following functions typically employ a Quicksort algorithm and 'binary chop' respectively, but ANSI X3.159 does not demand any particular methods of implementation.

qsort

■   #include < stdlib.h >
    void qsort (void * b, size_t n, size_t w, comparison);

> where comparison is a function call in the form:
>
> int (* f) (const void *, const void *);

The function rearranges the n pointers held in b such that the objects they point to (each of w bytes) may be accessed in ascending order. Specify which order by providing a function to compare the objects indicated by its arguments. Use a library function like strcmp() or write your own. The function should return a positive integer if the first argument points to the greater object, a negative integer if it points to the lesser, otherwise zero.

```
char Kids [ ] [6] = { "mo", "meeny", "eeny", "miny" };
int i, n = sizeof Kids / sizeof Kids[ø];
qsort ( Kids, n, 6, strcmp );
for ( i= ø; i<n, ++i )
    printf ( "%s ", Kids[i] );
printf ("\n");
```

```
eeny meeny miny mo
```

bsearch

■   #include < stdlib.h >
    void * bsearch (const void * k, const void * b, size_t n,
                                        size_t w, comparison);

> where comparison is a function call as defined for qsort( ).

The function searches the first n objects in a sorted array, b, each element of size w bytes, and compares them with the key indicated by k. Comparisons employ the function you nominate, the key being associated with first argument, the array element with the second. If a match is found, the function returns a pointer to the matching element, otherwise it returns NULL. If more than one element matches the key, one of them is pointed to, but which of them is unspecified.

sorted list

```
char Kids [ ] [6] = { "eeny", "meeny", "miny", "mo" };
char * Key = "meeny";
printf ( "%s\n", bsearch ( Key, Kids, 4, 6, strcmp ) );
```

```
meeny
```

DATE and TIME

For the functions defined in the time.h header file, there are two distinct representations of time:

- as a type, time_t
- as a structure, struct tm

As a type, time_t, time is represented as the number of seconds since the start of New Year's day, 1972, in Greenwich. The definition of struct tm is as follows:

```
struct tm                            range allows up to two
{                                        leap seconds
        int tm_sec;      /* seconds after the minute, 0-61 */
        int tm_min;      /* minutes after the hour, 0-59   */
        int tm_hour;     /* hours since midnight, 0-23      */
        int tm_mday;     /* day of month, 1-31             */
        int tm_mon;      /* months since January, 0-11     */
        int tm_year;     /* years since 1900               */
        int tm_wday;     /* days since Sunday, 0-6         */
        int tm_yday;     /* days since 1st January, 0,365  */
        int tm_isdst;    /* daylight saving time flag      */
};
```

asctime, ctime

■
```
#include <time.h>
char * asctime ( struct tm * t );
char * ctime ( const time_t * t );
```

Function asctime( ) returns a pointer to a string. The string contains an encoding of what is represented in the structure indicated by t. Function ctime( ) does the same thing, but for an argument of type time_t. The form of the encoding is:

Sun Nov 10 21:21:00 1991\n\0

```
struct tm MyBirthday = { 0, 0, 10, 28, 1, 30 };
printf ( "%s", asctime ( & MyBirthday ) );
```

```
Sun Feb 28 10:00:00 1930
```

clock

■
```
#include <time.h>
clock_t clock ( void );
```

Returns the time, measured in 'ticks', since the current process was started. The duration of a 'tick' depends on the implementation; to obtain the number of seconds, divide the returned value by CLOCKS_PER_SEC, which is a macro defined in the time.h header file. If the implementation does not provide a clock facility the function returns -1 (cast as type clock_t) .

```
i = clock ();
    process
j = clock ();
printf ( "%i secs\n", ( j - i )/CLOCKS_PER_SEC );
```

CLOCKS_PER_SEC according to ANSI x3.159-1989 but CLK_TCK is the name used in some implementations

difftime

■   #include < time.h >
     double difftime (time_t, *t2*, time_t *t1*);

Returns the number of seconds between the earlier time, *t1*, and the later time, *t2*.

```
Lapse = difftime ( Start, Finish );
```

gmtime, localtime

■   #include < time.h >
     struct tm * gmtime (const time_t * *t*);
     struct tm * localtime (const time_t * *t*);

Decodes information contained in the object pointed to by the argument, *t*, stores the expanded information in a structure of type struct tm, and returns a pointer to this structure. The results are based on Greenwich Mean Time or local time according to the function chosen; see your particular manual about the implications of GMT and local time.

```
p = gmtime ( & Start );
```

mktime

■   #include < time.h >
     time_t mktime (struct tm * *p*);

Encodes information representing local time, and held in the structure pointed to by *p*, then returns this information encoded as type time_t. Two of the fields, tm_wday and tm_yday, play no part in the encoding. Returns -1 ((cast as time_t)) if the function fails.

```
time_t Occasion;
Occasion = mktime ( & MyBirthday );
```

time

■   #include < time.h >
     time_t time (time_t * *t*);

Consults the computer's timer. Returns the current date and time encoded as type time_t. If *t* is not NULL, the result is also copied to the location *t* points to.

```
time_t TimeNow;
time ( & TimeNow );
printf ("Time is now %s\n", ctime ( & TimeNow ) );
```

```
Time is now Thu Dec 19 15:50:05 1991
```

strftime

A function for formatting the date and time held in a structure of type
struct tm as a string to your own design. A battery of about twenty
format specifiers is provided; each begins with a percentage sign on the
principles adopted in printf() and scanf() but using multi-byte characters.
The application of strftime() is sensitive to locale. See ANSI X3.159 for
details.

11

SUMMARIES

This chapter contains summaries of information designed for quick reference. It contains:

- Operator summary, including a table showing the relative precedence of operators.

- Syntax summary, showing all syntax diagrams included in the text

- Library summary, listing alphabetically the prototypes of all library functions except those concerned with multi-byte characters and foreign locales.

OPERATOR SUMMARY

High →	( ) [ ]	++	--	*postfix*	*infix* .	->	
←	! ~	+	* &	++ --	sizeof	*prefix*	
→	* /	%					
→	+ -						
→	<<	>>			*all the rest infix*		
→	< <=	>	>=				
→	== !=						
→	&						
→	^						
→	|						
→	&&						
←	||						
←	?:						
Low →	= *=	/=	%=	+= -=	<<= >>=	&= |=	=

precedence (vertical, left axis)   *associativity*

PREFIX OPERATORS

+	▶ + a	confirmation	
-	▶ - a	negation	
&	▶ & v	address of l-value	
*	▶ * p	pointee of (object pointed to by)	
~	▶ ~ m	ones' complement ~ `1 0` ⇨ `0 1`	
!	▶ ! m	logical *not* (1 if n *false*)	
++ --	▶ ++ i	increment (decrement) then use value	

KEY

v	*l-value*
i	*integral l-value*
a, b	*expressions*
m, n	*integral expressions*
p	*pointer*
w	*member name*

INFIX OPERATORS

*	▶ a * b	product
/	▶ a / b	quotient
%	▶ m % n	remainder
+ -	▶ a + b	sum (difference)
& | ^	▶ m & n	bitwise *and* (*or*) (*exclusive or*)
<< >>	▶ m << n	m shifted left (right) n positions
,	▶ a , b	evaluate & discard a, eval & retain b
> >= < <= == !=	▶ n > m	1 if comparison is *true*, otherwise 0
&& ||	▶ n && m	logical *and* (*or*)
=	▶ v = a	assign value of a to l-value v
+= -= *= /= %=	▶ a += b	short for a=a+b (*and similarly*)
&= |= ^ =	▶ n &= m	short for n=n&m (n=n|m) (n=n^m)
<<= >>=	▶ n <<= m	short for n=n<<m (n=n>>m)
.	▶ v . w	member w of structure v
->	▶ p -> w	short for (*p).w

POSTFIX OPERATORS

++ --	▶ i ++	use value, then increment (decrement)

OTHER OPERATORS

?:	▶ m ? a : b	if m=0 value is a, otherwise b
(*type-name*)	▶ (double) a	result is a double ('a' undisturbed)
sizeof	▶ sizeof v	size in bytes of object v
sizeof ( )	▶ sizeof (double)	size of every object of type *double*
( ) [ ]		( ) signifies *function*, [ ] signifies *array*

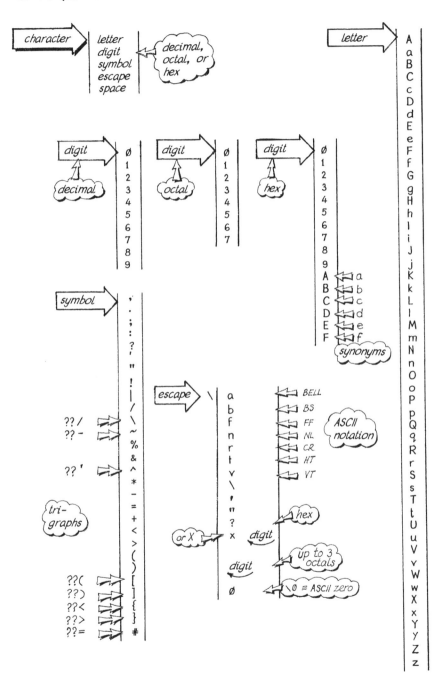

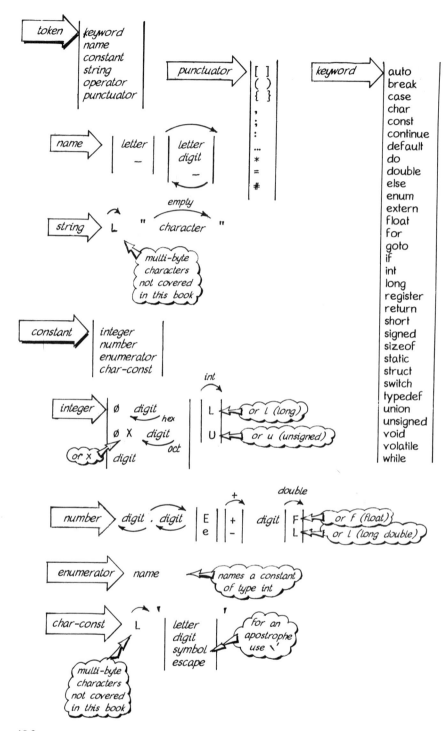

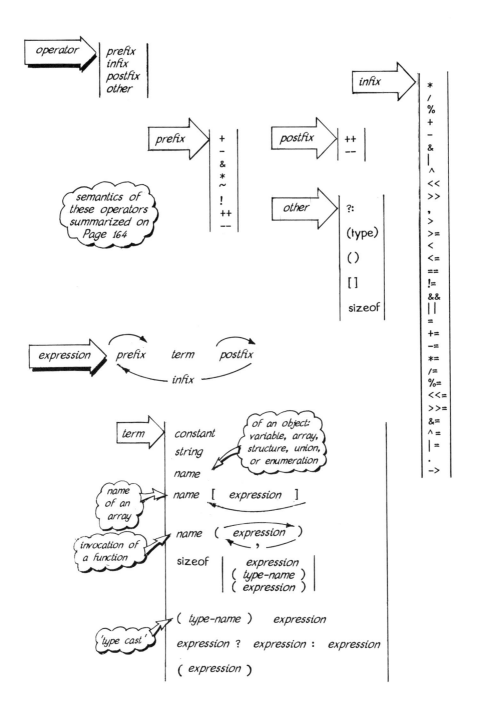

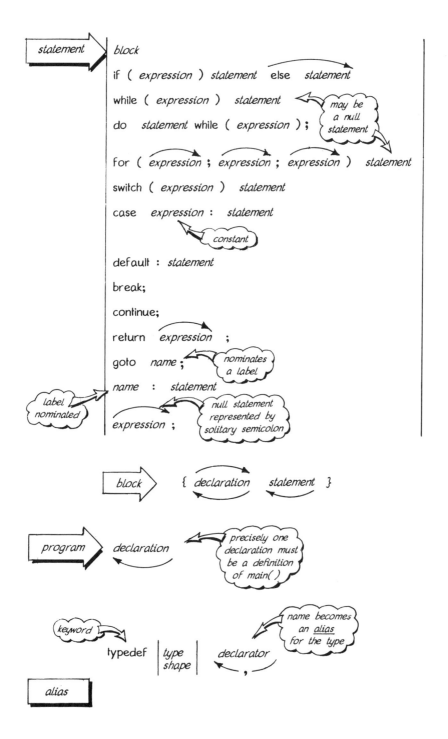

statement ⟶ block

if (*expression*) *statement* else *statement*

while (*expression*) *statement*

do *statement* while (*expression*) ;

may be a null statement

for (*expression* ; *expression* ; *expression*) *statement*

switch (*expression*) *statement*

case *expression* : *statement*

constant

default : *statement*

break;

continue;

return *expression* ;

goto *name* ;

nominates a label

name : *statement*

label nominated

expression ;

null statement represented by solitary semicolon

block ⟩ { *declaration* *statement* }

program ⟶ *declaration*

precisely one declaration must be a definition of main( )

keyword

name becomes an alias for the type

typedef | *type shape* | *declarator* ←— ,

alias

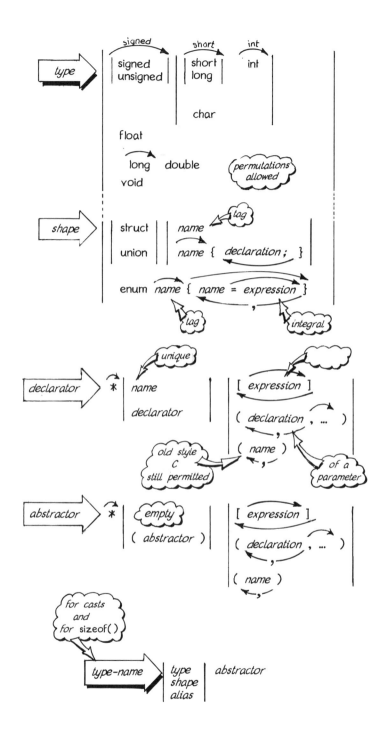

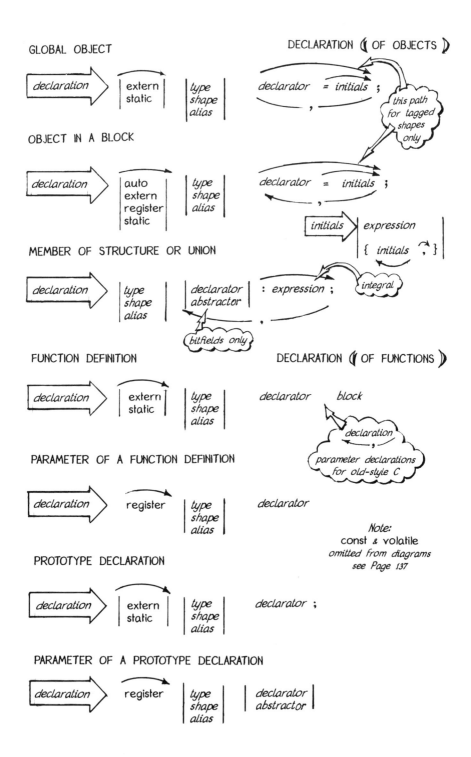

GLOBAL OBJECT

DECLARATION ❨ OF OBJECTS ❩

OBJECT IN A BLOCK

MEMBER OF STRUCTURE OR UNION

FUNCTION DEFINITION

DECLARATION ❨ OF FUNCTIONS ❩

PARAMETER OF A FUNCTION DEFINITION

Note:
const & volatile
omitted from diagrams
see Page 137

PROTOTYPE DECLARATION

PARAMETER OF A PROTOTYPE DECLARATION

Each directive must be on a line of its own
《 possibly extended by ⬚⬚ 》
preceding the program it is to modify

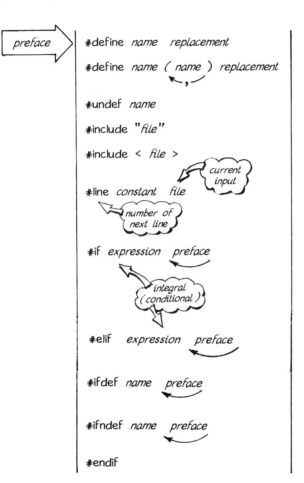

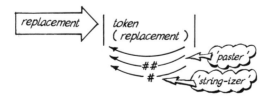

Return	Function (Prototypes of parameters)	Header	Page
a			
void	abort (void);	stdlib.h	172
int	abs (int *n*);	stdlib.h	180
double	acos (double *a*);	*math.h*	*181*
char *	asctime (struct tm * *t*);	time.h	192
double	asin (double *a*);	math.h	181
void	assert (int *expression*);	stdlib.h	172
double	atan (double *a*);	math.h	182
double	atan2 (double *y,* double *x*);	math.h	182
int	atexit (void (* *fun*)(void));	assert.h	172
double	atof (const char * *s*);	stdlib.h	178
int	atoi (const char * *s*);	stdlib.h	177
long	atol (const char * *s*);	stdlib.h	178
b – c			
void *	bsearch (const void * *b,* const void * *b,* size_t *n,* size_t *w, comparison*);	stdlib.h	191
void *	calloc (size_t *NumElts,* size_t *EltSiz*);	stdlib.h	177
double	ceil (double *d*);	math.h	180
void	clearerr (FILE * *s*)	stdio.h	166
clock_t	clock (void);	time.h	192
double	cos (double *ar*);	math.h	181
double	cosh (double *x*);	math.h	182
char *	ctime (const time_t * *t*)	time.h	192
d – f			
double	difftime (time_t *t2,* time_t *t1*);	time.h	193
div_t	div (int *num,* int *denom*);	stdlib.h	183
void	exit (int *status*);	stdlib.h	171
double	exp (double *a*);	math.h	184
double	fabs (double *d*);	math.h	180
FILE *	fclose (FILE * *s*);	stdio.h	165
int	feof (FILE * *s*);	stdio.h	166

Return	Function (Prototypes of parameters)	Header	Page
int	ferror (FILE * s);	stdio.h	166
int	fflush (FILE * s);	stdio.h	165
int	fgetc (FILE * s);	stdio.h	164
int	fgetpos (FILE * s, fpos_t * c);	stdio.h	167
char *	fgets (char * b, int n, FILE * s);	stdio.h	167
double	floor (double d);	math.h	180
double	fmod (double x , double y);	math.h	183
FILE *	fopen (const char * file, const char * mode);	stdio.h	165
int	fprintf (FILE * s, const char * fmt, ...);	stdio.h	168
int	fputc (int c, FILE * s);	stdio.h	164
int	fputs (const char * b, FILE * s);	stdio.h	168
size_t	fread (void * buf, size_t b, size_t c, FILE * s);	stdio.h	164
void	free (void * p);	stdlib.h	177
FILE *	freopen (const char * file, const char * mode, FILE * s);	stdio.h	165
double	frexp (double x, int * p);	math.h	184
int	fscanf (FILE * s, const char * fmt, ...);	stdio.h	169
int	fseek (FILE * s, long offset, int origin);	stdio.h	166
int	fsetpos (FILE * s, const fpos_t * p);	stdio.h	167
long	ftell (FILE * s);	stdio.h	167
size_t	fwrite (const void * buf, size_t b, size_t c, FILE * s);	stdio.h	164

g – i

Return	Function (Prototypes of parameters)	Header	Page
int	getc (FILE * s);	stdio.h	165
int	getchar (void);	stdio.h	165
char *	getenv (const char * Name);	stdlib.h	173
char *	gets (char * b);	stdio.h	168
struct tm *	gmtime (const time_t * t);	time.h	193
int	isalnum (int c);	ctype.h	185
int	isalpha (int c);	ctype.h	185
int	iscntrl (int c);	ctype.h	186
int	isdigit (int c);	ctype.h	185

Return	Function (Prototypes of parameters)	Header	Page
int	putc (int c, FILE * s);	stdio.h	164
int	putchar (int c);	stdio.h	164
int	puts (const char * b);	stdio.h	168
void	qsort (void * b, size_t n, size_t w, comparison);	stdlib.h	191

--- r ---

Return	Function	Header	Page
int	raise (int sig);	signal.h	175
int	rand (void);	stdlib.h	182
void *	realloc (void * p, size_t newsiz);	stdlib.h	177
int	remove (const char * file);	stdio.h	166
int	rename (const char * old, const char * new);	stdio.h	166
void	rewind (FILE * s);	stdio.h	166

--- s ---

Return	Function	Header	Page
int	scanf (const char * fmt, ...);	stdio.h	169
void	setbuf (FILE * s, char * b);	stdio.h	171
int	setjmp (jmp_buf saver);	setjmp.h	174
char	setlocale (int category, const char * locale);	locale.h	174
int	setvbuf (FILE * s, char * b, int mode, size_t sz);	stdio.h	170
void	(*signal (int sig, void (* hndlr)(int))) (int);	signal.h	175
double	sin (double ar);	math.h	181
double	sinh (double x);	math.h	182
int	sprintf (char * p, const char * fmt, ...);	stdio.h	168
double	sqrt (double a);	math.h	181
void	srand (unsigned int seed);	stdlib.h	182
int	sscanf (const char * b, const char * fmt, ...);	stdio.h	169
char *	strcat (char * s1, const char * s2);	string.h	188
char *	strchr (const char * s, int c);	string.h	189
int	strcmp (const char * s1, const char * s2);	string.h	188
char *	strcpy (char * s1, const char * s2);	string.h	187

Return	Function (Prototypes of parameters)	Header	Page
size_t	strcspn (const char * s1, const char * s2);	string.h	189
char *	strerror (int n);	string.h	190
size_t	strlen (const char * s);	string.h	187
char *	strncat (char * s1, const char * s2, size_t n);	string.h	188
int	strncmp (const char * s1, const char * s2, size_t n);	string.h	188
char *	strncpy (char * s1, const char * s2, size_t n);	string.h	187
char *	strpbrk (const char * s1, const char * s2);	string.h	189
char *	strrchr (const char * s, int c);	string.h	189
size_t	strspn (const char * s1, const char * s2);	string.h	189
char *	strstr (const char * s1, const char * s2);	string.h	189
double	strtod (const char * s, char ** p);	stdlib.h	178
char *	strtok (const char * s1, const char * s2);	string.h	189
long	strtol (const char * s, char ** p, int base);	stdlib.h	179
unsigned long	strtoul (const char * s, char ** p, int radix);	stdlib.h	179
int	system (const char * command);	stdlib.h	173

t

Return	Function	Header	Page
double	tan (double ar);	math.h	181
double	tanh (double x);	math.h	182
time_t	time (time_t * t);	time.h	193
FILE *	tmpfile (void);	stdio.h	170
char *	tmpnam (char * nam);	stdio.h	170
int	tolower (int c);	ctype.h	186
int	toupper (int c);	ctype.h	186

u - v

Return	Function	Header	Page
int	ungetc (int c, FILE * s);	stdio.h	165
type	va_arg (va_list p, type);	stdarg.h	176
void	va_end (va_list p);	stdarg.h	176
void	va_start (va_list p, name);	stdarg.h	176
int	vfprintf (FILE * s, const char * fmt, va_list ap);	stdio.h	169
int	vprintf (const char * fmt, va_list ap);	stdio.h	169
int	vsprintf (char * p, const char * fmt, va_list ap);	stdio.h	169

ILLUSTRATING C

BIBLIOGRAPHY

American National Standard for Information Systems
Programming Language – C, ANSI X3.159–1989

The Standard defines the dialect of C presented in this
book. National standards can be forbidding documents, and
expensive, but ANSI X3.159 is worth having if you are going
to program seriously in C. The document is beautifully
organized and the prose intelligible. It is not a tutorial text,
but appended to the Standard is a 'rationale' to explain
difficult paragraphs of the Standard and say why certain
library functions were included.

Kernighan, B.W, & Ritchie, D.M. (1988) *The C programming
language*, Second edition. (Prentice Hall)

Dennis Ritchie invented C; this book is its bible. The first
edition is dated 1978 and remained the only authoritative,
and certainly the best, book on C ((although not the
easiest to read)) until the second edition was published ten
years later. During the intervening decade there must have
been an enormous amount of feedback from readers. The
second edition shows every sign of professional
involvement in its authorship, responding to the feedback
and resolving the old ambiguities. The book is marked 'ANSI
C'. It is a joy to read.

Bakakati, N. (1989) *The Waite Group's Essential Guide to
ANSI C*, (Howard W. Sams & Co.)

This is a pocket-sized reference to ANSI C. It covers the
language and keywords, but most of it describes the
library. The description of each library function comprises
a short explanation of its purpose, its syntax, an example
call, a description of what it returns, and a list of names
of related functions. A useful reference for the practical C
programmer.

operating system, 4
operators, 8
  access, 129
  action of, 49
  arithmetical, 38
  assignment, 42
  bitwise, 39
  demotion & promotion of, 48-9
  incrementing, 43
  logical, 38
  precedence & associativity of, 47
  reference, 44
  summaries of, 46, 196
  syntax of, 38ff
  sequence, 43
organization, 65ff
output, 107ff

P

parameters, 8, 88
  as pointers, 82
  coercion of, 48
  counting of, 96
  names of, 21
parentheses, in macros, 68
Parlour trick, example, 86-7
parse trees, 90, 91
paster, 69
perror, 172
pointee, concept of, 80
pointer arithmetic, 84-5
pointer
  concept of, 80-1
  constant, 88
  declaration of, 81
  to functions, 88
pow, 180
power cables, example, 60
precedence, 47
preprocessing, conditional, 71
preprocessor, 34, 67
  purpose of, 66
print format, 110
printf, 168
program
  concept of, 2-3
  processing, 66
  syntax of, 36
promotion, 48
prototypes
  concept of, 38
  in header files, 70
punctuators, 67
putc, 109, 164
putchar, 109, 164
puts, 168

Q

qsort, 191
qualifier, 34, 73, 81
Quicksort, 62-3, 83

R

raise, 175, 182
random access, 122
realization, 4
realloc, 177
recursion, concept of, 24
register storage class specifier, 73-7
remove, 117, 166
rename, 118, 166
return statement, 36, 53
reverse Polish, example, 139-41, 148
rewind, 117, 166
ring structures, 154
Roman numerals, 56
Roses, example ring, 156

S

scan format, 112
scanf, 7, 169
scope,
  concept of, 74
  of declarations, 37
  of variables, 23
semicolon, 7
setbuf, 171
setjmp, 174
setlocale, 174
setvbuf, 170
shape, synonym for type
short type, 31, 32, 134
shortest route, example, 150-3
signal, 175
signed type, 31, 32, 134
sin, 181
sinh, 182
sizeof operator 45, 71, 145
spacing, see whitespace
specifiers, 31, 110, 113
sprintf, 168
sqrt, 181
srand, 182
sscanf, 112, 169
stacks, 138,
  dynamic, 146
statement, 3, 7,
  as a block, 36
  compound, 12
  syntax of, 36
static storage class specifier, 23, 73-7, 128